INWARDLY**DIGEST**

THE PRAYER BOOK AS GUIDE TO A SPIRITUAL LIFE

Library of Congress Cataloging-in-Publication Data

Names: Olsen, Derek A., author.
Title: Inwardly digest : the prayer book as guide to a spiritual life /
　　Derek Olsen.
Description: First [edition]. | Cincinnati : Forward Movement, 2016.
Identifiers: LCCN 2016024170
Subjects: LCSH: Episcopal Church. Book of common prayer (1979) |
　　Prayer--Episcopal Church. | Spiritual life--Episcopal Church. |
　　Episcopal Church--Liturgy.
Classification: LCC BX5945 .O47 2016 | DDC 264/.03--dc23
LC record available at https://lccn.loc.gov/2016024170

© 2016 Forward Movement
Second printing, 2017

ISBN: 9780880284325

Printed in USA

Forward
Movement

Praise for *Inwardly Digest: The Prayer Book as Guide to a Spiritual Life*

Too often, *The Book of Common Prayer* is open to a few familiar pages on Sunday and closed the rest of the days, with little regard to the deep, transformative spirituality inside. With humor, deep reverence, and academic insight that is anything but dry and boring, Derek Olsen reminds us of the breath of the Spirit, the lives of the saints, the love of Jesus, and the magnificence of God held in the words, silence, and worship of our *Book of Common Prayer*. Clergy and laity should read this to discover and re-discover the daring words and liturgies of our faith spanning eons and to engage the prayers and worship of our faith.

—LAURIE BROCK
Episcopal priest and author of *Where God Hides Holiness:
Thoughts on Grief, Joy, and the Search for Fabulous Heels*

Derek Olsen is the patron saint of the overlooked; campaign manager of the undervalued; tour guide to the taken for granted. His patient, scholarly watchfulness and his gift for rendering complex ideas in clear, concise prose make *Inwardly Digest* an insightful guide to *The Book of Common Prayer* and a sure and steady introduction to Anglican spiritual practice.

—JIM NAUGHTON
Founder of Episcopal Café and
partner of Canticle Communications

Written in an engaging style that is both conversational and informative, *Inwardly Digest* is a timely invitation to life in the Spirit sustained by the patterns and rhythms of the Prayer Book.

—FRANK GRISWOLD
25th Presiding Bishop of The Episcopal Church

⁓

With the spiritual foundation in *The Book of Common Prayer,* Derek Olsen shows how everyday Christians can grow closer to God through a "training regimen" that incorporates the spirituality of Anglican liturgy as a daily practice. In straightforward and accessible writing, Olsen provides a guide to Prayer Book spirituality for everyone.

—THE REV. SUSAN BROWN SNOOK
Episcopal priest and author of *God Gave the Growth: Church Planting in the Episcopal Church*

⁓

INWARDLY**DIGEST**
THE PRAYER BOOK AS GUIDE TO A SPIRITUAL LIFE

DEREK OLSEN

FORWARD MOVEMENT
CINCINNATI, OHIO

Dedicated to my three ladies:
Meredith, Greta, and Hannah

Table of Contents

FOREWORD

FOREWORD

There are all sorts of different ways of being Christian

I grew up Lutheran and had been working toward ordination in the Evangelical Lutheran Church in America when I felt a subtle tugging at my soul. As I explored this further, I found myself being pulled toward a different way of being spiritual than I had known in the Lutheran church. It was an older path, one that gave more credence to mystery and sacrament than I saw in my Lutheran environment, one more heavily populated by the psalms. I began praying with *The Book of Common Prayer* and found a liturgical and sacramental depth that answered the call that I felt in my heart. For me, this spiritual path was more authentic to who I had been created to be. After much agonizing and long conversations with my wife, I left the Lutheran church and the ordination process and found a home in The Episcopal Church.

Don't get me wrong—I have nothing against Lutherans, and I treasure the many things I learned and the many friendships I maintain with my Lutheran colleagues. It simply wasn't the path for me.

I had always intended to pursue a doctorate after seminary. Following my move to The Episcopal Church, I earned a PhD in New Testament for which I focused specifically on the connection between scripture and liturgy—how liturgies use scripture and are, in turn, informed by it. I never entered a discernment process for ordination in The Episcopal Church, nor did I take an academic job after graduation. In the final years of my academic studies, I found a good job doing computer work for a major corporation, and I remain there today.

These biographical facts make me a weird author for this kind of book. Most writers on spirituality tend to be priests or professors or both. I'm neither. I have the same training as a parish priest (including a full year serving a Lutheran parish complete with preaching, teaching, and counseling), and I have a doctorate in a spirituality-ish field. But nobody pays me to study; nobody pays me to pray. My days aren't spent in scholarship and pastoral work with dedicated time for prayer, but in working the day job, cooking dinners, and shuttling my daughters to and from their activities. The only ivory towers in my life are the ones I pass on my way to my older daughter's ballet studio!

As a lay theologian living an ordinary life, I am not under any illusions about the difficulties of balancing a spiritual life in addition to and in relation to all of the other demands in my life and on my time. Figuring out that balance is an important piece of the puzzle for me.

Yet I have found an answer. The spirituality informed by and grounded in *The Book of Common Prayer* leads me most directly into the depths of God. Out of the many possible ways that there are to be Christian, my focus in this book is Anglican liturgical spirituality. Those last three words are terms that we ought to get clear upfront.

Anglican comes from the name *Angles*. It pertains to one of the many Germanic tribal groups that invaded Britain during the Migration Era of the fourth through seventh centuries. These tribal groups took over the place and renamed it Angle-land, which eventually became England. Through a series of events, the Church of England developed and was characterized by a certain perspective on the faith—a way of being Christian—embodied within *The Book of Common Prayer*. As English-speaking people spread across the world, they brought Anglicanism with them. The Episcopal Church is the heir of the English state-supported church in the America colonies. Other groups with Anglican lineages have appeared in America since then, most having split off from The Episcopal Church at some time or another.

Liturgical refers to a set of spiritual practices that use established formulas to structure regularly occurring worship services. Or, as some of my Methodist friends like to kid me, it means that we use "wrote-down" prayers. It's more than that, though. The term liturgical brings with it a sense of patterns that we as individuals and as a church value. These patterns include the seasons of the church year and the rhythm of daily prayer as well as how services on Sundays are ordered. I'll let you in on a little secret: Most Christian churches are liturgical, even those that would be horrified at being called such. If a church uses some sort of regular pattern when the congregation gathers for worship, then they are using a liturgy. Of course, in the Anglican tradition, we have moved quite a bit up the liturgical scale. Not only do we have liturgies and patterns, but we also embrace them as a basic principle of our spiritual practice. And that is where we are going to start. The first section of this book wrestles with the whys, hows, and wherefores of being liturgical, investigating the principles and logic of such a decision.

The word spirituality gets thrown around a lot these days, particularly in church circles, but often the word is dropped without any sort of explanation. What is spirituality? How does it relate to being spiritual? In one way, the answer is simple: Spirituality refers to a set of thoughts, ideas, feelings, habits, and practices that lead us deeper into the reality of God. Spirituality is an intersection of these things in a more or less systematic way that helps us live our faith, get more out of it, and share it with the people around us, aiding us—with God's help—to open and align our lives alongside God's own hopes for this world.

At the heart of Anglican liturgical spirituality is *The Book of Common Prayer*. Some of what I say here can and should apply to any book of common prayer. However, since I am an Episcopalian living in the United States, I will focus specifically on the prayer book authorized in my particular part of the Anglican Communion, the Episcopal *Book of Common Prayer* officially adopted by the Church in 1979. My contention is that the prayer book has at its heart a pattern for Christian living, a rule of life that represents a deeply authentic and well-trodden path toward Christian maturity.

Now—does this mean that this book is only for Episcopalians? Actually, no. My belief is that the Anglican tradition and The Episcopal Church hold a treasure in trust for the larger Church, for that great mystical body of believers that transcends organizational structures and denominational lines. That treasure-in-trust is the liturgical life that flows from the prayer book with its balance of classic Christian elements: the Calendar, the Eucharist, and the Daily Office (Morning & Evening Prayer). I hope that any liturgical Christian will find this book to be a resource for their spiritual journey whether they use *The Book of Common Prayer* or not.

The title for this work comes from a prayer that is as old as the prayer book tradition itself. Near the beginning of the

English Reformation, an assembly of bishops created a new prayer book to be used by the whole country, replacing the Latin masses of the Roman Catholic Church and the many Reformation-inspired forms that were springing up. The leader of these bishops was the Archbishop of Canterbury, Thomas Cranmer. He had been experimenting with and composing English-language liturgies for many years, but King Henry VIII steadfastly refused to allow public services in any language other than Latin. Once Henry died and his young son, Edward VI, took the throne, Cranmer and his colleagues had the opportunity they had been hoping for: to present the English people with liturgies in their own language, liturgies in continuity with the services they had heard all of their lives (whether they had understood them or not), infused with a renewed focus on scripture.

While many of the prayers had been translated from the Latin sources, many others were newly composed and underscored the theological principles of the reformers. The brief prayer (or collect) for the Second Sunday of Advent was one of Cranmer's new compositions:

> BLESSED Lord, *which hast caused all holy scriptures to be written for our learning: grant us that we may in such wise hear them, read, mark, learn, and inwardly digest them, that by patience and comfort of thy holy word, we may embrace and ever hold fast the blessed hope of everlasting life, which thou hast given us in our Saviour Jesus Christ.*[1]

At the heart of these words is a desire for the scriptures to take root in human lives. This encapsulated the reformers' hope: to instigate a renewal of Christian life in England,

1   Joseph Ketley, ed., *The Two Liturgies, A.D. 1549, and A.D. 1552: With Other Documents Set Forth by Authority in the Reign of King Edward VI* (Cambridge: Cambridge University Press, 1844), p. 42.

grounded in the scriptures and mediated by the liturgies of the Church. This hope remains with us today. While the language has changed a bit, this prayer is still with us. Its position has shifted around a bit—it's appointed for a Sunday just before Thanksgiving now—but the longing embodied within it remains just as keenly felt now as centuries ago when it was first written.

It is still my hope, an Anglican hope, that the authorized liturgies of the Church serve as a vehicle to connect us to the deep wisdom of the Christian tradition, to its scriptures and teachings. By living the liturgies week by week, day by day, we do—literally—hear and read the Word of God. Eventually, with practice, we come to mark and learn the scripture. But it's that next step of the prayer that is critical: It's not enough to just learn holy scripture. We need to make it a part of ourselves, part of our being.

We have to inwardly digest it.

And that's my hope here. I'm trying to give you a pathway to the riches of our prayer book so that you can understand them more deeply. I am trying to infect you with some of my love for these texts—and not just the words on the page but the energies that can spring from acting them out in your life.

One last note—this book contains a lot of "we" and "us" language; hopefully not much "I" and "you." That's not just a stylistic convention. Rather, it is born out of the conviction that this whole spiritual business that we're engaged in is a group activity. We don't—we can't—do it by ourselves and, indeed, trying to do it solo is frequently one of the warning signs that we're going off track. Instead, we practice our spirituality within a community of other people who are alternately supporting us, challenging us, frustrating us, and reminding us what authentic love looks like. This book took shape within the context of several such overlapping communities without which it could not have happened and without which it would have been a much shorter and poorer work.

The most basic community that enabled it to happen is, of course, my family. My wife, Meredith, is an Episcopal priest as well as being a wonderful mother, a wise friend, and a faster runner than I'll ever be. She has put up with and pushed back on most of the thoughts in this book in one way or another, and they are stronger and richer for it. Our two delightful daughters, Greta and Hannah, relentlessly remind me to "keep it real" verbally and otherwise. Without the support of my family, none of this would have been possible.

The team at Forward Movement has been tremendous. Executive Director and Pamphlet Baron Extraordinaire Scott Gunn helped me hash out the shape and direction of this work. Richelle Thompson, Melody Wilson Shobe, and Nancy Hopkins-Greene were steadfast editors who helped improve the structure and content of the work in spite of my resistance. Michael Phillips has an incredible process for coming up with compelling and fitting cover art, and Carole Miller has a keen eye for detail and consistency in layout. And, of course, Jane Paraskevopoulos and the rest of the staff that authors rarely interact with keep the ship righted and moving forward.

Lastly, this book has already been profoundly shaped by its readers. Over a decade ago, I started a semi-anonymous blog and gave it the obscure, unpronounceable, and unspellable name of *haligweorc*. Hey, it made sense at the time. The blog was a creative outlet for me to write and think about things that had absolutely nothing to do with my doctoral dissertation. Over the years, the blog became a community of readers, writers, and responders who have helped me grow in my writing and my thinking. While many of the ideas in this book were informally worked out first on the blog, some of them achieved a more concrete form because of relationships created through it. Part of the first chapter grows out of a post spurred by Jim Naughton when he was still running the online *Episcopal Café*. Parts of the seventh chapter started life as an address to the Society of Catholic Priests at the instigation of David Cobb and Robert Hendrickson.

Once the book concept became more clear, I blogged much of it as I went, and I owe a debt of gratitude to all of the readers who commented and improved what I wrote. In particular, Barbara Snyder, Christopher Evans, and Nicholas Heavens have been there from the start. Susan Loomis, too, continually pushed me to write more clearly and to remember for whom I was writing. Brendan O'Sullivan-Hale and Holli Powell, hosts of *The Collect Call* podcast, read and improved the chapter on collects. In addition to my Internet comrades, Brooke Watson and Steven Dalle Mura (my uncle-in-law) commented on every page in order to make this a better and more accessible work.

And finally, dear readers, I invite you to continue the conversations—in your homes, your parishes, and your Internet communities. I've renamed my blog to the more user-friendly *St Bede Productions* (www.stbedeproductions.com), and you're always welcome to join us there.

Derek Olsen, PhD
Feast of Saint Bede

CHAPTER 1
FUNDAMENTALS

Keeping the Main Thing the Main Thing

My wife is, among other things, a coach with our local running club. Runners come to her and complain that they don't feel like they are making progress. Her first question is, "What's your goal?" Whether it's maintaining a certain pace for a number of miles, setting a new personal record for a given race, or losing a few pounds, there has to be a goal. Otherwise the idea of progress is a futile one! Whether they have a goal or not, she then asks to see their running log. Well—they haven't filled it out. Or they have, and it shows sporadic workouts scattered across a couple of weeks. Or the log shows consistency but no differentiation between types of workouts. With the log in hand, she can coach the runners to develop training plans that will help them get to their goal. She helps the runners establish a connection between their daily and weekly training and the accomplishment of their longer-term goal. Then they understand: The training has to be tailored to the goal.

The practice and metaphor of physical training has been connected with the process of spiritual development since the ancient world.[1] It takes the same kind of discipline and consistency to progress in the spiritual life as it does in physical fitness. Indeed, the technical term for the theory and practice of spiritual development is "ascetical theology" taken from the Greek word *askesis* that simply means training. Paul taps into the language of physical training (and running specifically) when he speaks to the Corinthians of his own self-disciplines: "Do you not know that in a race the runners all compete, but only one receives the prize? Run in such a way that you may win it. Athletes exercise self-control in all things; they do it to receive a perishable wreath, but we an imperishable one. So I do not run aimlessly, nor do I box as though beating the air; but I punish my body and enslave it, so that after proclaiming to others I myself should not be disqualified" (1 Corinthians 9:24-7). Paul reminds us that we have to have a goal. Not only that, but also we have to understand and believe that our training is directly contributing to our attainment of that goal.

There is a disconnect between the way most people approach their spiritual lives and how they approach a project like getting in shape to run a marathon. When you're working on such a project, there are concrete tasks to accomplish; there's a goal to work toward, and success can be measured by progress against that goal. We don't tend to think of prayer and meditation in the same way; you can't see it taking shape—you cannot check off the workouts or mark off the dates on the calendar as the big day approaches. Yet just because spirituality cannot be easily measured does not mean that there aren't steps toward progress. Anglican spiritual writer Martin Thornton reminds us that there is one true test of an effective spiritual practice: Does it make me a more loving person?[2]

The use of "training" language doesn't work for everyone; it's not the only metaphor that the Church has used for this kind of work. If it doesn't work for you, consider other metaphors. For example, one can speak of relaxing into the person of God, an approach that doesn't use the language of effort and progress. This path recognizes that a relationship with God isn't something we have to create; it already exists. It frames spiritual growth as a process of clearing away impediments that prevent us from experiencing this relationship as fully as possible. Another classic metaphor is that of healing. We are sick with sin and need to be restored to full health in our relationship with God and with all of creation.

I am using the training language because it has a long and significant history in the Church. I also think it is a concept that connects with many people in today's world. Use the other metaphors if they work better for you. These three perspectives share three implicit assumptions: 1) God already loves us and is reaching out to us in a variety of ways, 2) the state that we are in now needs to be transformed by God, through God, and toward God, and yet 3) we have a role in this process as well. At the very least, we have to be attentive to the action of God's graces leading us toward love and the practices of being more loving.

At the end of the day, this is what we are created for. We have been created in the image and likeness of God. At the beginning of our making, before even the first cells of our bones were constructed, God framed us in his own image. A God-shaped pattern lies at the heart of our being. As scripture and tradition have revealed again and again, God's own character is rooted in love, justice, mercy, and fidelity. The psalms struggle to use the immensity of creation to describe the character of God: "Your love, O Lord, reaches to the heavens, and your faithfulness to the clouds. Your righteousness is like the strong mountains, your justice like the great deep; you save both man and beast, O Lord" (Psalm 36:5-6). These same attributes of love, justice, mercy, and fidelity were woven into our being before the cords of our sinews were knit. Where are they now? As beings created to love and serve God and one another, are we in touch with this fundamental pattern?

Truthfully, we fall far short of the promise of God's pattern for us. We don't consistently manifest the characteristics that have been built into us. This is the result of sin. Through our own choices, through the choices of others, through the choices that society makes and heaps upon us, we lose sight of who and what we are. We invest ourselves in stories at odds with God's story, stories about riches and success and fame where what matters is getting ahead. Or perhaps our stories are about needs and hungers and habits where what matters is quieting the cravings...until they kick up again. We invest ourselves in patterns of life, in ways of living, that are skewed from the pattern that God has laid down for us, patterns grounded in something other than love and faithfulness.

One central point of Christian spirituality, then, is to recall us to ourselves. It is to reconcile us to the God who loves us, who created us in his own image, and who cared enough for our redemption to take frail flesh and demonstrate the patterns of love, mercy, and justice in the person of Jesus Christ—patterns that led him through the cross to resurrection. In Jesus, in God's ultimate act of self-revelation and of self-emptying for our sake, we have been called back; we can get in touch with the "us" that God originally created us to be. Therefore, the true test of a Christian spirituality is whether it helps us address this question and accomplish our goal: Are we free to love and to be who God created us to be?

But we can't stop there, either. The Christian enterprise isn't just about us individually. While God cares deeply about the redemption of each one of us, there is a much bigger scope in view here. God wills the redemption of all humanity, of all creation. Our spiritual work isn't just about being the best we can be—it's about participating in God's monumental effort to reconcile all creation back to the patterns of love, justice, mercy, and fidelity, back to the goodness that it had once and can have again.

To put it another way, Paul reminds us again and again in his letters that we have been baptized into the Body of Christ. He means this in a mystical sense—that we are connected to the life, death, and resurrection of Jesus—but he means it socially as well—that we are connected to the community of all the others who have been connected to Jesus as well, the Church. But being incorporated into the Body is the beginning of the process, not its end. It's not enough to be grafted into the Body of Christ if we don't share in the Mind of Christ, which is laid out in the Christ-hymn of Philippians: "Let the same mind be in you that was in Christ Jesus, who, though he was in the form of God, did not regard equality with God as something to be exploited, but emptied himself, taking the form of a slave, being born in human likeness. And being found in human form, he humbled himself and became obedient to the point of death—even death on a cross..." (2:5-8). Ephesians reminds us that this is the point of the whole exercise; Christian spirituality isn't just about you. Rather, your spiritual success is tied to everyone else around you. Indeed, that's the point of the Church: "To equip the saints for the work of ministry, for building up the body of Christ, until **all of us** come to the unity of the faith and of the knowledge of the Son of God, to maturity, to the measure of the full stature of Christ. ...But speaking the truth in love, **we** must grow up in every way into him who is the head, into

Christ, from whom **the whole body**, joined and knit together by every ligament with which it is equipped, as each part is working properly, promotes the body's growth in building itself up in love" (4:12-13; 15-16, *emphasis added*). We are not on this journey alone; our own spiritual maturity is tied up with how we model and encourage that maturity in others. Any spirituality or spiritual exercise that cuts us off or makes us feel superior to those around us is not being rightly used.

Thus, the goal of Christian spirituality is to bring the whole Body of Christ to Christian maturity. We do this by cultivating that maturity in ourselves, modeling it for others, and encouraging them in their own path. We build up the Body by using the gifts that we have been given. No matter how it may appear, Christianity is a team sport.

If that's the goal, then how do we get there? How do we measure our progress toward it? Well, this is a little more subjective. It is not like running; I can't see how I'm doing in the same way that I glance down at a running watch to check my pace or look at the path behind me to see how far I've come.

As Thornton suggests, the most reliable guide is an honest appraisal of how we treat those around us. Are we treating the inevitable provocations of daily life with anger and resentment or with patience and compassion? When I sit and ponder how my spiritual life is going, one of the best measures I know is to consider how my wife and kids might rate me. Am I being a more thoughtful and patient husband? Am I responding to their demands on my time in appropriate ways? And not just them. How would my coworkers answer the same questions?

The habits of devotion foster in us the habits of virtue. We are transformed—slowly and with a certain amount of inevitable backsliding—gradually toward the Mind of Christ. As disconnected as worship and virtue might appear from one another, both the wisdom of the Church and our own experience will confirm it. I remember once being angry at my wife over some petty household argument—which I can't even remember now—and thinking that I couldn't bear to pray Evening Prayer. I knew that once I prayed, I would have better perspective and be more centered—and I would have to acknowledge that she was right!

I also want to offer a word of caution concerning another kind of measurement. Sometimes we get the sense that the point of spiritual devotions (or even church services and sacraments) is to feel uplifted or inspired. We say it "worked" if we felt the Spirit moving or if we felt a spiritual high. I am a firm believer in the presence and the movement of the Spirit. I have discerned it in liturgical worship, in free-church worship, in the sacraments, and outside of them as well. And yet I have also felt emotional states that seem much like the Spirit that passed quickly or were the result of some kind of emotional manipulation. You cannot manipulate the Spirit, and you can't manipulate long-term formation. The point of a solid devotional practice is not momentary surges of emotion; long-term formation and transformation is measured in years and decades. Sometimes good and worthwhile devotional practices will inspire us—and sometimes they may feel more like work for long stretches of time.

As we continue to think together about spirituality, I want you to keep all of this in the back of your mind: We are doing this for a reason. There is a purpose to all of this. There is a goal. We want to connect back to the God who calls us each by name. We want to align our priorities with his priorities. We want to make our individual stories part of his greater, larger, deeper story. We want to be transformed to be as he is, so that we might love as he does so that, so graced, we might better understand and express his love for us and for all of creation.

My wife tends to get annoyed when I just go out and run. "But what are you trying to accomplish?" she'll ask me. "I dunno," I respond. "I just need to get out there for a while." She is trying to remind me that taking a run around the block to clear my head is fine. But if I am running with the idea that it is part of a whole-life plan to stay fit and healthy, this sort of aimless occasional activity really isn't moving toward that goal. Those who embrace this fitness thing as a lifelong discipline have in-seasons and out-seasons. They train for specific events to help them stay motivated, and above all, they have three interlocking tools to bring it all together: a set of workouts with a clear function and purpose, a training plan that works with their schedule, and a coach who alternately encourages them to work harder and to ease off as necessary.

These three tools—effective exercises, a training plan, and a coach—are just as essential for cultivating the spiritual life. We find our effective exercises within *The Book of Common Prayer*. Between its covers are a variety of different rites and devotions that give us the building blocks for a healthy and well-rounded spiritual life. We will talk about these specifically in the next section and throughout the rest of the book.

The training plan for the spiritual life is often called a "rule of life." *The Book of Common Prayer* contains an implicit rule of life and, I would suggest, using the book properly is an endeavor of claiming and incarnating this implicit rule of life. However, just like a lot of fitness plans, it is not something you can jump into all at once. It's best to work into this rule of life as you figure out how to integrate it into the demands of a busy modern life. Putting together a rule of life will help you do this. On one hand, like a training plan, it will give you a clear sense of what you need to do on certain days to get in the habit and to prepare you for the next steps. On the other hand, it will also prevent you from getting burned out if you try to take on too much at once. In my experience, when I try to adopt a complex, involved training scheme all at once, I find that I'll keep up with it for a week or so, then it will all crumble, and I'll stop doing any of it! A good rule of life should guard against this. Each season you should review it, see what should be added, adjusted, or dropped. It will free you from the anxiety of needing to take on everything "right now" because it reminds you that more can be added later once you have a good routine established.

The best way to put together a rule of life, though, is in conversation with someone who knows what he or she is doing. The best athletes put together their training plans with the help of their coach. It's always helpful to have someone outside of your own thoughts, hang-ups, and excuses who can more objectively tell you when you need to work harder and when you need to go easier on yourself. This is the role of a spiritual director.

A good spiritual director will work with you, ask you direct and pointed questions (maybe ask to see your training log!), and help you put together a rule of life that will help advance your spiritual fitness, moving you on to your goals. Often your priest can help you with this—at least in the beginning stages—but some congregations and some dioceses have specifically trained people who have been doing this for a long time. If you are planning to be serious about your spiritual fitness, it makes sense to look for a spiritual director who can give you the direction that you need.

So let's dive in, and see how *The Book of Common Prayer* gives us this set of exercises that can help us shape an effective training plan for our spiritual lives.

The Book of Common Prayer

The Book of Common Prayer 1979 is the official worship resource for The Episcopal Church. On one hand, it stands in the tradition of the English and Scottish books of common prayer that stretches back to the middle of the sixteenth century. And this tradition flows from the great stream of the historic Western liturgy that can be traced to the Apostolic Age with notable periods of formation in the sixth and eighth centuries. On the other hand, *The Book of Common Prayer* is also influenced by the recent ecumenical Liturgical Renewal Movement fostered by the Roman Catholic Second Vatican Council (1962-65) that re-energized liturgical scholarship by looking at the fourth century—the earliest period of church history for which we have solid liturgical documentation. So it is a book with a very old heritage that has been updated with the best modern thinking about what the Early Church was up to.

The Book of Common Prayer stands at the very center of Anglican spirituality. It gives us our core spiritual exercises. Furthermore, it relates them to one another in a sensible fashion, providing a baseline implicit rule of life. As we unpack this, let us start with three fundamental statements about the prayer book from which everything else proceeds. First, the prayer book is best understood not as the Sunday service book, or even as a collection of services, but as a system of Christian formation. Second, this system with its interlocking cycles has a coherent spiritual purpose. Third, this system as enshrined in the successive books of common prayer is an essential part of what it means to participate in the Anglican tradition.

THE PRAYER BOOK SYSTEM

A well-rounded fitness plan doesn't just have one kind of exercise. Instead, there are different kinds of runs; some focus on speed, others focus on distance. And these, in turn, interact with other kinds of exercises—weight training and stretching and cross-training. Some exercises are best done in groups where you receive the support and participation of others. Some can—and perhaps should—be done by yourself. The prayer book is no different. There are a variety of services in it; some can be done by yourself, some require other people, and still others are intended to gather the whole community to do them right.

When we consider the Table of Contents of *The Book of Common Prayer*, we note that—broadly—there are three general kinds of services. First, there are those that take us on a life-cycle arc from birth to death and are chiefly of a pastoral nature (meaning that there's a particular event or life-experience that is bringing the priest and the people together at that moment). Thus, there are services that take us from Thanksgiving for the Birth of a Child to Baptism (infant baptism being typical, if not the norm), to Confirmation to Marriage to Reconciliation of a Penitent to Burial. Second, there are services that order our worship on a regular repeating basis. The liturgical round is made up of three components: the liturgical calendar where we reflect upon our central mysteries through the various lenses of the seasons of the life, death, and resurrection of Christ and in his continuing witness in the lives of the saints; the Daily Office where we immerse ourselves in the scripture and psalms; and the Holy Eucharist where we gather on holy days to most perfectly embody the Body of Christ and receive the graces that the sacraments afford. Third, there are the services for ordaining and consecrating the clergy of the church: deacons, priests, and bishops. (Sometimes these are conceptually grouped together and called the Ordinal.)

Of these three kinds of services, the second (the regular repeating ones) constitute the theological, spiritual, and practical heart of the prayer book. These are the Daily Offices (consisting of Morning Prayer, Noonday Prayer, Evening Prayer, and Compline) and the Holy Eucharist (also called Holy Communion). However, they are dispersed through the book in such a way that their importance, their various elements, and their relationship are not easily identified. Grasping the content and nature of these services is the key to understanding the spiritual structure offered by the prayer book.

If the standard by which you measure the services of the church is Sunday morning, you might wonder why they are grouped together in this way. After all, one of the big shifts in the current prayer book is that Eucharist is the standard Sunday service while Morning Prayer used to be the primary one. It appears that one displaced the other, and functionally that is the case, but when we take a big step backward and get a bigger picture historically, we realize that this is a set of false options.

Indeed, the Sunday morning either/or is a relatively recent occurrence. The first Anglican prayer books replicated the Sunday morning pattern of services that they inherited from the Western liturgical tradition: Morning Prayer followed by the Great Litany followed by the Eucharist. All three were done one after the other. After the Reformation, the piece that got dropped was the consecration of the Eucharist itself: worshipers would do Morning Prayer, the Litany, and the Holy Communion service through the readings, sermon, creed, and prayers but then would stop. (Sometimes the Eucharist was only consecrated three or four times a year.) It wasn't until the late nineteenth century that a prayer book gave the option of doing either Morning Prayer or Holy Communion. So the either/or had classically been a both/and.

If these services represent the basic exercises, how do they fit together? What is the implicit rule of life here?

The heart of the prayer book system is described in the first sentence of the first real section of the prayer book called Concerning the Service of the Church:

> The Holy Eucharist, the principal act of Christian worship on the Lord's Day and other major Feasts, and Daily Morning and Evening Prayer, as set forth in this Book, are the regular services appointed for public worship in the Church (p. 13).

Here in this sentence are the three key items that we identified above. The establishment of "the Lord's Day and other major Feasts" is determined by the Calendar; the Holy Eucharist and daily Morning and Evening Prayer alternate as central public services. The Eucharist is the central exercise for the feasts; the Daily Office is the central exercise for all of the other days.

Like the natural world, *The Book of Common Prayer* has seasons. However, rather than pointing to agricultural potential or lack thereof, the prayer book constructs time around the person of Jesus in a set of seasons referred to as the temporal cycle. These include seasons such as Advent and Lent. The sanctoral cycle (which celebrates the saints) is superimposed upon the year as a succession of static days mostly independent of the seasons. The way that the prayer book orders time, then, is supposed to tell us something about our priorities. Time itself is provided with a Jesus-colored lens.

Now we move to contemplate the Holy Eucharist and Daily Office. The liturgy of the Western Church—especially liturgy that partakes of a monastic spirit—can be described as (among other things) a disciplined and bounded encounter with scripture. That is, under the early medieval monastic ideal—lifted up as a worthy pattern in the preface to the first prayer book in 1549—the scriptures were read in their entirety every year in the services of the Daily Office. The Eucharist could then cherry-pick small sections of text (known as pericopes) at its leisure, firm in the knowledge that—thanks to the constant repetition of scripture—the congregation would immediately recognize the proper text and recall its literary context.

Thus, the process of reading, hearing, and becoming familiar with scripture is located in the Daily Office with a special emphasis on the psalms. In Morning and Evening Prayer, the psalms—the garden from which the fruit of all the other scriptures may be plucked, as Athanasius put it—would be repeated regularly (weekly, monthly, or following the prayer book's seven-week cycle), and the bulk of scripture read through every year or two depending on how many lessons were used at Evening Prayer. This is fundamentally catechetical—it teaches. This pattern grounds us in the stories, the laws, the histories, and the laments of the people of God that illuminate and inform our own experiences. The biblical canticles within the Daily Office serve an important function too. They aren't just praise-bits stuck in with the "real" material; rather they are lenses and orienting devices to help us interpret the readings—especially the Song of Zechariah, the Song of Mary, and the Song of Simeon, canticles that have been part of the Offices for well over a thousand years.

The Eucharist, then, as it rolls through the seasons, offers us not only a weekly (or more frequent) experience of the grace of God but also allows us to hear and experience the Good News in several major modes: expectation, joy, enlightenment, penitence, celebration—the principle Christian affections. If the Office is primarily catechetical, the Eucharist is primarily mystagogical. That is, it leads us by experiences of grace into the mystery of God and the relationship that God is calling us into with him and with the entire created order through him.

The final aspect of the prayer book system is that the Calendar, the Office, and the Eucharist all form us for a continual practice of personal prayer. While the prayer book gives us the words for our common prayer, these words likewise offer models for how we converse with God in our private and passing moments. This then is the prayer book's rule of life. But how, specifically, does such a rule of life help us get to the end goal of Christian spirituality?

THE SPIRITUALITY OF
THE PRAYER BOOK SYSTEM

The purpose of any spiritual system is to bring the practitioner and their community into a deeper relationship with God—to create a family of mature Christians. Through their increasing awareness of who God is, how much God loves them and all of creation, they translate the love they have been shown into concrete acts of love and mercy in the world around them. Different spiritual systems use a variety of strategies to accomplish this. One of the classic ones—referred to in Saint Paul's direction to "pray without ceasing" (1 Thessalonians 5:17)—is the recollection of God. The idea here is that if we can continually keep in mind the goodness of God, the constant presence of God, and an awareness of the mighty works of God on behalf of us and others, then we will more naturally and more completely act in accordance with God's will and ways. Continual recollection is nearly impossible, but there are methods to help us in this habit.

A primary goal of liturgical spirituality—that is, spirituality that is grounded and formed by regularly repeated fixed patterns of prayers, scripture, and ritual actions—is to create a disciplined recollection of God. Thus, if we specifically pause at central points of time—morning and evening; noon and night; Sundays and other holy days—to reorient ourselves toward God and the mighty acts of God, whether recalled to us through the scriptures or experienced by us through direct encounters with the sacraments, then this discipline will lead us toward a habitual recollection of God.

In the liturgical round, *The Book of Common Prayer* gives us specific moments to stop and orient our time and ourselves around the recollection of God. As a result, one of the most important parts of the book is the Daily Office section that provides forms for prayer at morning, noon, evening, and night. These prayer Offices are our fundamental tools for disciplined recollection; they provide the foundation for our spiritual practice. This foundation, then, is punctuated by the Eucharist on holy days (at the least). And, conceptually, this is how we should view Sundays—not the day of the week on which we go to church—but as a Holy Day that recurs on a weekly basis.

Committing ourselves to living out these patterns is what makes us a prayer book people. I can call myself a runner, but I can't earn that title unless I get out there and run. If I run once or twice a month, I am not really a runner, even if I want to be one—or want to see myself as one. The title is earned by doing it; it doesn't matter if I'm fast or slow, the point is whether I actually run. It's the same way with the prayer book. We have these cycles to use, to inhabit, if we want to be a prayer book people, a liturgical people. There is a big difference between dipping into it every once in a while and committing to live within its patterns.

While this sounds awfully churchy, it's actually not. Indeed, this liturgical structure was mediated into the prayer book tradition by a spiritual devotion for the laity that was widely embraced by regular people who lived outside of churches and monasteries. The idea of the Daily Office was originally a regular communal practice. By the end of the fourth century, the Daily Office was transitioning into a monastic practice and began to be less of a feature in lay life. By the medieval period, it was expected that the laity would be at Matins (Morning Prayer) and Vespers (Evening Prayer)—as well as Mass—on holy days. Thus, regular folks would only attend Morning and Evening Prayer a few times a month. However, a new spiritual practice grew up that took the monastic pattern as a model but adapted it to the lives of lay people.

The rise of lay literacy in the high medieval period brought with it the Books of Hours. These were the central devotional books used by laypeople (men and women alike), and they contained a cycle of Offices that followed the basic structure of the monastic and priestly Office but with fewer psalms and greatly reduced seasonal variations. It offered regular folks a way to join in the Church's great cycles of prayer but in a manner that did not require retiring entirely from the world. They could read or say these abbreviated prayer hours and still lead their lives. On the eve of and during the English Reformation, the Latin Books of Hours and the English-language prymers that replaced them held an important place in the devotional lives of upper- and middle-class lay Christians who prayed these Offices on a daily basis. The Daily Offices that appeared in our initial 1549 *Book of Common Prayer*—and in every subsequent book—are equally derived from these lay prymers as well as the Sarum breviaries (the Daily Office books used by priests and monastics in England at the time).[3] This Daily Office pattern in the prayer book is often described as taking the books of the clergy and allowing the laity to use them. However, it is just as fair— and perhaps more accurate—to say that these prayer book

Offices were the regular devotions of the laity with more room provided for the scripture and the psalms.

Why is this particular point important? Because it gives us the proper perspective: the Daily Office isn't a clergy thing that gets dumped on the laity, but a habit, a lay thing, that was maturing as scripture became more accessible to an English-reading public.

THE PRAYER BOOK SYSTEM AND THE ANGLICAN TRADITION

This pattern of prayer—the Daily Offices prayed twice a day and the Eucharist at least weekly if not more frequently—is the common heritage of the Christian Church. The Eastern Orthodox churches have it; the Roman Catholic Church has it; the Anglican churches have it. All of these churches understand that not everybody is going to be doing all of this praying all of the time—and that's okay. However, in the Eastern and Roman Catholic traditions, the Daily Offices (referred to as the Divine Praises and the Liturgy of the Hours respectively) as daily practices are virtually the province of clergy and monastics. Lay people, for the most part, are not aware of them or encouraged to do them except when they might appear publicly on Sundays or important feast days. Indeed, Roman Catholic spirituality since the time of the Reformation has emphasized daily Eucharist to the point that any other kind of daily service would be considered odd by the laity. The Anglican tradition is the only one that has consistently insisted by means of the prayer book that clergy and laity alike participate in this cycle of worship, formation, and transformation on a daily basis. I say by means of the prayer book advisedly: Our books insist on it, but that doesn't mean that the people have always practiced it and that the clergy have always taught it.

However, many of the reform movements within Anglicanism have been anchored by a call back to the prayer book system of prayer and devotion. We see it with the Caroline Divines; we see it with the Oxford Movement; we see it with the Victorian English Revival. We even see it with the lifelong Anglicans John and Charles Wesley. The prayer book system is part of the method that earned the name of Methodism.

Can you be an Anglican without engaging, practicing, knowing, or caring about the prayer book system? Of course. Millions of Anglicans do it every day! But can you be an Anglican deeply engaged in the art and practice of Anglican spirituality without grappling with this system? As the prayer book represents a major strand of Anglican DNA, inattention to its rhythms and structure results in a severely restricted enjoyment of the Anglican experience. This is the homeland of Anglican spirituality. Even when Anglican churches and their flocks have not been diligent in this practice, living daily in the words of *The Book of Common Prayer*, there is value in realizing that it exists, seeing it as a devotional ideal, and understanding our own efforts within the sweep of the larger picture of the Church's spiritual work, past and present.

Basic Principles for Liturgical Worship

Liturgical worship can be both daunting and confusing for those encountering it for the first time. And that is to be expected. It has its own internal rules and logics; once you get an idea of what these are, then it makes more sense. However, not all of these internal logics are obvious or self-evident; there are people who have been worshiping in this way their whole lives who may not be aware of them either.

Think again of running: It's something that most people have done to one degree or another all of their lives. Yet when someone chooses to take up running as a central part of an active lifestyle, they often need to re-learn some of the fundamental principles like posture, hydration, and structuring different kinds of runs for a better overall effect. Can you run without learning these things? Sure. You can strap on a pair of shoes and pound the pavement a few times a week without this knowledge. But you will achieve your goals more quickly and more safely—and with less pain—if you take the time to learn some basic principles.

ADORATION

Modern American secular society is a transactional society. As a result, children absorb the principles of commercial transactions at a young age: If you want something, you have to pay for it; if you pay for something, you'd better get it. As a result, it's no surprise that many of us start out with a vending-machine model of God. As a child, I remember getting a sense that if I prayed for something, I should get it—if I didn't get it, God either didn't like me or wasn't being fair. I outgrew this perception, of course, as all do who have prayed for God to give them a pony. Nevertheless, I think many of us still have a vaguely transactional sense of worship. That if we are faithful and diligent in our attendance, God somehow owes us—as if we were building up credit to be used when we get stuck in a jam. Or, on the flip side, attendance at worship is a bargaining chip to be held over God's head. ("Do this thing for me, and I'll start going to church/I'll go to church a lot more/I'll never miss church.")

It doesn't work like that.

When we consider the principles of liturgical worship, it's helpful to take a quick look at the various ways in which we address God. Different traditions break down the aspects of worship and prayer in various ways, but one of the most common schemes (and the one referenced in the prayer book's catechism) identifies seven types: adoration, praise, thanksgiving, penitence, oblation, intercession, and petition.[4]

I see adoration and praise as interrelated because of what is driving them—nothing but God. Praise is worship directed toward God for no other reason than rejoicing in the person and presence of God. It is not bribery to get something; it is flat-out joy in the Lord's presence. Adoration is one step closer still: It is relaxing in the direct presence of God.

Thanksgiving is driven primarily by past events. This is when we give thanks for what God has already done for us (and with us and through us) and for the wonder, majesty, and delight of God's creation.

Oblation is prayer driven by our response to God and God's works: At the heart of oblation is offering. Specifically, we offer ourselves—as well as our works— to God to be united with his will and works. I see this as related to thanksgiving but the next logical step beyond it.

Penitence, intercession, and petition are different from the others because they are all asking for something. In penitence, we acknowledge (and bewail) our sins and ask God for forgiveness. In intercession, we ask God for things on behalf of others, recalling individuals, groups, and ultimately all creation to God's memory—and our own. In petition, we make requests to God based on our own needs.

The liturgical worship of *The Book of Common Prayer* contains all seven of these elements in different balances at different points. All forms of Christian worship have these seven aspects to various degrees. One of the strengths of liturgical worship is that the balance between these elements is stable.

Within the Eucharist and the Daily Office, the first three—adoration, praise, and thanksgiving—predominate. That's not to say that the others don't have a place and don't appear, but these liturgies emphasize the praise of God and rejoicing in God's presence. The fundamental and primary purpose of liturgical worship is praise and adoration. It's about celebrating the relationship; it's about experiencing the vastness of who and what God is. It's not flattery with an eye to scoring something off the Big Guy at a time to be named later. God does not need our praise; God is not subject to our manipulation.

FORMATION

Having said that the primary point of worship is the praise and adoration of God, I'm going to turn that around on us. The praise and adoration of God is and must be our primary purpose in worship—but God doesn't need it. God is not made greater for our praise; God is God perfectly well without us. We are the ones who need to be reminded—we're the ones who have to have the Gospel held before our eyes lest we forget and forsake it. So, despite God being the fundamental aim of our worship, if we are to speak of benefit at all, we do it for our benefit.

As a result, the way we worship has to accomplish its aim but also must be formational to those of us who participate in it. It needs to draw our minds and hearts to God. It needs to facilitate a lively encounter with the Holy One whom we praise. It needs to give us the tools for understanding what it means to be in the midst of holy things, holy people, and the holy presences within holy places. It needs to feed our sense of the sacred so that, once we have returned to more ostensibly secular living, we may spy out the presence of the holy woven in the warp and weft of the world around us and within us. In worship we are given the signatures, the characteristics, the tastes of God in a deliberate sense so that we are more able to recognize them when and where we least expect them.

There is a danger in realizing that worship is for us: That is when formation usurps the purpose and becomes the primary focus. When the nave is turned into a lecture hall or when worship becomes an exercise in consciousness-raising, we have lost sight of God. Edification, formation, is an important secondary purpose of worship but, whenever it moves into primacy, we move into an idolatrous self-worship where we take the center rather than the Living God.

No less idolatrous, of course, is when worship becomes its own end, and its aesthetic qualities and technical performance edge out adoration. Worship too consumed by its own elegance is a worship of ourselves and the works of our own hands. I say this not because I don't like beautiful and elegant worship—indeed, I say it precisely because I do. Beauty and holiness are essential aspects of worship done well; care, precision, and planning are essential for worship to be what it can be. And yet whenever our focus is turned from God, we have substantially missed the mark because the purpose of the worship has gone awry.

The true formation found in worship consists of orienting the soul toward God and aligning us within God's vision of reality. In worship, we are turned to God in praise and adoration and are given to see the rest of creation as fellow worshipers hymning God with their very being. This is the edification that we need. Whenever worship moves toward ostensible edification, it loses its primary focus—God—and, in doing so, loses its power to orient us beyond ourselves in him. Thus, edification is an important secondary aspect of worship, but if it ever threatens to take primary place, then its very value is undermined.

REPETITION

Liturgical worship is founded on the principle of repetition. There are patterns and habits that make us who and what we are. The shape of worship shapes our character; the texts of worship pattern our priorities; the ways of relating to one another performed in the liturgy rehearse principles for engagement outside of worship as well. Worship is—literally—habit-forming. And it's supposed to be. We don't repeat certain words or prayers or texts because we are unable to think of anything else or have no other substitutes; we repeat them because we believe they are important and worth repeating over and over again.

Modern brain science tells us that an action has to be repeated daily for roughly forty days for it to become a habit. My martial arts teachers tell me that the Chinese reckon daily practice for one hundred days as the small accomplishment, 1,000 days as the middle accomplishment, and 10,000 days as the great accomplishment—and that no one should presume to teach without the middle accomplishment at least (roughly three years of daily practice) on the grounds that they have not yet achieved sufficient understanding.

Repetition happens in a few different ways in the prayer book system. The first is the repetition of services. Morning and Evening Prayer truly are the bedrock of the system; their daily, weekly, and yearly repetition shapes us like nothing else. The Eucharist and the sacraments of the Church become the punctuation of this ongoing rhythm.

The second is the repetition of texts and actions. The same texts and the same body of texts are rehearsed over and over. Some—like the Lord's Prayer and the Apostles' Creed—are repeated multiple times a day. Some—like certain psalms and canticles—are repeated several times a week. Some—like our Eucharistic Prayers—are repeated at least once a week. The Psalter is run through monthly or in a seven-week cycle; scripture itself—or at least a fulsome quantity—is covered every year or two. As we gather in corporate worship, our rituals of greeting, responding, and reconciling with one another are patterns of relating designed to help us see Christ and find the holy in the other.

Repetition teaches in a variety of ways; it is not just a matter of gaining information or training a skill. One of the most fruitful teachings of repetition comes through exhaustion: In martial arts training, constant repetition of an act or form wears out the muscles—no matter how strong they may be—and forces the body to learn efficiency. Our body learns something in a special way when the muscles are burdened, deadened, and ultimately desensitized by repetition; at a certain point the neuromuscular motion breaks down, and the repetition becomes an act of will—the will guiding and sustaining it as the body finds on its own a minimal efficiency that enables the motion to continue. It is then that the deepest levels of learning occur. At this point, it's no longer a matter of being fun or enjoyable or even good exercise—it's passed purely into the realm of discipline.

What are our expectations of our spiritual practices? Do we expect them to be fun or enjoyable or a good spiritual stretch? What happens if we come to them and find them no longer fun? We speak of a discipline of prayer because the repetition of the liturgical round requires discipline. It requires commitment to the concept of repetition even when we don't feel like we're getting anything out of it.

VARIATION

But repetition on its own can get a bit boring. Even worse than being boring, repetition without allied aspects and disciplines can become rote and stagnant, allowing the mind and focus to wander and reducing the formative texts and actions to mechanical and thoughtless motions and mumblings. As a result, the liturgical round has principles of variation built into it. Variation—a break from the routine, a deliberate alteration in the pattern—not only keeps our attention and keeps us mindful but can also break open new vistas into prayers and practices that we thought we already knew.

The seasons of the liturgical year are one of our chief vehicles of variation. As the seasons highlight different aspects of the Christian Gospel, liturgical texts are required or omitted; the *Gloria* disappears in Lent, the *Pascha Nostrum* appears in Easter. These changes may be slight, but they subtly alter our experience of worship. Sometimes we don't notice any effect on us. At other times, they may catalyze a new understanding of God, life, and everything. At the least, the changes through the seasons—whether those be textual or the ornamentation of the worship space or the kinds of music chosen (when there is music)—communicate something of the unique character of the time.

One of the most constant sources of variation is found in the scripture texts deployed in worship. The psalms and lessons prescribed by the lectionary are just as much a part of the liturgy as the prayers. The lectionaries present scriptural pieces—stories or prophecies or teachings—that combine to communicate the deep meaning of the season in which they are placed. The changing psalms give us something new in the otherwise stable structure of Morning and Evening Prayer. Variation is the spice for repetition that helps us keep our minds and hearts engaged.

Again, we can see the parallels to running. If you train like it is in-season all of the time, you're going to injure yourself. Instead, you push hard in some seasons; you cut back in others. You add in speed workouts on the track or hill-repeats in the weeks before an important race; you do fewer in the off-season when you're just maintaining your general level of fitness. More rest days and long runs give the body what it needs without undue stress on the various parts.

Some people need more variation than others. I also think some times, places, and cultures tend to need more or less variation than others. Modern westerners on the whole prefer a higher level of variation in liturgies than we see in other times and places. The prayer book is helpful here in both respects: It offers ways that variation can be introduced but also controls just how much can be altered so that the benefits of balanced repetition are not completely lost.

CONTINUITY

One of the most beautiful images from the Book of Revelation is the image of the cosmic chorus encircling the celestial throne of God and the Lamb in chapters 4 and 5. Revelation gives us a sense of the whole world oriented in a continuous outpouring of praise in the presence of God. Holding this image in mind, we gain the sense that our worship only appears to begin and end. We temporarily join our voices to the unending chorus of praise. We slip in and out of that eternal song. Whenever we pray and worship, whether we are in a crowd of thousands, together with only a few, or if we are in our room alone, our prayer and worship is never strictly an individual thing. Because of this greater praise, our personal prayer and praise is always corporate because our worship contributes to the whole.

Liturgical worship helps us remember this because we are not just joined in the principle of prayer—we are also united with the whole in its practice. The liturgy gives us a tangible sense of continuity with the rest of the Christian family across both space and time. When we use the words of *The Book of Common Prayer*, we are sharing common words with all those in our church. Not only that, but we are also praying in union with Anglicans across the world. Our prayer joins us across space and connects us with the Communion of Saints through time as well. We share practices with all those who have used books of common prayer across the past five hundred years. We share with all those who came before, and we bear witness to the prayer and praise of the Church stretching to the time of the apostles. Indeed—language aside—the Eucharist from the seventh-century Leonine sacramentary (one of the oldest surviving liturgical books) would seem pretty familiar to anyone used to the Eucharist from our American prayer book dating from 1979.

STABILITY

This great continuity across time leads us to the last principle—stability. Despite the passage of ages and the many cultures it has moved through, the liturgy has provided a coherent and continuous pattern of understanding, communicating, and living the Gospel. Indeed, *The Book of Common Prayer* as a whole has been prayed over generations and centuries.

The prayer book is an authentic expression of the historic Western liturgy that has nourished millions who have come before us. It is an authentic expression of the English devotional experience. The importance of this is not that it's English, of course, but that it is a rooted, embodied, and inherited tradition that has been embraced and passed on by a diverse group over centuries—not just dreamed up by a few people last week. Furthermore, the prayer book is an authentic expression of historic Anglican liturgy that balances reform of Western norms with scripture and the theological and spiritual practices of the Early Church.

Because of this long period of use, because of its proven ability to form Christians, the prayer book system commends itself to our use. Repetition and formation work best when we commit ourselves to a given pattern of practice. The prayer book offers us a stable set of practices capable of sustaining the spirit across decades, through highs and lows, enthusiasms and doldrums.

Basic Disciplines for Liturgical Worship

THE NEED FOR DISCIPLINES

On my more optimistic days, I have faith in the formative power of the liturgy. Much of the work of the liturgy on the soul occurs passively. That is, it's a matter of trusting the process. We may not feel it working on us, but following the prayer book system, being in the liturgies, participating in the prayers, will have a long-term effect whether we realize it or not. General wisdom is that eighty percent of success is simply showing up—and that certainly seems to apply here.

However, at the end of the day, just being there isn't enough. There are people who live in these liturgical cycles yet who seem not to be transformed and changed by them, who can exhibit the baser tendencies of human nature unaltered by their liturgical practice.

Showing up is important—but it isn't enough.

In a central scene from *The Godfather: Part III*, the aging mafia boss Michael Corleone meets with the fictional Cardinal Lamberto. In speaking about the nature of things, the cardinal takes a stone out of a fountain. Although the rock has been sitting in water for years, the cardinal breaks it open to reveal that it is completely dry inside. He then says to the crime boss, "The same thing has happened with men in Europe. For centuries, they have been surrounded by Christianity. But Christ has not penetrated it. Christ does not live within them."[5]

Showing up is important—but it isn't enough.

I don't want to be a rock. I want to be a sponge. I want to be permeated and saturated by my environment. I want my insides to be touched as much as my outsides. I don't want to simply experience the cycles of the liturgy; I want to be altered and transformed by them.

If eighty percent of success in the liturgy is just showing up, than the other twenty percent may well be about making it count, about opening up the insides. This is where we get to the disciplines that can enhance and amplify our liturgical practice. These are the long-term habits that help us open our minds and our hearts to what is going on around us, that crack open our shells and enable the waters of life to seep within us and change us. As we discussed earlier, it may be helpful to think about these habits from an active perspective: These are the things that we do to cooperate with God's transforming grace. Alternatively, you may resonate with a more passive construction: These are the things that help us stop resisting God's embrace and help us relax into the person of God.

I will focus here on six disciplines that can help us delve deeply into our liturgical worship: participation, attentiveness, memorization, diligence, stability, and intentionality.

PARTICIPATION

When we come before the Lord to worship, when we prepare ourselves to once again take the plunge into the unending choruses of praise to God and to the Lamb, it means fully committing. If we're there to praise, then let every part of us join in the praise. Check the psalms. Does it really say, "Let the sea thunder and all that is in it; let the field be joyful and all that is therein. Then shall all the trees of the woods fold their branches over their trunks and just stand there stoically while everyone else is singing as if they're too cool to join in (perhaps in a slightly ironic way)."[6]

I didn't think so. And yet, I see this almost every week at worship.

During colonial times, two people appeared at the front of the church to make worship happen: the priest and the clerk or reader. If you go into some of our oldest Episcopal churches that still have their original furniture, you might see a two-level pulpit: The priest stood in the upper part while the clerk stood in the lower. The priest was, well, the priest, and he would say the priest parts. The clerk was a layman, and his job was to lead the speaking parts for the people. On one hand, this setup has benefits—with the clerk leading, participants knew when to say what they needed to say. And, in a time where the congregation had varying degrees of literacy, it was always helpful to have at least one person who could read. On the other hand, it also became entirely too easy to sit back and let the clerk do his thing instead of seeing him as the leader for our thing. The Victorian liturgical scholar Walter Frere speaks unfavorably of this duet between the priest and the clerk or, later, the priest and the choir. In both cases, the congregation sat in as the audience while someone else performed their parts. In his book, *Principles of Religious Ceremonial*, Frere describes this—quite rightly—as a low-point for liturgy.

We have inherited *The Book of Common Prayer* so that we can pray together in common. The fact that the Anglican tradition has always provided access for the whole people to the whole service speaks volumes about what we understand participation to be. When the prayer book says "People," it doesn't intend a token representative but the whole body. Thankfully, the clerk phenomenon has not been a big part of Episcopal worship in recent years, but the point still stands: The prayer book tradition is a participatory tradition. The intention has always been that the congregation should be engaged intellectually, spiritually, and verbally in what is going on.

Participation does, at the minimum, three things. First, it is much easier to engage and remain engaged in the act of worship when we are verbally involved. The acts of listening, responding, rolling the words around in our mouths connect us to what is going on around us. Second, our verbal participation represents an assent to the content of the words. When we join in, we are affirming what is being said—we believe it, or at least have an understanding that this is what the Church teaches and that we are committed to it, even as we may wrestle with some phrases. In fact, that is what "amen" means—it's a Hebrew word meaning so be it or yes, indeed! Third, participation both signals and creates a rapport with the people around us. We don't come to public worship in the church by ourselves and for our own sake. Public worship is corporate worship in the most literal of senses. We form a body, the Body of Christ into whom we were baptized. As we come together, we are separate members of the Body of Christ joining back together, re-forming the Body in a simultaneously spiritual and literal sense. When people stand silent in such a gathering, their actions call into question their relationship to the rest of the Body.

Participation in singing is a slightly different story, but the same principles should be kept in mind. Not everyone sings—or sings well—I understand that. There are different patterns of participation of singing in worship. Some folks are better singers than others. Some are shy. Some don't read music or don't read it well enough to feel comfortable joining in from the beginning of a song—particularly if it's a new one. Some guys might think it unmanly (and they would be totally wrong on that count). Some people were raised in churches where singing isn't common or is frowned upon—whether officially or by long-standing custom.

After pointing out the myriad instructions to sing parts of the service from the psalms to the prayers to the creeds to the hymns, Victorian scholar John Henry Blunt in the *Annotated Book of Common Prayer* confidently concluded, "The devotional system of the Prayer Book is, therefore, a singing system; and the Church of England is what the Mediaeval, the Primitive, and the Jewish Churches were, 'a Singing Church.'" As framed notices in choir rooms across the world will attest, the great early African theologian Saint Augustine of Hippo really did say that, "To sing is to pray twice" (once with the words, and again with the beauty of the voice raised in song).

The goal should be for the whole congregation to join in song at the congregational singing parts—service music and hymns alike. That means as congregants, we have a responsibility to raise our voices and join them with those around us—even if we do so softly. But we aren't the only ones who have a say in this situation; the musicians and worship planners can have an impact here as well. Some music—particularly some of the pop styles of recent years—works better for individual performers than large groups. A wide vocal range from high to low notes, complex rhythms, and jumps in pitch are hard for the average congregation to sing and to sing well together. The choice of the music can sabotage the intention to participate even if it is entirely inadvertent on the part of the musicians.

Participation in the service, whether in the sung or the spoken parts, is an important part of aligning yourself with the intention and the purpose of the liturgy. That is not to say that there aren't other modes of participation—not all participation is active participation—but vocal participation in conscious consonance with the body around you is a hallmark of Anglican liturgy at its best.

In some churches, parts of the service music may be sung by the choir in English, Latin, or another language. Is it possible to fully participate if this is happening? After all, the language may not be one you understand, and your neighbors might frown on you trying to join in with the choir. All is not lost here. As we will discuss a bit later when we tackle the Eucharist, the *Gloria in Excelsis* (Glory to God in the Highest) and the *Sanctus* (Holy, Holy, Holy) are themselves songs that scripture places in the mouths of the angels. They both represent and embody that ceaseless chorus of praise that we are privileged to join at least temporarily.

We can participate fully even when someone else is doing the singing if we do two important things: First, we participate by engaging the meaning of what is being sung. We can still roll the words around in our minds if it is a part of the service music that we know. In most churches, if the music is in a language other than the mother tongue of the congregation, a translation usually is (and certainly should be) provided. Second, we need to revel in the beauty. We sometimes forget that beauty is an apt attribute of God and that our worship communicates God and proclaims the Gospel with a greater authenticity when beauty is placed in its service. A good choir can metaphorically transport us, conjuring sonically the whole celestial realm and its heavenly chorus with whom we join in praising God.

ATTENTIVENESS

If intentionality is about keeping ourselves focused on the big picture, then attentiveness is the related-but-different discipline of keeping our eye on the little picture. It is the discipline of remaining in the present and being attentive to what we're doing, the words we're hearing, the words we're saying, the rite that we're experiencing. Attentiveness is remaining in the moment.

Most of us like to think we're pretty good at this already. Alas, it only takes a brief experiment to show us how wrong we are. Go ahead. Make the exercise of remaining in the present as simple as you can. Cut out all distractions and attempt to sit in silence for five minutes; remain attentive and present by counting your breaths up to ten and starting over again. If you are like me, it won't take too long before your mind is flitting all over the place. You realize that you stopped counting a while back, or you discover that you finished planning your grocery list while you counted to twenty-five. This phenomenon is aptly described by Zen teachers as monkey mind. You discover that however disciplined you *thought* your thoughts were, they dash around like a hyper little primate at the drop of a hat.

Here's the thing: Our struggle with being present in the moment doesn't just arise when we are trying to sit in silence and count breaths. It is a challenge all of the time. The counting of breaths just helps us to notice the problem more clearly. Hence the need for attentiveness. And, as much as I'd like to blame it on mobile devices, the Internet, or TV, spiritual writers have been wrestling with the issue of attentiveness since at least the fourth century and likely earlier. So, how do we cage the little monkey for as long as we need so that we can pray, sing, and join in the worship of God?

This requires a multi-pronged approach. The first and most basic step is to recognize that the situation exists in the first place. When you are in a service and you realize that your mind has wandered, gently but firmly direct it back. Don't beat yourself up about it. Your mind will only use that as an excuse to go wandering off again about what a failure you are. As frequently as you find yourself wandering, just direct yourself back.

One of the few bodily gestures inserted into English canon law also provides an opportunity for attentiveness. In 1603, canon 18 enjoined that everyone present should make "due and lowly reverence" at the name of Jesus—that is, bow the head. At the parish where I learned this custom, it was explained as an honoring of the Incarnation. As a result, the head was bowed whenever the names Jesus, Mary, or the saint of the day were said, each reminding us of God's incarnational presence in the world. I find that this sort of brief physical response helps me to pay better attention—to listen harder and to focus more clearly on the task at hand.

When praying alone from a book or saying the Daily Office by yourself, another tactic for retaining attentiveness is to engage as many senses as possible. Reading silently gives your mind ample opportunities for wandering. The act of reading aloud greatly improves the experience: You get the lips moving, and you hear the sound of your own words in addition to the passing of the mind over the letters. Adding in further physical gestures—like bowing or crossing yourself or kneeling—may help.

A fifteenth-century devotional for English nuns recommends that attentiveness is much improved when you remember yourself to be in the presence of Jesus and imagine him close by you.[7] If you hold in mind that you are speaking your words of praise directly to him, the feeling of being in conversation can help keep you more attentive.

The same devotional also makes a broad statement, noting that inattention in saying the Office is related to inattentive habits outside of the Office as well. I think I would rather say it the other way—habits of discipline outside of worship help us be more disciplined within it. As far as habits of discipline go, there is none better than a daily bout of breath meditation.

Simply sitting in silence for ten to twenty minutes, counting your breaths to ten, then starting over again, is a very useful tool for learning your mind more deeply, getting a handle on your inner life, and gradually soothing the hyper little monkey that seems to live there.

I have heard some people express concerns over such a practice because it is Buddhist rather than being properly Christian. To my mind, that is as silly as a wrestler saying that he couldn't do push-ups because they're a football exercise. Just as push-ups are a universal fitness exercise, breath meditation in various forms, under various names, and taught in various ways is a universal tool for spiritual fitness. While it may be best known in modern America as a Zen practice, breath meditation has been part of Christian spiritual practice at least since the time of the fourth-century Desert Fathers and Mothers, if not before. Breath meditation is also an excellent foundational discipline if you choose to explore the tradition of contemplative prayer.

At the end of the day, attentiveness touches deep chords around the practices of an intentional, incarnational life. The principle of incarnation takes seriously the reality of God, the ongoing presence of Christ, the movement of the Holy Spirit within our normal, daily, earthly life—described by Julian of Norwich as the "full homely divinity" rightly celebrated in our Anglican tradition. If we are not able to be fully present in the present of each moment, then these daily incarnations, these moments of God's self-revelation, will slip past us, unnoticed as our minds flit from past to present to imaginary worlds of our own making.

MEMORIZATION

While I am tempted to file this discipline as a subset of attentiveness, it's important enough to earn its own section. We are more attentive in corporate worship when we can follow along, and, while we are a people of the book, that doesn't always mean we have to be stuck in the book! One of the glories of worship conducted in the tradition of the prayer book is that so much of it repeats, both daily and weekly. As a result, over time, it will become ingrained in your memory.

When my elder daughter was quite small—maybe four or so—I was concerned about her lack of attention during church; she would frequently color when I wanted her to pay attention (but since she was being quiet, I didn't make a fuss). Then, one day, I noticed a strange sight: of her own volition, she went into our parlor, lined up her stuffed animals in front of a small organ bench topped with a cross she'd swiped from somewhere, and began doing church complete with most of Eucharistic Prayer A! I learned two very important things from this: Attentiveness may come in a variety of forms (especially in the young), and memorization occurs naturally with the prayer book rite.

It is easier to be attentive to words that are already a part of us. When we pray alone, it is easier to stay focused on prayers we already know. It's easier to stay focused on the words the priest is praying if we are praying them silently along with her. Memorization can happen by osmosis—indeed, it's easiest if it happens that way—but the passive acquisition of the liturgy is only enhanced when we set out to actively acquire it as well.

As in acting, make sure you know your own lines first. Memorize the congregational parts of the Eucharist. Make sure you know the fundamentals: the basic responses, the Kyrie, the Gloria, the Creed, the Confession, the Post-

Communion prayers. Then, the central canticles of the Office: the Song of Zechariah, the Song of Mary, the Song of Simeon. Other pieces will suggest themselves to you from there.

We will talk about this later, but the collects of the prayer book represent a great distillation of our tradition. And when I say tradition, I mean that our prayer book includes collects from the time of the Church Fathers—that is, the writers and thinkers from the first four centuries of the Church's existence—to the present, with many of the Sunday collects having their origins in the sixth or seventh centuries. Taking time each week to commit the collect to memory will place you in living conversation with these spiritual and theological gems.

I have found that the more I memorize (or the more that memorization happens to me), the more I understand the interrelation of our liturgical language. For instance, I remember the first time I realized that the words "…walking in holiness and righteousness…" in the General Thanksgiving at Morning and Evening Prayer come from the Song of Zechariah ("…holy and righteous in his sight…"). Then, a while later, reading an alternate history book set in post-Civil War America by a favorite (Jewish) sci-fi author, I was astounded to see a character make proclamation that was full of prayer book language.[8] The Author's Note confirmed that most of the speeches in the book had been adapted from actual addresses of the period, and, without having to look it up, I recognized from the rhythms and the rhetoric a nineteenth-century prayer book Episcopalian connecting with his audience through words familiar to them all. Sure enough, upon Googling it, I found that the proclamation was an adaptation of one by Jefferson Davis, Confederate president—and Episcopalian.[9]

Indeed, this is how the real fruits of memorization occur. Little bits of the liturgies will float up unannounced. Maybe

it is sparked by a couple of words put in combination by
a colleague or a snatch of song—they strike a chord with
something buried in your memory. Often, my most fruitful
theological thoughts and connections occur in this way as my
subconscious mulls over something I've memorized without
being quite aware of it. Moments like these move us closer to
the habitual recollection of God, that end to which liturgical
spirituality directs.

DILIGENCE

This one is pretty obvious but it still needs to be said. We are
talking about habits, formation, the process of constructing
an abiding Christian character through the discipline of
regular worship that leads toward the habitual recollection of
God. This can't happen without diligence. Acts don't become
habits if they're not practiced on a regular, repeating basis.
American historian and philosopher Will Durant offered this
summary of Aristotle's ethics: "We are what we repeatedly
do. Excellence, then, is not an act, but a habit."[10] The same is
true of spirituality. It is not an act (or, alternatively, if we don't
want it to *be* an act); it must be a habit.

A devotion like the Daily Office does its work in a period
measured by decades, not moments or occasions. We can't
pray it occasionally and expect it to bear fruit. Likewise,
treating corporate worship as a once a month, drop-in-if-the-
mood-strikes affair fails to train us in the paths of holiness
that weekly attendance does.

This is not to try to set up a New Legalism. There was a
letter that started floating around Europe and the Middle East
at some point in the sixth century, originally composed in
Latin and eventually translated into virtually every medieval
local language. It was allegedly written by Christ himself in

heaven and dropped through the clouds into Jerusalem, and it is filled with dire warnings against anyone who didn't go to church on Sundays and who did any sort of secular work.[11] In countries where people did work, it threatened plagues, famines, and widespread disasters. I am happy to say that several councils and church leaders denounced this crude attempt at social control, including Saint Boniface, the eighth-century, English-born Apostle to the Germans who had stern words for those who circulated it. Yet the mentality of the letter appeared in law codes across Europe and persists in modern day. We don't go to church on Sunday lest God blast us; rather it is both our duty and delight to worship together the God who formed us, who loves us, and who was willing to become incarnate and suffer bodily for our redemption and reconciliation.

At its most basic, the discipline of diligence is about priorities. To what degree are we willing to spend our most precious coin, that which we can neither earn nor hoard: our time? The way we choose our activities reveals our priorities above all else. Any relationship worth having must be nurtured with this precious commodity, and our relationship with God is no different.

As the father of two active children, I know how difficult it can be to carve out time. In our time-strapped age, schedulers of sporting events and dance rehearsals think nothing of seizing the Sunday morning time slot. While creative use of the available options (like Saturday or Sunday evening services) can help negotiate this treacherous turf, sometimes decisions have to be made. And on those mornings with no good alternatives when ballet wins (I'm looking at you, mandatory *Nutcracker* dress rehearsal), do we have the persistence to substitute a family act of worship in lieu of the full-on corporate experience?

To tell the truth, I am sometimes envious of my priestly wife and clergy friends for whom praying the Daily Office is (or could be or should be) part of their paid work. As a layman, I can only imagine my boss's response to a request for paid prayer time. Instead the Offices have to be fit into carefully carved out niches of time that occur between child care and house work and relationship maintenance and regular employment. I will freely admit that sometimes those carefully carved niches collapse; sometimes the time I think I have disappears. There are days when the set prayer just doesn't happen. On those days, I try to at least glance over the psalms for the day, and if that doesn't happen, at least hit the memorized highpoints of the Office, and if that doesn't happen, at least a quick prayer of apology. In the grand scheme of things, at least feeling guilty about missing the Office is itself an act of diligence.

While holding up the importance of diligence, we also have to approach the spiritual life as a marathon, not a sprint. This is a lifelong path we tread. There will be seasons of our lives where time is easier to find or harder to find. There will be periods when blocks of time come more freely and periods when it will not. This, too, is part of the ebb and flow of incarnate life. Our goal is to be as diligent as possible given the conditions in which we find ourselves.

STABILITY

While we talked about stability under the basic principles of liturgical worship, it has to be discussed as a discipline as well. In this sense, stability means rooting yourself within a set of liturgies. It means defining the center of your spiritual practice.

When I was considering graduate school, I sat with a mentor and agonized over a variety of choices, largely around which theological discipline should be my focus. After letting me go on for a while, my mentor stopped me. "It's actually very simple," he said. "What do you want to be formed as?" It was, of course, the perfect question for me at that moment. Before embarking into the process of intellectual formation, I had to consider what I wanted my fundamental tool set and perspective to be at the end of the process. Historians and theologians and textual scholars may all look at similar material; what makes them who they are and what establishes their disciplines is what questions, perspectives, and skill sets they bring to that material.

The same is true here too.

What do you want to be formed as? What will be your tool set and perspective for engaging life in God?

The prayer book offers one perspective. But it is hardly the only one. Christianity offers a wide array of spiritual tool sets, some complementary to one another, others more exclusive. There are a variety of Roman Catholic schools of practice as well as Orthodox ones; the Protestant array is even larger. Once we head outside of Christianity, there is an even broader set of possibilities. In the face of the vast multitude of options, one possibility is eclecticism, a sort of cafeteria spirituality where we take a bit from here, a bit from there, and not too much of any one thing. In the modern, consumer-driven marketplace of twenty-first century America, this option seems popular and is the hallmark of the spiritual but not religious set.

But what do you want to be formed as?

The trouble with eclecticism is that its specialty is forming spiritual dilettantes. Saint Benedict starts off his famous rule for monks with a description of different kinds of monks that turns out to be a parable of sorts. One kind of monk is the sarabite. Benedict says: "With no experience to guide them, no rule to try them as gold is tried in a furnace, [they] have a character as soft as lead. Still loyal to the world by their actions, they clearly lie to God with their tonsure. Two or three together, or even alone, without a shepherd, they pen themselves up in their own sheepfolds, not the Lord's. Their law is what they like to do, whatever strikes their fancy. Anything they believe in and choose, they call holy; anything they dislike, they consider forbidden."[12]

I hear this passage, and then I think about my own spiritual journey—the way that I wander and flit, trying out a devotion here or a practice there, and sometimes being earnest about something for a few weeks until the novelty wears off. "Their law is what they like to do, whatever strikes their fancy. Anything they believe in and choose, they call holy." It seems Benedict has put his finger on the spiritual seeker trend. Benedict is giving us a warning, born out of decades if not centuries of monastic practicality. It is fine to search, but if we expect to find transformation of self and transformation of character, we need to find something and stick with it; we need to find something and, instead of shaping it to conform with what we think we want, allow it to shape us toward what we need.

Benedict's rule cannot do this for us—we're not monks. As Episcopalians, however, the prayer book is the next best thing.

When I sit at my desk, I can look up and see two bookshelves crammed with various liturgical works and prayer books from a host of traditions past and present. As much as I love these resources, looking through them, and being inspired by things I find in them, I have a home base in *The Book of Common Prayer.*

What do you want to be formed as?

I want to be formed as an Anglican. More than that, I want to be formed as an Episcopalian. And that means dedicating myself to the patterns and poetries of practice embedded within the prayer book. I can use other sources too, but the prayer book is the center around which everything else is arranged. I rely on a variety of liturgical materials from different sources to supplement and embellish the texts of the prayer book, but my primary toolset and perspective for engaging life in God remains the prayer book. That's the kind of stability that enables transformation of life.

INTENTIONALITY

The final discipline is intentionality. Think of this as focusing our attention on the big picture. It's not enough to simply show up; we also need to hold in our minds the reason why we're showing up. God is not made greater through our worship of him; God is already greater than that. While we worship God for our own purposes, we would do well to remind ourselves of what those are and to carry them into worship with us. But we don't simply come to worship to fulfill an obligation or to gain another bargaining chip with God. Rather, we come because God is worthy of praise, and in the very act of praise and adoration, we recall to ourselves and those around us who God is and what God has done for us.

Before we participate in any act of worship—whether alongside hundreds of others or by ourselves—we would do well to stop and fix in our minds what we are about to participate in. We are here to worship God. We are here to enjoy the presence of God and to participate in the process of communicating with God alongside and in communion with a great company who have praised him through the ages. Beyond that fundamental principle shared by all forms of liturgical worship, the various liturgies have their own purposes. Be aware of what it is you are about to do. Focus on the general intention of the service in which you will participate.

Furthermore, worship is part of a pattern of orienting ourselves toward God and aligning our stories, beliefs, and principles with God's. As we consider the general intentions of the service, we also want to connect these general intentions with what is going on with us. The liturgies tend to speak in generalities—we thank God for blessings, we lift up concerns. As part of being intentional, as we take a moment to consider the big picture, we should also take a moment to consider the specific intersections between the language of the liturgy and the events of our lives. What are those specific things we are thankful for? What are the actual concerns burdening our hearts and minds?

I'll talk more about the general intentions of the various services later in the book. But briefly, specific intention is the practice of holding in mind a particular aspect of the service that touches on something going on in our lives at that moment. For instance, if someone has just died, we might choose to participate in a Eucharist holding them in mind, recognizing that—as the Eucharist connects us with the whole communion of saints—we are thankful for their place in our lives. We are comforted, knowing that our connection with them through the Eucharist has not ended but that we share the same banquet table with them. Or, if we have been touched by a particular joy as we approach the Daily Office, we might hold that joy before us as a concrete example of those things for which we praise and thank God.

Next Steps

Just as a runner needs to have the right kind of shoes, a good training plan, a set of achievable goals to shoot for, and sense of how all of these things relate to one another, these are the basic tools and techniques for an informed and engaged approach to the spiritual life from the Anglican perspective. Sure, there is more to it than just these things we explored— some we will discuss later in the book, and some we won't. Nevertheless, these are fundamentals that will help you understand and get the most out of the spiritual depths in *The Book of Common Prayer*.

Now that we have covered the fundamentals of the prayer book's implied rule of life, we have identified three particular components that fit together; the Calendar of the Church Year, the Daily Office, and the Holy Eucharist. In the following chapters, we will take a look at these three elements. Each of these topics will get three chapters. In the first chapter of each section, I'll give a basic orientation to help you understand the prayer book's perspective on the element. In the second chapter of the section, I'll look at the text of *The Book of Common Prayer* itself and point out where that element appears. In the third chapter, I will focus on an aspect of that element that has a particular pertinence for the Anglican tradition. There is no way that we can cover everything about these topics—indeed, we will barely scratch the surface! However, this way of approaching the topics provides a solid sense of how the prayer book tradition understands the core elements of liturgical spirituality.

NOTES

1   The letters and essays of the Roman Stoic author Seneca, the Cynic epistles attributed to Diogenes and Crates, and the *Discourses of Musonius Rufus* all pick up on this theme.

2   Martin Thornton, *English Spirituality*. (London: SPCK, 1986), pp. 21-23.

3   You'll see this term, *Sarum*, pop up at various points. Sarum is the Latin name for the English Diocese of Salisbury. In the late medieval period, Salisbury was a major center of book production; as a result, the liturgical books produced for the cathedral and the churches of the diocese spread far beyond the regional borders. Because of its wide diffusion, most English worship before the Reformation was according to the Sarum Rite. The texts of these liturgies are broadly continuous with the common Latin liturgies of the West, but there were some peculiarities in the lectionaries and the ceremonial also found in North France and Brittany. Thus, Sarum refers to this English, pre-Reformation, Latin-language heritage.

4   The discussion of these seven principle kinds of prayer in the catechism is on pages 856-857 of *The Book of Common Prayer*.

5   *The Godfather: Part III*.

6   Psalm 96:11b-12 (*The Book of Common Prayer*, 726). Paraphrased.

7   This devotional is called *The Myroure of Oure Ladye* and is a fascinating work written to explain to the sisters of a Brigittine monastery the meaning of their Latin services in Middle English. It gives us a unique insight into the lives of late medieval nuns and how they approached their lives of prayer.

8   Harry Turtledove, *How Few Remain: A Novel of the Second War Between the States*, (N.Y., N.Y.: Ballentine, 1997), p. 468.

9   The proclamation adapted was Jefferson Davis' proclamation of a fast day on February 26, 1862.

10 Will Durant, *The Story of Philosophy: The Lives and Opinions of the World's Greatest Philosophers* (New York: Garden City Publishing, 1926), p. 87.

11 This text is referred to as "The Sunday Letter" or "The Letter from Heaven." The English versions of it and background information are found in Dorothy Haines, ed. and trans.*, Sunday Observance and the Sunday Letter in Anglo-Saxon England* (Anglo-Saxon Texts 8: Brewer, 2010).

12 RB 1:6-9. All citations from the Rule are from Timothy Fry, ed., *RB 1980* (Collegeville, Minn.: Liturgical Press, 1980).

SECTION 1
THE CALENDAR

CHAPTER 2
THE ESSENCE OF THE CALENDAR

Pick up a prayer book from a church pew and—keeping it closed—look at the edges of the pages. There will usually be a thin section of dark edges a little past one-third of the book. That's where the service for Holy Eucharist appears. The pages are worn and dirtied from use. The rest of the pages are usually fairly clean in comparison. That's because no one is looking at them on a weekly basis the way they are the Eucharist.

If you were to look for the cleanest pages of the prayer book, they would be at the very front—where the Calendar and the Church Year are listed—and the very back—where the lectionary tables appear. Clergy and worship leaders consult these pages every once in a while to make sure they are ordering things correctly, but on the whole, most people are not aware of these sections. Despite the apparent lack of interest, the way we as prayer book people order time impacts us on a daily basis. It regulates how the church worships, what hymns we sing, and what parts of scripture we hear.

Think for a minute about how humans reckon time. Genesis 1 gives two reasons for the creation of the celestial bodies—the sun, moon, and stars: Light is the second purpose.

The primary is that they may "be for signs and for seasons and for days and years" (1:14); they are time-keeping devices first and foremost. Some aspects of time are built into the fabric of the created order. The revolution of the earth gives us a day divided into light and dark with a particular point (noon) where the sun hits a high-point and all the shadows go away. The journey of the earth around the sun gives us a year with intermediate points at the solstices and the equinoxes. Additionally, the moon gives us periods of twenty-nine-and-a-half days. Astronomers could add a few more, I'm sure, but these are the big ones.

I bring this up for a particular reason: Notice just how much of our timekeeping doesn't show up here! Hours, minutes, weeks, months: None of them follow natural indicators. Time as we experience, measure, and mark it is a social construct more than anything else. The way we reckon our years (*Anno Domini* [Year of Our Lord] 2013, 5774 years from the giving of the Law, 2766 *Ab urbe condita* [from the founding of Rome]), the way we structure our weeks, the way we subdivide our days reflect choices about what things are worth reckoning. Even more socially conditioned are days, times, or seasons that we observe as particularly memorable. The government proclamation of a day off work, whether it be Labor Day, or the Queen's Birthday, or Corpus Christi, says something about what a country values.

This is just as true of the Church as any other social grouping. We tell time in particular ways for particular reasons. Much of the order of time in the secular world revolves around business—originally around agricultural demands and more recently by the work week and the punctuality required by a mechanized society. On the other hand, the Church's time is primarily structured to orient us toward God. At points, Church time adopts the secular ordering; in other points, it adapts it, and in a few places, it explicitly contradicts the wider reckoning. In some areas, the relationship is not one way—the secular culture's time has itself been shaped by the Church's traditions. We will explore what these mean in relation to the system of spirituality laid out in *The Book of Common Prayer*.

Before we get to our particular time-keeping system, let's focus on the inner workings of the two main aspects of the Church Year. In particular, I want to talk about the Christian year from two different perspectives. The first relates to its connection with our doctrine; the second relates to its connection with our emotion. We grasp the Church Year most completely only when we see both aspects and when the two are understood to be complementary parts of a whole.

LIVING THE CREED

Our doctrine—our beliefs—are stated in the Apostles' Creed and the Nicene Creed. What exactly are the creeds, and what are they for? Stated briefly, the creeds are a relatively quick overview of what the Church believes and teaches. The Apostles' Creed plays an important role in baptisms because, for almost two thousand years, it has been used in the Western Church to show that the person being baptized (or their sponsors) knew and assented to the beliefs of the organization they were joining. The Nicene Creed is a slightly longer form modeled on an Eastern baptismal creed. It was hammered out between the fourth and eighth centuries by bishops from across the Church in an effort to address how we understand the interrelations between Father, Son, and Holy Spirit. This is the creed that we say or sing during Eucharist.

Modern churchgoers are sometimes a little unclear on the purpose of the creeds. In a culture that emphasizes thinking for ourselves and is suspicious of organizations telling us what to believe, creeds seem like an anachronism. We are left with the question: What do we do with the creeds in modern time? Most often, people have one of three perspectives about the creeds. They are a laundry list of ideas, a set of thoughts disconnected from real life. They are litmus tests for true believers that can and should be used to separate out the sheep from the goats. Or, some say, the creeds are something to be transcended and left behind—sort of a starting place on the road of faith that can be left on the wayside once we are further along in our journey. None of these options capture the full role and purpose of the creeds in the life of faith. I believe that our major problems with the creeds are because we have disconnected them from their proper function: The creeds are a framework to guide our reading of the scriptures. Some of the greatest problems and heresies of the Early Church came about not in spite of the reading of scripture but precisely because of it! That is, the scriptures can be read in many different ways, from many different angles. Once we acknowledge—as we must—that scripture contains both literal and metaphorical material, one of our chief tasks is to determine which is which. The creeds represent a set of interpretive boundaries. They don't tell us what to believe about everything but rather nail down certain points of controversy and render a clear judgment on the Church's perspective.

It's worth emphasizing the "points of controversy" notion. I have often heard questions and concerns about why the life and ministry of Jesus is not discussed in the creeds. It's not because the Church didn't think these were important; rather, it's because there weren't fundamental arguments about it. The orthodox and heterodox alike believe that Jesus lived, taught, and worked wonders. There was no controversy about these things and hence no need for clarification.[1]

Rather, the creeds address specific points of controversy that have practical implications both for theology and for Christian living. For instance, when we confess that God is the creator of the heavens and the earth, we confirm our belief that the creation of the material world came about through God who is the father of Jesus Christ and not some evil, lesser god who sought to trap the spirits and souls of humanity in flesh. This is in deliberate contrast to a dualistic impulse that saw all spirit as good and all matter as evil and was convinced that no good God would get tangled up in material things. But that's precisely what we believe. Not only did God get tangled up in material things, but God also took the material world so seriously that he became incarnate within it. But that conviction begins with the belief that God is the God of creation and that creation is not what we need to be saved from.

Too often, we only note what the creed says—and lose sight of the mistaken interpretations that it prevents. We get so caught up in arguing about what the creeds say that we forget that they are also shutting down other lines of interpretation that can have disastrous pastoral consequences and skew our understanding of and relationship with God.

So what does this all have to do with the Christian Year?

Quite simply, one aspect of the Christian Year is that it is a temporal embodiment of the interpretive doctrines of the creed. Almost every line of the creeds has a corresponding feast or fast. In observing these feasts and fasts, the Church has an opportunity to explore and explain exactly what the terse lines of the creed are—and are not—trying to say. For those who feel a little wary about the creeds, this facet of the Church Year should, actually, come as good news. What the creeds state quickly and sparsely, the feasts explore at more leisure. The traditional liturgical materials of these feasts reflect a more poetic, meditative approach that gives greater nuance and the opportunity for deeper reflection about the meaning of the event, person, or concept celebrated by it.

Let me give you an example. The feast of the Epiphany concludes the season of Christmas and begins an emphasis on how Christ revealed himself and was revealed to the world. The Early Church connected the feast of Epiphany with three different biblical events: Matthew's story of the Magi arriving to honor the infant Jesus, John's story of the wedding at Cana identified as "the first of his signs" (John 2:11), and the Baptism of Jesus by John in the Jordan, which is mentioned in all four Gospels. While these Gospel stories were eventually expanded to their own Sundays, an anonymous liturgist operating perhaps in the sixth or seventh century wove these narratives into a single antiphon as a way of driving to the heart of the feast:

> This day is the Church joined unto the Heavenly Bridegroom, since Christ hath washed away her sins in Jordan; the wise men hasten with gifts to the marriage supper of the king; and they that sit at meat together make merry with water turned into wine. *Alleluia.*[2]

Using the central notion of the wedding feast, the doctrine of the Incarnation is made even more relational as the wedding of Christ and the Church by means of the sacrament of Baptism. The first miracle of Christ reflects the joy of the banquet, and the gift-bearing Magi hint at the inclusion of the Gentiles into God's promise of reconciliation. This is the sort of liturgical play that helps us return again to the creeds with greater appreciation.

Of course, with the simplification of the church services that occurred during the Reformation, we lost sight of many of these liturgical gems, but the last century has seen a renewed interest in their perspective and they can be found in several devotional resources like *Saint Augustine's Prayer Book*.

THE SEASONS AND
THE RELIGIOUS AFFECTIONS

Doctrines—like those revealed in the creeds—are an important part of the Christian faith. They are less important for their own sake and more because they help us get a clearer sense of the relationship that we are developing and the identity of the Triune God to whom we relate. More than being an exercise in right thinking, the Christian faith has been described as a particular pattern of deep emotions shaped over time.

Emotions are tricky things, and the language that we use to talk about them is not always clear or precise. Feelings, having feelings, and listening to your feelings is—and must be—an important part of the religious life as well as the whole process of self-discovery. However, we have all seen forms of religion that rely upon emotional manipulation, using guilt or a feigned joy. But emotions, like thoughts, are often fleeting things over which we have little control; they arise within us, and we respond to them, express them, give vent to them, or suppress them. The affections are more than this; they are more like emotional habits, patterns of feeling that we choose and cultivate. There is a difference between feeling anger and choosing to live out of an attitude of anger; similarly, there's a difference between feeling gratitude and choosing to cultivate it as a way of being. The Christian affections, as identified by theologian Don Saliers in his work, *The Soul in Paraphrase*, are gratitude, holy fear and penitence, joy and suffering, and love of God and neighbor.[3]

In what may seem like a paradox, an important part of this "feeling" work is about ideas, thoughts, and doctrines. Just as what we know about a person may influence how we feel toward them, what we know and the ideas we hold about God shape our feelings in our relationship with the Divine. Because of this interrelation between thinking and feeling, the affections are a constellation of beliefs, doctrines, and feelings that are shaped and reinforced by language that not only provokes emotions within us but also offers us images and descriptions of reality that help us understand what living out these perspectives looks like.

When we examine the emotional atmosphere of the seasons of the Church Year, we recognize that each season provides its own particular entrée into one or more of the affections. Lent disciplines us toward penitence; Easter explores holy joy. Advent teaches us about hope and expectation; Christmas also returns to joy—but from a slightly different angle than Easter. These seasons give us an opportunity to concentrate on an affection, to cultivate it, and to understand it more thoroughly. Recognizing the seasons as affectional frameworks also helps free us from a particular kind of seasonal guilt.

Sometimes, I'll catch myself rejoicing in the spring air and newly warm sunshine and feel badly that I am enjoying myself so much during Lent. Conversely, holidays—particularly Christmas and Easter—can be difficult for those who have recently lost loved ones or who experience familial conflict at these times, contradicting the joyous intent of the Church's celebrations. If we understand the seasons as training opportunities rather than emotional straightjackets, we can free ourselves from this unnecessary guilt. It's okay to feel something different—to experience a whole range of emotions despite an affectional intention of the season. Neither our emotions nor the affections should be restricted by the seasons. Rather, we focus upon particular affections as we move through particular seasons in order that these patterns may become features of our long-term way of being in the presence of God.

The seasons cultivate particular affections in a variety of ways; several factors converge to create the emotional tenor of a season. The liturgical color often provides an initial clue to the season's character. The bright white colors of Christmas and Easter give visual cues as do the darker, more somber hues of Advent and Lent. The use of unflowered greens in Advent and an absence of floral decoration in Lent provide further visual indicators of the Church's mood as you glance around the sanctuary. Music, too, changes. In the great cathedrals where multiple services occurred at the same time and where the chancel organ played a supplemental role (rather than a dominant role as now), its tones were often suppressed during Advent and Lent. More telling is the use of certain musical elements. The *Gloria in exclesis* is one of the Church's great songs of rejoicing, and its absence is one of the ways that the Church communicates tone. The *Gloria* is used at any occasion in Christmas and Easter but not at all in Advent and Lent. The traditional rule that it is used only on Sundays (and not weekdays) in green seasons elevates Sundays within these seasons of patient endurance. The canticles at Morning Prayer also help shape the season's mood. One of the more subtle means for creating a season's mood is in the selection of the biblical readings in both the Office and the Eucharist. For instance, Isaiah's prophecies of the coming Messiah have been a feature of Advent since its creation while Lamentations is a consistent feature of Holy Week.

The prayer book gives us free reign on many of these things. Although seasons, readings, directions on canticles, and other elements appear in the prayer book, there are no directions on things like colors or floral decorations. Rather, denominational practice, parish tradition, and the type and color of vestments on hand inform how various congregations choose to celebrate the seasons.

All of these elements combine to focus us on certain ideas, doctrines, and feelings that contribute to the composite character of an affection. And the affections together with their sometimes complementary, sometimes sequential movements between love and holy fear, penitence and joy, form the basic grammar of the Christian way of being.

LITURGY, HISTORY, AND THE POWERFUL PRESENT

In one sense, the Church Year unfolds like a Gospel, following the life of Christ. Advent reflects the waiting of God's people for the coming Messiah. Christmas focuses upon the birth and Incarnation. Epiphany combines manifestation and ministry to explore the character of Jesus in both word and works. Lent begins the turn to the cross, which is intensified in Holy Week. Easter features the Resurrection and the presence of the Risen Christ in the midst of his people until the Ascension. The coming of the Spirit at Pentecost initiates a new period for the Church, and the later ministry of Jesus that unfolds from that point is dually informed by both the Spirit and the Resurrection. Finally, Advent once again reflects the waiting of God's people for the coming Messiah, but this time as the one who comes to preside over the final consummation of all things as judge of heaven and earth.

The danger with only seeing the year like this, though, is that we can view it as a panorama of historical remembrances. To do this is to miss something important. The Church Year is *kerygmatic*—an act of proclamation in and of itself. It proclaims not just the past but also the present power of the Risen Christ and professes both presence and power in our very midst. At Christmas we pray, "O God, you have caused *this* holy night to shine with the brightness of the true light…" and "…you have given your only begotten Son…*to be born this day* of a pure virgin…" (*The Book of Common Prayer*, pp. 212, 213). During Christmas we pray, "…you have poured upon *us* the *new light* of your incarnate Word…" (*The Book of Common Prayer*, p. 213). We don't say, *a long time ago you did some things that we now remember fondly*. No! This night, this day, us, new light, in our very midst!

We see the same language, emphasis, and themes in the second collect for Easter—"O God, who made this most holy night to shine with the glory of the Lord's resurrection" (*The Book of Common Prayer*, p. 222). These themes reach full crescendo in the Church's great song of rejoicing, the *Exultet*, which is one of the high points of the Easter Vigil. Scooping up the great biblical images of redemption in the Exodus from Egypt and the Resurrection of Christ, they are united in our present moment as the faithful stand in a darkened church, staring at the single paschal candle, our own pillar of flame. The deacon sings:

> This is the night, when you brought our fathers, the children of Israel, out of bondage in Egypt, and led them through the Red Sea on dry land.

> This is the night, when all who believe in Christ are delivered from the gloom of sin, and are restored to grace and holiness of life.

> This is the night, when Christ broke the bonds of death and hell, and rose victorious from the grave.

> How holy is this night, when wickedness is put to flight, and sin is washed away. It restores innocence to the fallen, and joy to

those who mourn. It casts out pride and hatred, and brings peace and concord.

How blessed is this night, when earth and heaven are joined and man is reconciled to God (*The Book of Common Prayer*, p. 287).

This isn't about the past: It's about now. The mighty acts of God in the past and the great promises of God that will reach their full fulfillment in the future are bound together in this sacred moment—and our present expands to encompass them both.

The Church Year isn't just a catechetical exercise (although it does that). It is a means of accessing the power and the promise of God now! This is why the Anglican fathers fought the Puritan attempts to get rid of the Church Calendar: They recognized that this cycle is a means of tapping into the mysteries that God offers us in the sacramental life.

COMMEMORATING THE SAINTS AND HEROES OF THE FAITH

The temporal cycle that celebrates in time the high points of the creeds and, in doing so, the main movements in the life of Jesus, is mirrored by the sanctoral cycle that celebrates Christ and his Church in and through the heroes of the faith. The temporal cycle operates along two major axes: incarnation and redemption. That is, the seasons of Lent and Easter focus our attention on how God acts to redeem us; the seasons of Advent and Christmas along with attendant feasts involving Mary and John the Baptist focus us on God becoming human. The best way to think about the sanctoral cycle is not as some other separate thing that gets plopped on top of the temporal cycle as an occasional interruption. Rather, the sanctoral cycle is the logical next step from the temporal cycle that flows from the life of Jesus and shows us the fusion of both redemption and incarnation as they intersect within human lives. The sanctoral cycle shows us the promise and potential of humanity reconciled with God; it gives us vivid examples of redeemed humans who incarnated Christ in their very flesh to the wonder of the watching world.

Some people are a bit wary of the sanctoral cycle. And that's understandable. There is a wide range of attitudes within The Episcopal Church and within Anglicanism as a whole toward the heroes of the faith and how we decide to remember them in church. A lot of this has to do with the way that the Roman Catholic and Eastern Orthodox churches honor these heroes and Episcopal desires to emulate, learn from, or reject what it is that they do. Some Episcopalians are fine with the sanctoral cycle and are perfectly comfortable using the "s-word" (saints). Others are much more leery of it and see the notion of saints as inherently troublesome and problematic. The prayer book and associated material tries to respect the diversity of opinion while still providing for liturgical celebration of these heroes. We're not going to solve the difference of opinion here but, instead, will try to use the principles of the prayer book to wrestle with the topic in a way that helps us touch the heart of it: the intersection of the dual mysteries of redemption and incarnation.

A BAPTISMAL ECCLESIOLOGY: WHERE THE RUBBER MEETS THE ROAD

The best way to untangle this matter, it seems to me, is to cut to the heart of the matter. It starts with Baptism. One of the real achievements of our prayer book is its embrace of the sacrament of Baptism and the restoration of its place as one of the two great sacraments of the Church. You won't spend very long around arguing Episcopalians without somebody referring to the Baptismal Covenant or even tossing out the phrase "baptismal ecclesiology."

But what is baptismal ecclesiology and why does it matter?

Baptism joins us to Christ. Using the image of drowning, Paul speaks of us dying in the waters of Baptism with Jesus and rising from them, sharing in his new risen life (Romans 6:1-11). This is the moment when we get plugged into the life of God. It can be seen as an individual and individualistic event—me and Jesus. And yet, that's not how the New Testament or the Church talks about it. It's not just me and Jesus—it's me and Jesus and everybody else who is likewise plugged into Jesus. It is all of us who are connected by Christ into the life of God. That's the heart of what the Church is: all those who are fellow travelers with us by virtue of Baptism. The Church is defined by Baptism. We fail to see the Church properly if we are only looking at the clergy. Or if we're only looking at the people who decide to show up to our church on Sundays. A real, robust baptismal ecclesiology takes seriously that everyone who is, was, or will be baptized shares in a common bond, the union with Christ, without regard to church attendance or denominational lines. Furthermore, Paul's insistence that baptismal life is a sharing in Christ's risen life means that we don't see the line between the living and the dead quite so starkly either.

I fear, despite all of our talk of a baptismal ecclesiology, that we tend to have a parochial view of the Church. And I mean that in two different senses of the word. I mean it in the word's negative sense when parochial is used to mean short-sighted and narrow. I also mean it in the word's most literal sense as it relates to the parish we go to on Sundays. We tend to think of Church as restricted to the people we see around us—and that's a mistake. If we take Baptism seriously, we have to see Church not only as the people within our walls but also the folks in the church down the street (even if we don't agree with them on some things), all the folks who don't actually attend our church or any church, and the whole host of those who have gone before us that we see no longer. If the act of Baptism replaces our life, plugging us into the life of God in some fundamental, meaningful way—however we understand that—then the dead share the very same life that we do. We are all bound together into the energies of God. What we do with the dead, how we understand them, and our relation to them finds focus liturgically in two days at the start of November: the Feast of All Saints and the Commemoration of All Faithful Departed, historically called All Souls. If we want to do the sanctoral cycle right, we have to start with these two days and what they mean for us.

ALL SAINTS AND ALL SOULS

To approach this topic from a prayer book perspective, the place we have to begin is one of humility. We don't have all the answers here, and that's okay—we have enough to get by on. The first thing to note is that, despite what you might think, the Bible doesn't spend very much time at all talking about death or what happens after we die. Christian tradition has filled in the gaps with a whole lot of stuff and often in some fairly imprecise, rather sketchy, and often downright contradictory ways. Some of our most treasured notions about what happens when we die are more products of cultural myths than anything rooted in scripture and historic Christian teaching. Frankly, that's part of what makes this discussion a bit tricky—we are touching on treasured notions. It is certainly not my intention to harm anyone's faith or pass judgment on what you were taught, formally or not. As a result, I will stick closely to the words and intentions of the prayer book.

In the Proper Preface for the Commemoration of the Dead, we say, "for to your faithful people, O Lord, life is changed, not ended" (*The Book of Common Prayer*, p. 382). That declaration is the foundation upon which everything else is built. Because of our faith in the Resurrection and the promises of Baptism, death is a shift—not an end. From that fundamental recognition, the prayer book then makes reference to two general groups: the departed and the saints. Most often, these are verbally placed right next to each another. For instance, in the various forms of the Prayers of the People, we routinely mention both the departed and the saints in close proximity: "Give to the departed eternal rest; *Let light perpetual shine upon them.* We praise you for your saints who have entered into joy; *May we also come to share in your heavenly kingdom*" (Form III, *The Book of Common Prayer*, p. 387) and "We commend to your mercy all who have died, that your will for them may be fulfilled; and we pray that we may share with all your saints in your eternal kingdom" (Form IV, *The Book of Common Prayer*, p. 389) and "For all who have died in the communion of your Church, and those whose faith is known to you alone, that, with all the saints, they may have rest in that place where there is no pain or grief but life eternal, we pray to you, O Lord" (Form V, *The Book of Common Prayer*, p. 391). Too, we have sets of fixed prayers (Commons) appointed for the Dead and for the Saints. But how do we interpret these two groups? Are they distinct or does one flow into the other?

I suggest that the prayer book is being deliberately vague on these points. The clearest statement that I can find that sheds light on this comes from the Prayers of the People in the Rite I Eucharist, which reflects the language that we inherited from classical Anglicanism: "And we bless thy holy Name for all thy servants departed this life in thy faith and fear, beseeching thee to grant them continual growth in thy love and service; and to grant us grace so to follow the good examples of all thy saints, that with them we may be partakers of thy heavenly kingdom" (*The Book of Common Prayer*, p. 330). This language affirms that the saints of God are partakers of the heavenly kingdom and also envisions a process of growth that is not ended by physical death. The pattern that is laid out here reflects a classical threefold division into the Church Militant—we the living; the Church Triumphant—those departed who currently enjoy the fullness of God's presence; and the Church Expectant—those departed who do not yet experience the full presence of God but who will, as that process of growth is played out and as God's promises in Baptism and Eucharist are fully delivered in the final consummation of all things.

Keeping these categories in mind, the feast of All Saints celebrates the mighty deeds of God in and through the Church Triumphant; the feast of All Souls recalls to us the Church Expectant who shall yet enjoy that final consummation.

Now we get to the tricky part: If we are saying that we have two buckets—who goes where, and why?

Well, that's complicated.

BACK TO BAPTISM

The Church uses two primary definitions for the term saint. The first definition is a general one with biblical roots; Paul consistently uses the saints to refer to the whole people of God.[4] Those who have been joined to Christ in Baptism are holy ones (which is the same word as saints in Greek) because they have become part of a holy whole. Thus, there is a general sense that saint is appropriate for every member of the Church.

But there is also a more specific use of the term that the Church has used for centuries: A saint is a person who manifests Christ to the world. A saint is a person in whom and through whom Christ can be seen. In a sense—like the icons that represent them—the saints can be seen both as windows and as mirrors. The saints are windows because the light of Christ flows through them, and their primary purpose is not to reveal themselves but, in their transparency to the Divine, reveal the heart of God. The saints are mirrors because they offer us an opportunity to see ourselves as we could be—to show us what life in the service of Christ looks like. Just as we might glance into a mirror before a big meeting, the saints reveal when we still have spinach stuck in our teeth, when and where we fall short of living a life glowing with God.

The saints represent the goal for us. What we receive in the spiritual patterning of the prayer book, in the spiritual patterns of the Church at large, is a sacramental path to discipleship. Baptism, Eucharist, Confirmation, and Reconciliation (confession) are tools that lead us ever deeper into discipleship where we hear and answer God's call to follow, to learn, to love, to die, to truly live. The saints model Christian maturity in a variety of ways. These ways take many forms in a host of situations, but the central qualities never stray far from the pattern of Jesus himself: faith, hope, love, mercy, justice, and peace.

Paul, positively influenced by the Stoic teachings of his day, understood that the true transmission of the faith could only be partially accomplished through language; the deeper patterns required examples. Hence, a critical part of his proclamation is captured in this simple (but not easy) call: "Be imitators of me, as I am of Christ" (1 Corinthians 11:1). There is an inherently incarnational element in the call to imitation. It contains the recognition that the essense of people cannot be reduced to their thoughts or their teachings or even their virtues in an abstract sense. Instead we learn from the whole embodied reality with which they engaged the world. The saints are mediators of the faith to us because, as Paul wrote, they call us through themselves to imitate Christ and to learn from him what it is to be holy, what it is to be fully human.

Imitation of the saints means learning lives. Some of the earliest literature about spirituality and teaching spirituality did not appear in the form of treatises or doctrinal essays. Instead, they wrote lives. The fathers of the nascent monastic movement writing in the fourth century presented their ascetical theology in narrative form. Athanasius, the fiery bishop of Alexandria, gave us the life of Antony. Jerome, the ascerbic monk and translator best known for translating and editing the Latin (*Vulgate*) Bible, gave us a number, including the more fantastical lives of Paul the Hermit and Malchus as well as the more historically grounded life of Epiphanius and the various examples and remembrances in his letters of people with whom he had lived and to whom he had ministered. Even the first great writings on Christian spirituality sought to retain a connection with lives and stories. John Cassian's great work is a dialogue that weaves oral teachings with human lives; Sulpicius Severus, another early writer, likewise offers a mediation of eastern monasticism to the West by means of a dialogue about ways of life and means of imitation.

What I'm getting at here is that when we deal with the saints—particularly using the second, more particular, sense of the term—we are working within the realm of Incarnation. How is Christ made manifest in material means to heal and redeem the world? An answer is in the lives of those called to follow him. We, in turn, learn Christ in and through them.

To return again to the prayer book and to Baptism, the Baptismal Covenant lays out a set of ideas that have always been implicit in Baptism and in discipleship. The Baptismal

Covenant asks: fidelity to the Church's creeds (particularly the Apostles' Creed), persistence in the Church's worship and gatherings, the practice of repentance, spreading the Good News of what God has done in Christ, humble service to Christ in the person of all humanity, striving for justice, peace, and respect for all. These promises are not new but reflect facets of discipleship that the Church has taught through the ages. Some individuals embrace these promises more concretely than others. Some embody them more profoundly than others. These are our exemplars of Christian maturity, these are the stewards of the virtues, from whom we learn Christ and imitate him in them. To the degree that they model the more excellent way, they deserve to be set apart and held up by the Church.

And, in making that connection, we come full circle to the issue of the two buckets—the saints, the departed, and who goes where. The good news, of course, is that it's not our decision. We can't put anyone into these buckets—that is God's work. And, at the end of the day, even the metaphor of buckets fails as being overly concrete. Here's what we can say: God knows his own far better than we ever will. Recognizing that fundamental truth, no Church or ecclesiastical body has ever said (or at least not properly or wisely) that it can state the contents of the buckets. Even when Churches declare saints, they are not attempting to identify the whole population of the holy. There are far more who enjoy the fullness of the presence of God than we can imagine. And, if God's ways are true to what we find in scripture and in tradition, some of those enjoying that nearer presence will come as quite a shock to us! No, the most that Churches can—and should—do is to state that there are strong positive signs that certain individuals are among the blessed. Not so that whole company can be catalogued, but so that we have a sense of whom to hold up as exemplars and representatives of the holiness and spiritual maturity to which all of us are called.

Now, what may these strong positive signs be? I'd like to focus on the one that makes us the most nervous. In Late Antiquity and through the medieval periods, one of the key signs of sanctity was identified as miraculous power. The saints could be known and identified because they were agents of supernatural power. For most of Christian history, in fact, sanctity was something declared on the local level by people who were convinced that one who was dead was still serving as an agent of God's power in their community. Bishops might ratify this by proclaiming a feast, and pilgrimage centers would spring up as healings or apparitions or other manifestations occurred. When the Roman Catholic Church centralized the process of sanctity in the mid-fourteenth century—in a way that the Christian East never did—it incorporated this principle in the famous criterion requiring two documented miracles. To this day, this is the part of the process that makes many modern people uncomfortable. Significantly, among the various Anglican churches who recognize saints, no such criterion exists. Rather than getting bogged down in the whole question of miracles, it's more useful for our purposes to ask, not how and to what degree it gets fulfilled, but why this criterion is important in the first place.

Truthfully, it's all about connections. The point about miracles originally was that it established proof that the saint was hooked into the life of God and was serving as a conduit of God's grace and power to the local community. Furthermore, most of the miracles that are described in the medieval lives of the saints aren't terribly original. A disciple of Saint Benedict might do something that Elisha did, or healings and meal multiplications mirror what Jesus did. What were these people doing, just copying scripture?

No. They were, in fact, *imitating* scripture. When the saints either performed or were thought to have performed biblical sorts of miracles, it confirmed that they were participating within a continuity of sanctity that points directly back to scripture and to Christ himself. The Christian life—the holy life—was about embodying scripture, not only by following its guidelines but also in receiving the same graces the biblical personages enjoyed. Imitation of the saints and imitation of the scriptures ultimately point to the imitation of Christ who is the source and pattern of both the saints and the scriptures.

It's one thing to show evidence of holy power when you're alive—it's another to do so when you're dead. Because this is precisely proof that you're not dead, at least not in the usual sense. And that's precisely the difference between secular culture and church culture. The secular culture has days that celebrate certain individuals—Presidents' Day, Martin Luther King Day, and so forth—and they do it to celebrate important historical figures who are a significant part of our national story. They are dead, gone, and fondly remembered. It's not so with the Church. When we remember the saints, we're remembering those around us whom we see no longer but who are still fellow workers with us in the kingdom of God. Recovering a true baptismal ecclesiology requires the recognition that this baptismal connection is not severed by physical death. The prayer book encapsulates this notion in these two collects:

> Almighty God, by your Holy Spirit you have made us one with your saints in heaven and on earth: Grant that in our earthly pilgrimage we may always be supported by this fellowship of love and prayer, and know ourselves to be surrounded by their witness to your power and mercy. We ask this for the sake of Jesus Christ, in whom all our intercessions are acceptable through the Spirit, and who lives and reigns forever and ever. *Amen* (*The Book of Common Prayer*, p. 250).

O God, the King of saints, we praise and glorify your holy Name for all your servants who have finished their course in your faith and fear: for the blessed Virgin Mary; for the holy patriarchs, prophets, apostles, and martyrs; and for all your other righteous servants, known to us and unknown; and we pray that, encouraged by their examples, aided by their prayers, and strengthened by their fellowship, we also may be partakers of the inheritance of the saints in light; through the merits of your Son Jesus Christ our Lord. Amen (*The Book of Common Prayer*, p.504).

The proper theme here is fellowship, connection, and continuity. The saints pray for us, love, and remember us, just as we love, remember, and pray for those we see no longer. The celebration of saints' days gives us an opportunity to honor and thank those who pray for us, to lift up their examples before our eyes, and to point back to Christ himself who gave them gifts of grace and courage in their trials.

Just as the seasons of the Church Year foreground the great religious affections that motivate us as Christians— love, joy, penitence, hope, etc.—the saints show us what these affections look like lived out in incarnate lives. Some favor one or two affections over the others, but each one of them helps us get a better sense of what Christian maturity looks like. As the seasons show us different facets of Christ, so the saints demonstrate for us what his message of love, hope, and redemption is like in different times and places. By living with and praying the temporal calendar and sanctoral calendar in the prayer book, we find ourselves formed by and drawn into the life of Christ and his saints. Praying through these times and seasons shapes us in their image and incorporates us into their midst.

CHAPTER 3
THE ANATOMY OF THE CALENDAR

The Calendar is most clearly laid out in a section at the beginning of *The Book of Common Prayer*. After this initial material, several other parts relate back to it and assume its patterns. In particular, the Collects, the rites provided for special days, and the lectionaries depend on the shape of the year laid out in the Calendar.

The Calendar of the Church Year

1. Principal Feasts (p. 15)

2. Sundays (p. 16)

3. Holy Days (pp. 16-17)

4. Days of Special Devotion (p. 17)

5. Days of Optional Observance (pp. 17-18)

[List of Fixed Feasts and Days of Optional Observance by Month] (pp. 19-30)

The Titles of the Seasons, Sundays and Major Holy Days observed in this Church throughout the Year (pp. 31-33)

The first few pages of this Calendar section provide the liturgical rules governing the various days of the year. These provide general rubrics for figuring out what to celebrate on a given day. Next, we have a section that lays out the months from January to December and identifies which fixed feasts fall on which days. Lastly, we have a list of titles that specify how we name the various liturgical occasions of the year.

For the most part, this section does a good job of ordering your services, but there are a few oddities worth noting that affect both how we order things and how we understand the wider Church Year.

First, the normative unit of time throughout this section is the day, and therefore seasons are given short shrift. Notice that there is no section here that describes seasons of the Church Year. That's not to say they are absent; the names of the seasons are mentioned throughout the Calendar section and they are used as structuring devices in the titles listed on pages 31-33. However, the seasons are assumed rather than explained.

Indeed, many people assume that the colors of the liturgical seasons and the practices around them are listed out somewhere. There are plenty of such lists—but none of them appear in the prayer book.

Second, the Calendar section begins with three paragraphs that discuss the movable date of Easter. The third paragraph emphasizes that "the sequence of all Sundays of the Church Year depends upon the date of Easter Day" (*The Book of Common Prayer*, p. 15). However, it doesn't actually tell you that there are tables later in the prayer book that help you figure out when Easter falls each year and the impact that Easter's placement has on the other feasts around the Easter season (Ash Wednesday, Ascension, Pentecost) as well as how this placement affects the First Sunday of Advent. These tables, which had formerly been joined to the Calendar rules, are now found in the back of the book:

Tables for Finding Holy Days

There is much in this section that seems fairly arcane—like the specific rules for determining the date of Easter—but there are also some nuggets that will help you with planning that involves the Church Calendar. The Table to find Easter Day is a straightforward list: You look up the year, and it tells you the month and day on which Easter falls and whether it's a leap year or not. Once you have that information, you can turn the page, and look up that month and day in the next table, the Table to Find Movable Feasts, and it will provide the number of Sundays after Epiphany, the month and days for Ash Wednesday, Ascension Day, and Pentecost, the Numbered Proper that the Sunday after Trinity Sunday will start with, and the month and day of the First Sunday of Advent. In a sense, this table reinforces an important theological point in a practical way: So much of what the Church does is oriented around Easter, and the Church's gaze must remain on Easter to know how to properly order everything else.

There is also an explanation of the funny letters and numbers listed in the monthly tables on pages 19-30. If you look at page 22—the month of April—you will see four columns going across the page. The first only appears sporadically and gives a number. This is the Golden Number related to finding Easter Day—feel free to ignore it.[5] The second gives the days of the month. The third is a repeating string of letters going from A to G; these are the Sunday Letters. This column can be handy if you want to know what holy days fall on a Sunday in a particular year. By finding the letter of the current year on the table at the top of page 881, you can learn which letter will represent the Sundays throughout the year. The fourth column gives the title of the occasion with feasts in bold type and optional days in regular type.

Third, the focus of the Calendar section is on establishing precedence. That is, it helps to identify what days are more important than other days. Most of the Church's holy days have a fixed date; they occur on the same date on the Calendar every year. For instance, the Presentation of Our Lord is always on February 2, and the Annunciation is always on March 25. But, as you know, Sundays fall on different dates every year, and since Easter is a Sunday (and a rather variable one at that), precedence helps you to know what to celebrate when Sundays and holy days overlap one another. Thus, if the Presentation of Our Lord falls on a Sunday, what do you celebrate in church? The holy day or the Sunday? Or, conversely, if the Annunciation happens to fall on Good Friday, what do you do?[6] The precedence table doesn't necessarily help you figure out what to do or pray in all cases, though. It turns out that a certain amount of useful material on the Calendar is hidden within the section of the book devoted to the Collects:

The Collects for the Church Year

Concerning the Proper of the Church Year (p. 158)

Collects: Traditional

[Collects for Sundays of the Church Year] (pp. 159-185)

Holy Days (pp. 185-194)

The Common of Saints [for Days of Optional Observance] (pp. 195-199)

Various Occasions (pp. 199-210)

Collects: Contemporary

[Collects for Sundays of the Church Year] (pp. 211-236)

Holy Days (pp. 237-246)

The Common of Saints [for Days of Optional Observance] (pp. 246-250)

Various Occasions (pp. 251-261)

The initial section on the Proper of the Church Year gives us two important principles:

The Sunday collect is used throughout the rest of the week unless there's a holy day.

"The Collect for any Sunday or other Feast may be used at the evening service of the day before" (*The Book of Common Prayer*, p. 158).

Then, a variety of notes get tucked between the collects. There are three kinds of notes: 1) notes that identify when certain optional movable days occur, 2) notes that give additional directions on how to handle a tricky part of the Calendar, and 3) notes that direct you to other services within the book.

The Calendar section mentions Rogation Days and Ember Days but never explains what they are or when they fall. While the what never does get explained, the when is provided by italicized notes like the one on page 160 following the Collect for the Third Sunday of Advent: "Wednesday, Friday, and Saturday of this week are the traditional winter Ember Days" (*The Book of Common Prayer*, p. 160).

Page 161 gives an example of the second kind of procedural note: The italics on both sides of the title for the First Sunday after Christmas provide more detailed instructions for how to negotiate the three holy days that fall after Christmas and what to do if one of them lands on a Sunday.

On page 166 after the title for Ash Wednesday, we find the third sort of note. This one directs you to a proper liturgy for the day in another part of the prayer book. Essentially, these notes are present for the major days of the redemption cycle that ground the seasons of Lent, Holy Week, and Easter that are gathered together toward the middle of the book:

Proper Liturgies for Special Days
>Ash Wednesday (pp. 264-269)
>
>Palm Sunday (pp. 270-273)
>
>Maundy Thursday (pp. 274-275)
>
>Good Friday (pp. 276-282)
>
>Holy Saturday (p. 283)
>
>The Great Vigil of Easter (pp. 285-298)

All of this sounds very confusing. This is because there is no piece dedicated to tying it all together. Allusions and references are made to a wide variety of concepts around the Calendar, but these references assume a big picture sense of the whole that the prayer book never actually provides. In order to understand what the mechanics are and how the mechanics flow into our spirituality, we need to take the time to construct the big-picture view that is implied but never stated explicitly.

THE SHAPE OF THE CALENDAR

Competing Calendar Schemes

The Calendar as we currently have it stands in the midst of three different schemes. First, we have the historical Western Calendar that has been in use since it solidified around the seventh century. This is the structure that informs liturgical and spiritual writing up through the middle of the twentieth century. Second, we have the revision and simplification of that Calendar influenced by the Liturgical Renewal Movement and enshrined in the Roman Catholic reform of the Calendar at Vatican II in 1969. While most of the historical pattern was retained, it was reoriented; the reforms superimposed on the Calendar an idealized view of fourth-century practice that focused on Easter, Sunday, and Baptism, simplifying and sometimes suppressing features that didn't seem to work well with these emphases. Third, the Calendar of the Revised Common Lectionary has now superseded the lectionary originally printed in the prayer book, which reinforces the process of simplification and the application of modern principles to an ancient system.

The Eucharistic Lectionary that shaped the Calendar of the first prayer books was the one-year lectionary used by the English Sarum Rite. This lectionary was one of several floating around Western Christianity in the years before the Reformation and is similar in most respects to the Roman Catholic lectionary formalized at the Council of Trent—the first time that the Roman Catholic Church set forth a single uniform liturgy.[7] (There are a few differences in readings at the beginning of the Season after Pentecost and in some other places.) This one-year lectionary that we held largely in common with the Roman Catholics and those Lutheran groups who retained lectionaries had an important influence in the formative years of the prayer book. As we will note later on, specific references to some of the lectionary readings are tucked away in our collects and hearken back to this old system.[8]

The Roman Catholic council, Vatican II, was a watershed moment for the Western Church as a whole. One major change that had wide-ranging ecumenical impact was the move away from a one-year Eucharistic Lectionary to a three-year cycle. When the 1979 prayer book was being prepared, several Protestant denominations were at work on a common lectionary based on the Roman Catholic model. The lectionary originally authorized and printed in the prayer book was a product of this process. However, it was not the endpoint.

The Revised Common Lectionary (RCL) was released in 1994 by the Consultation on Common Texts, a broad body containing members from The Episcopal Church, Anglican Church of Canada, the Evangelical Lutheran Church in America, the conferences of Roman Catholic bishops of both America and Canada, and many other Christian bodies. Content-wise, it is very similar to the earlier version put in the prayer book—but not the same. Not only have some of the readings changed, but also the lectionary's ecumenically based sense of the Church Year has some differences from the prayer book's Calendar. Finally, in 2006, the General Convention of The Episcopal Church voted to replace the lectionary printed in the prayer book with the Revised Common Lectionary. As a result, we have moved from a one-year lectionary to a three-year lectionary to a different three-year lectionary with slightly different readings and a slightly different shape. Thus, one of the things that we contend with are the slight differences and gaps between the prayer book and its Calendar and the Revised Common Lectionary and its Calendar system.

Some General Principles

Broadly speaking, the emphasis on Easter, Sundays, and Baptism has certain practical effects on the Church Year. There are two major meta classes of feasts: feasts of our Lord Jesus Christ and feasts of the saints. As a general principle, feasts of our Lord take precedence over feasts of the saints. The occasions of the temporal cycle are feasts of our Lord, as are the fixed holy days that celebrate events in the life of Jesus and his mother. Likewise, all Sundays are also feasts of our Lord.

So far, so good. As a set of general principles this works pretty well. However, there's a twist in here that never gets fully explained: In the section devoted to Sundays, three feasts of our Lord get special treatment and take precedence over a Sunday. Why these three? Well, this is the complicated part that the book doesn't explain.

Certain seasons are more protective of their Sundays than others. Basically, the Sundays within seasons that have a distinctive theological character are higher-ranking feasts of our Lord than the fixed holy days that fall within them. Here's a list of the order of precedence that may help:

1. Easter Week/Holy Week
2. Sundays of Easter
3. Sundays of Lent
4. Sundays of Advent
5. Holy Days: Feasts of the person of our Lord Jesus Christ
6. Sundays of Christmas
7a. Sundays of Epiphany
7b. Sundays of the Season after Pentecost
7c. Holy Days: Feasts relating to our Lord Jesus Christ
7d. Holy Days: Feasts of the Saints

You can see what's tricky here—there's a distinction between two different sorts of feasts of our Lord that get treated differently in different seasons. Basically, nothing will ever replace a Sunday in Easter, Lent, or Advent. When it comes to Christmas, Epiphany, and the Season after Pentecost, it depends. The more important feasts (Holy Name, the Presentation, and Transfiguration) do trump the Sundays; other feasts offer you an option. If a Holy Day of either sort falls in Epiphany or the Season after Pentecost, it is left up to discretion as to whether the Holy Day is transferred a day or two or whether its collects and readings are used on the Sunday in place of the Sunday collects and readings.

What we're really fussing with here is a delightful blend of incarnation and redemption. All Sundays celebrate the Resurrection; all Sundays remind us of our redemption wrought through Christ's Resurrection. Many of our holy days are rooted in the Incarnation; they offer specific examples of what it means for us that God took on our flesh or, conversely, that Christ incarnates himself in the very flesh of those who love him and follow him in the way that the first apostles and his mother did. Yes, all Sundays and holy days have a blend of both incarnation and redemption, but the way we celebrate the various occasions can help us reflect on them as we travel through the year.

Which is better to do when a feast falls on a Sunday in a green season: celebrate the season or the holy day? That depends—I would think it is better to celebrate the specific feast of our Lord (the fixed holy day) over the general feast of our Lord (the Sunday) and to give way to the most important of the sanctoral festivals: the dual feast of Saint Peter and Saint Paul, the feast of Saint Mary the Virgin (liturgists can debate whether it should properly be classed as a sanctoral feast or a feast of our Lord), and the feast of Saint Michael and All Angels.

While we are speaking about general principles, I'll note that the fourth section discussed in the Calendar identifies a different kind of day from the others. Sections one through three and section five (Principal Feasts, Sundays, Holy Days, Days of Optional Observance) are about precedence: What feast gets celebrated should a conflict arise. Section four fusses with a completely different issue. Rather than being concerned about *what* to observe, it focuses on *how* to observe. This section gives us ascetical directions. And they are fairly simple—fasting (eating less food than usual) or abstinence (refraining from a kind of food, usually four-footed flesh meat and poultry) are proper on Fridays that aren't celebrations.

You might ask what this is doing here if it doesn't seem to relate to the topic at hand. It does, in that it balances the importance of Sundays and the fullness of the faith. If we celebrate every Sunday as a festival of the Resurrection—as we should—we also need to keep Fridays as a reminder of the crucifixion. While Sunday should always receive the higher acclaim and the greater focus, we risk falling into danger if we celebrate a resurrection disconnected from a crucifixion, a liturgical theology of glory without a corresponding theology of the cross.

Advent

Advent focuses on one chief affection: watchful expectation. But, as the monastic reformer Saint Bernard expounded in one of his sermons for the season, we explore it in three different directions:

> We know that there are three comings [advents] of the Lord. The third lies between the other two. It is invisible, while the other two are visible. In the first coming he was seen on earth, dwelling among men...In the final coming all flesh will see the salvation of our God, and they will look on him whom they pierced. The intermediate coming is a hidden one; in it only the elect see the Lord within themselves, and they are saved. In the first coming our Lord came in our flesh and in our weakness; in this middle coming he comes in spirit and power; in the final coming he will be seen in glory and majesty (Bernard of Clairvaux, *Sermo 5, In Adventu Domini*).

The multiple senses of Advent allow it to be the perfect season to both begin and end the Church Year. Taking the first sense, seeing it as the time in which God's people waited for the birth of the long-promised Messiah, Advent serves as the perfect time of preparation for Christmas. Taking it in the third sense, seeing it as the culmination of the year and, indeed, of this present age itself with the coming of Christ as Lord and Judge, Advent serves as the perfect conclusion to the Church's Year. This third sense was the dominant sense of the season for a long time. Gregory the Great, reforming pope and highly influential author at the end of the sixth century, particularly connected Advent with the second coming; many of the classic hymns of Advent reflect this perspective: Charles Wesley's "Lo! He comes, with clouds descending" (*The Hymnal 1982*, 57; 58), the old Latin "Hark! A thrilling voice is sounding" (59), Philipp Nicolai's "Sleepers, wake!" (61; 62), the old Latin "O heavenly Word, eternal light" (63; 64) and Laurentius Laurenti's "Rejoice! Rejoice, believers" (68) to name but a few in our hymnal. Music lovers who are familiar with the "Dies Irae" ("O Day of Wrath") from requiems may be surprised to learn that this text was originally composed as a sequence for Advent. While Gregory's homilies focus on the dread associated with the appearance of the Judge, some of these hymn texts remind us to balance this perspective with a hearty dose of Christian hope. Both Laurenti and Nicolai use with good effect the parable of the wise and foolish bridesmaids to remind us that the coming of the Lord is our summoning to the marriage feast of the Lamb, not just to judgment.

Some modern authors have attempted to downplay Advent as a penitential season and have suggested that rejoicing at the coming of the Bridegroom is a more fitting attitude. They would also like us to see Advent as a pre-baptismal period, another forty-day stretch of catechesis leading to initiation

at the feast of the Baptism of Our Lord on the Sunday
after Epiphany. While the elements of rejoicing shouldn't
be suppressed, Advent does ask us if we stand ready for
the coming of the full presence of God. For myself, I find
this question to be the most fruitful. When I consider the
Baptismal Covenant in light of the Advent proclamation that
a holy God comes to dwell with a holy people, I inevitably
find myself falling short. I turn to penitence, less because the
season is an inherently penitential one and more because of
the realities that the season lays bare. If you are fine with the
Four Last Things: Heaven, Hell, Death, and Judgment—the
traditional themes for preaching during the season—then, no,
it doesn't have to be a penitential season at all. As for me, I'm
not quite there yet!

Even as we consider Bernard's third aspect of the season,
though, it is also tempered by the second coming that he
mentions. During this season we focus on our own watchful
expectation for Christ to be born within us. The coming of
the Lord does not have to be as dramatic as the entrance on
the clouds in Wesley's hymn; the affection of the season seeks
to cultivate in us an inward watchfulness, spurring us to get
our house in order for the coming King. Philip Doddridge's
"Hark! The glad sound!" (*The Hymnal 1982*, 71, 72) neatly
captures this second aspect, focusing on the inward experience
of Advent.

The final weeks of the Season after Pentecost begin
ramping up the theme of the Last Judgment flowing into
the first few weeks of Advent. The shift to the Nativity
is heightened by the beginning of the "O" antiphons on
December 17; while they don't appear in the prayer book
per se, they are explicitly broken out in Hymn 56, indicating
which verse should be used at Evening Prayer with the Song of
Mary on each day.

Christmas

The Christmas season lasts a spare twelve days, but at least half of them are prayer book feasts—if the two possible Sundays are included! The season begins on Christmas Day, December 25, and runs up to the eve of Epiphany. It is a season of rejoicing that focuses on the Incarnation and on the mystery of Immanuel: God with us. Yet, the rejoicing of the season is tempered a bit by the character of the holy days that, very early on, became associated with Christmas. This season is one of the most complicated in terms of rubrical gymnastics because there are four fixed holy days in a row, any one of which could be a Sunday in any given year: Christmas Day, Saint Stephen, Saint John the Evangelist, and the Holy Innocents. A note in the collects section establishes that if a Sunday happens to fall on any of the latter three days, that day and any successive day are pushed back by one. (For instance, if Sunday falls on the day after Christmas, the 26th is celebrated as the First Sunday after Christmas, the 27th honors Saint Stephen, the 28th honors Saint John, and the 29th honors the Holy Innocents.)

These holy days have been attached to Christmas for a very long time; they tend to put some perspective on the joy of Christmas. Saint Stephen is referred to as the *protomartyr*—the first of the martyrs. He is the first of Christ's followers to suffer death because of the faith, and the story is consciously told to mirror the death of Christ himself. Saint Stephen's death is recorded in Acts 7. Parallel to Jesus, Stephen commends his soul to God and forgives his persecutors—the young Paul among them. Historically, the liturgies of the Church have focused on two aspects of the feast of Stephen. First, like Jesus, Stephen's prayer at his death is effective: Paul is himself converted, and this conversion is greatly attributed to Stephen's prayer. Second, both prayers and hymns catalogue a number of antitheses or dramatic and ironic reversals between the Nativity and the death of Stephen: Christ was born to the world, but Stephen died to the world; Christ conferred life, Stephen endured death; Christ descended to humanity, Stephen ascended; Christ came to earth, Stephen went to heaven, etc. The underlying reminder here is that while Christ came to share the life of God with the world, the way to share most deeply in the life of God is none other than the way of the cross.

Next, we celebrate Saint John, apostle and evangelist. The only apostle not to suffer a martyr's death, the connection between John and Christmas comes preeminently through the famous opening of his Gospel—which has been read at the third Eucharist of Christmas ever since we have records of such readings. No other Gospel account captures quite so effectively the sense of incarnation as John's Prologue (John 1:1-18), and the high point of that passage is verse 14: "And the Word became flesh and lived among us, and we have seen his glory, the glory as of a father's only son, full of grace and truth."

The third holy day is the feast of the Holy Innocents, which, like Stephen, gives Christmas a darker turn. While it commemorates an event from Matthew's Gospel (2:16-18), its inclusion in this cluster of feasts around the Nativity itself underscores that we know the full story: Innocence is no guarantee of safety, and the innocent Lord of Life—himself an infant at this point—will in his own turn be condemned to die.

The next feast of Christmas is more benign even if it celebrates an occasion that may seem an odd liturgical moment: the feast of the Holy Name. This is a feast of the person of our Lord and, as such, should be celebrated even if a Sunday falls on this day. It's also our first octave day of the year. Under the pre-Reformation systems, certain important feasts would be celebrated for a whole week afterward—

liturgically, if not otherwise—and Christmas was certainly one of them. Thus, January 1 falls the week after December 25—seven days after, but eight if you begin counting with Christmas itself. What's interesting about this day is that, in addition to being the octave of Christmas, it also celebrates a biblical event: the circumcision of Jesus, which, as with any good Jewish lad, occurred a week after his birth as recorded in Luke 2:21. The ceremony of circumcision also included the naming rite. Our current prayer book prefers the more delicate "Holy Name" rather than former books' "Circumcision of our Lord." More than just recording a biblical event, this feast reminds us of an important corollary to the fact of the Incarnation: It explicitly reminds us of the scandal of particularity—that Jesus was born as a specific person in a specific culture. Circumcision brought him into God's covenant with the children of Abraham, locating him within a people, affirming and confirming his Jewish identity.

The doctrine of the Incarnation sometimes gets short shrift because the season dedicated to it is so brief and falls at a time that is often given over to travel, family, and holiday celebrations rather than church. Nevertheless, it is one of the most important doctrines of the faith, and it can be—and has been—argued that Anglicanism in particular has a special affinity with Incarnation. Indeed, the statement of the Incarnation was one of the greatest stumbling blocks of Christianity in its first few centuries. People could embrace a God who loved them. People could get behind a God who worked wonders, even the Resurrection. But the idea that a God, a divine spirit-being, would stoop to sully himself with matter—fallible, corruptible, imperfect, decaying matter—was crazy talk to the dominant Neoplatonic perspective that said that spirit was better than and fundamentally opposed to both body and matter. And yet this is what the Church insisted upon, even in the face of a variety of potential explanations of how spirit and matter stayed appropriately separate in the person of Jesus. Instead, the Church chose, and defended, and fought for Incarnation: the belief that God cares about us enough to become one of us. This is the miracle of Christmas: God took on humanity so that we might take on divinity. This, in and of itself, totally apart from crucifixion, totally apart from resurrection, is a fundamental act of God reconciling humanity and all creation to himself. Of course, crucifixion and resurrection are also part of the equation but take on greater and deeper meaning for the fact of the Incarnation. They mean more when we acknowledge that it was a truly human Jesus who suffered, died, and was raised than if it was a spiritual projection that only seemed to suffer.

Epiphany

One of the principles observed and standardized in the mid-to-late twentieth-century Calendar reforms is the notion that seasons tend to begin and end with feasts. As a result, it is often said that the feast of Epiphany concludes the Christmas season. In one sense, this is true—in another it is not. On one hand, if you count out the famous "Twelve Days of Christmas" by modern reckoning, they will end on January 6, the Epiphany. On the other, if you count them out following the standard classical method (counting the day you start with), the twelve day period ends on January 5. According to the prayer book's list of feasts (*The Book of Common Prayer*, p. 31), Epiphany is the first entry under the Epiphany Season while the Second Sunday after Christmas day closes out Christmas proper.

Whether there is such a thing as the Epiphany Season is a point of some debate. According to the prayer book, there is an Epiphany Season; according to the Roman Catholic reform of the Calendar, Christmas runs through the Sunday after the Epiphany and everything after that is Ordinary Time designated as Sundays after Epiphany. The Revised Common Lectionary attempts to split the difference; it retains the title, Season of Epiphany, yet breaks into an Ordinary Time sequence after the Second Sunday after Epiphany, beginning with the Third Sunday and thus functionally siding with the Roman Catholic removal of the season. With the Episcopal adoption of the Revised Common Lectionary, we find ourselves in the odd situation of keeping the season yet losing its character.[9]

The original point of the season is that it was about epiphanies. Epiphany comes from the Greek word meaning manifestations or showings-forth. Actually, many of the medieval calendars retained the Greek name of the feast, *Theophany*, which means manifestation of God. The point here is that the Epiphany season focused on the ways that the divinity of Christ was revealed to the world. The season as a whole was about how God was made manifest in the person of Jesus and how he was shown to be both fully human and fully divine. As a result, the Gospel readings of the period cycled through the first miracles in each of the Gospels and some of the earliest teachings of Jesus. These were all understood as different ways that Christ made himself known to the world.

So, why does the issue about a season of Epiphany matter? What's the point?

Perhaps it illustrates the ways in which we accept an over-simplification of our Calendar. The Roman Catholic reforms and the Revised Common Lectionary that follow them attempt to make the Church Year more tidy; they place it into neat classifications. According to these schemes, there are two cycles in the temporal sequence: one celebrates incarnation, the other celebrates redemption. The first includes the preparatory season of Advent, then the festal season of

Christmas; the second includes the preparatory season of Lent, then the festal season of Easter. Everything outside of these is relegated to "Ordinary." I resist this, though, because it feels just a little bit too tidy. If God's work of reconciliation is packaged into these two boxes, we lose shades of meaning through which these two interact with and interpenetrate one another. Retaining an independent Epiphany season recognizes that the earthly ministry of Jesus contained redemptive moments possible through his incarnate nature and that redemption includes more than simply crucifixion and resurrection—as central and important as these are.

There's one more oddity that ought to be mentioned. In accordance with the concept that feasts should begin and end liturgical seasons, the Revised Common Lectionary created a feast to conclude the Season of Epiphany, that is, Transfiguration Sunday. This actually makes quite a bit of sense if the theme of the Epiphany season is manifestation. The Transfiguration is, indeed, one of the more dramatic manifestations of Jesus' two natures in the Gospels. In hindsight, it seems ironic to create a new feast to underscore the meaning of the season after having functionally gutted it by turning it into Ordinary Time. Furthermore, the prayer book already contains a feast of the Transfiguration on August 6. The prayer book's original solution was to offer the feast without the name—the Gospel reading was of the Transfiguration and the collect mentioned it, but the day itself was simply referred to as The Last Sunday after the Epiphany. Now, with the official adoption of the Revised Common Lectionary, its status and title is unclear.[10]

When we turn to *The Hymnal 1982* during Epiphany, a couple of hymns helpfully lift up the themes of revelation and incarnate redemption. Caelius Sedulius wrote a very long poem on the life of Christ in the fifth century, sections of which have been used as hymns since the early medieval period. One of these is "When Christ's appearing was made known" (131, 132), which does a great job of connecting the various manifestations celebrated liturgically in the early part of the Epiphany season. Both Martin Luther's "When Jesus went to Jordan's stream" (139) and the nineteenth-century "'I come,' the great Redeemer cries" (116) emphasize the redemptive power of Christ's incarnate ministry. Finally, "Songs of thankfulness and praise" (135) unites the idea of manifestation along with the redemptive acts of the Incarnate Christ, making it, in my mind, one of the very best vehicles for communicating the heart of the Epiphany season.

Lent

The season of Lent engages the affection of penitence. During Lent we consider ourselves from two vantage points. The first concerns the human tendency to sin—individually and corporately. Sin is a reality of human existence. The other unavoidable reality of human existence provides the second vantage point: death. Lent opens with Ash Wednesday's stark acknowledgement of the reality of death. Lent isn't about being morbid or punitive, tearing ourselves down, or whipping ourselves into a lather of self-condemnation. It is, rather, about reality. It is about taking honest stock of who and what we are in the face of eternity and in the face of God. We are limited; we are fallible. In our short lives, we make choices that lead us deeper into separation and chaos—cutting ourselves off from those who love us and whom we would love. Lent is a deliberate exercise in owning up.

The Ash Wednesday liturgy has four particular parts that focus our attentions at the start of the season. The first is the exhortation to a holy Lent. It sets forth briefly the idea of Lent, noting its dual role as a season for baptismal preparation and a season for corporate repentance. After the history lesson, it points us to the particular disciplines of the season and identifies elements of a holy Lent: "by self-examination and repentance; by prayer, fasting, and self-denial; and by reading and meditating on God's holy Word" (*The Book of Common Prayer*, p. 265). Thus, we confront the reality of our inner lives, we do things that help us love God and neighbor, and we re-center ourselves on the vision that God has for the world and our place within it.[11]

The second component of the Ash Wednesday service is the imposition of the ashes. This is a liturgical moment of great power—and should be allowed to speak for itself without piling up a bunch of words around it. Some of my most poignant and important memories of Lent are from this part of this service. I remember my first Ash Wednesday as a parent when I carried my infant daughter to the rail and saw the priest put the ashes on her forehead. The contrast, the paradox, between her youth and the mark of mortality affected me deeply. Some may think this inappropriate, but I recall the many churchyards I have wandered, looking at gravestones and seeing markers for children (and often their mothers). The reality of mortality offends our sensibilities but to deny it plays into our fantasies.

Alternatively, I remember one year when I assisted in the chancel, imposing ashes. As I moved around the altar rail, I found myself facing three figures—in the center was an elder of the congregation, his eyes closed, face to the sky, arms outstretched, gripping the hands of his wife on one side, his best friend on the other. For the previous nine months, I had been visiting him weekly as he wrestled with an aggressive cancer that had turned terminal. We all knew this Ash Wednesday would be his last. For him, this moment was a solemn embrace of sister Death in the company of the Church, the whole Body of Christ gathered around him.

Here, though, lies one of the brutal truths of Ash Wednesday: This man from my congregation was not closer to death than anyone else in the room. All of us are but a breath, a heartbeat, a moment away from death. The difference between us was his awareness of his situation. He knew and chose to face the truth of his mortality, a truth about which most of us would prefer to remain blissfully unaware.

From this point in the service we move to the third component, Psalm 51, the greatest of the penitential psalms. In these words, we are given an example of full disclosure before God. The psalmist is under no illusions about his interior state; there is an honesty here that we may find uncomfortable but which speaks directly to the presence, reality, and power of sin in our lives. I think the prayer book purposefully gives us this psalm at the beginning of the season. We receive it as a model of penitent prayer. We may not feel every bit of what the psalmist says, but it gives us direction and guidance for the deep self-examination to which we are called. And, as we pray it and gaze within ourselves, we may indeed find ourselves drawing closer to the psalmist's perspective than we might have first thought.

The fourth part is the Litany of Penitence, which also spurs us to self-reflection. Its beginning mirrors Jesus' summary of the law that classically began Anglican Eucharists, including the Rite I Eucharist in our current prayer book. It still starts the Penitential Order that is especially appropriate in this season (the Rite I version is p. 319; Rite II, p. 351). Jesus encapsulates God's Law in Mark's Gospel in this way:

Jesus said, "The first commandment is this: Hear, O Israel: The Lord your God is the only Lord. Love the Lord your God with all your heart, with all your soul, with all your mind, and with all your strength. The second is this: Love your neighbor as yourself. There is no commandment greater than these" Mark 12-19-31 (*The Book of Common Prayer*, p. 351).

By putting this section of scripture at the beginning of Holy Eucharist, the architects of the early prayer books gave this passage a special place in our understanding of what God requires of us and what righteousness looks like: loving God, loving neighbor. This is us as God wants us to be.

The Litany of Penitence starts out with a frank acknowledgement that we are in clear and deliberate contrast:

> We have not loved you with our whole heart, and mind, and strength. We have not loved our neighbors as ourselves. We have not forgiven others, as we have been forgiven.
>
> *Have mercy on us, Lord* (*The Book of Common Prayer*, p. 267).

A lot of us are uncomfortable talking about sin, sometimes because we have come from traditions that seemed to overemphasize it. But the prayer book lays out clearly the definition of sin. Sin is the failure to love. When we have failed to love—in thought, word, and deed—we have departed from God's intention for us and for creation. The rest of the litany identifies and helps us recognize concrete ways that we have done this. Having set out the main thesis up front, we are offered further examples of failures to love in which we may find ourselves. Again, the purpose here is not self-flagellation but honesty about who and what we are. The litany confronts us with the reality that we fail to be the people God created us to be. It gently recalls us to that high vocation, reminding us of that second question of the Baptismal Covenant: "Will you persevere in resisting evil, and, whenever you fall into sin, repent and return to the Lord?" (*The Book of Common Prayer*, p. 304).

In these ways, Ash Wednesday sets the proper tone for the rest of the season. It is not a period of punishment but a sober, honest opportunity to look at ourselves as we are: frail, fallible, and mortal. We need God's grace. We need God's love. And we need to live that grace and love for the rest of the world to see. Lent is our time to look into ourselves and our communities and to pray for the strength, the courage, and the assistance to live our Baptism like we mean it. In a work such as this, I would be remiss if I did not offer the reminder that Lent is a perfect time to recommit ourselves to the regular practices of the faith—including the praying of the Office and attendance at Eucharist. These are not great ascetic works— they are actually fairly easy—but are more useful in the long run than attempts at greater feats of penitence. As we move more toward the habitual recollection of God, we are also recollecting ourselves—who we are in the face of the God who created us and loves us (no matter what!).

Of all the seasons that were altered in the twentieth-century reforms, Lent was changed the most. The best way to look at the historic Calendar is that it saw Lent as a graded movement into practices of penitence. That is, it started off easy, then, at designated points, ramped things up as the season progressed. The season began with Septuagesima on the Sunday ten weeks out from Easter, creating a three week Pre-Lenten period. Then Ash Wednesday hit with the liturgy of the ashes. The Lenten liturgical round started on the First Sunday of Lent. Then Passiontide moved the bar higher two weeks before Easter. Finally, Palm Sunday kicked off Holy Week. So, there were a series of four grades that moved us deeper into Lent and its exercises. However, this process did not fit within the twentieth-century emphasis on idealized fourth-century baptismal practices. In the move to realign the Lenten experience with the fourth-century catechumenal process, the principle of grading was rejected, and the Lenten experience was reduced to a period of forty days beginning with Ash Wednesday. The pre-Lenten season was trimmed away; Passion Sunday was merged with Palm Sunday to make Holy Week even more distinct. The Revised Common Lectionary does not recognize Holy Week as a distinct season—it is the final week of Lent. The prayer book, however, does give Holy Week its own heading equal with Lent so we will consider it separately although recognizing its intrinsic Lenten character.

The intention of the twentieth-century renovation of Lent is not entirely clear without the catechumenal liturgies contained in *The Book of Occasional Services*. Within the Pastoral Services, a set of liturgies is provided for those to be baptized at the Easter Vigil. On the First Sunday in Lent, the candidates for Baptism are enrolled; on the Third Sunday, they are given the Apostles' Creed (though the Nicene Creed can also be used); on the Fifth Sunday, they are given the Lord's Prayer. I have only experienced a catechetical Lent once—and that was in the context of a Roman Catholic college chaplaincy (I sang in their choir). It was a moving experience to share the Lenten journey with those preparing for Baptism, and it did give that Lent a deeper character. On the other hand, I have never seen this process take place within an Episcopal Church. While the prayer book envisions and provides resources for a return to adult baptism and its communal celebration during Easter, our evangelism seems to have fallen behind our liturgies. The potential is all too often left on the table. We have trimmed away some of the traditional richness of the season to make room for another facet of the season that, all too often, is lacking.

On a practical liturgical note, the Lenten liturgies receive a more austere tone. The *Gloria in exclesis* is not sung; alleluia is not said.[12] If a Hallelujah does appear in a psalm, the word can simply be omitted. Penitential options are provided for the opening of the Eucharist and as the invitatory antiphons at Morning Prayer. Sundays are always feast days (which is why we speak of Sundays *in* Lent rather than Sundays *of* Lent), but it's appropriate that the rejoicing be a bit more subdued. (And, of course, on Sundays you may—within moderation—indulge in those things that you have given up for Lent.)

The veiling of images, statues, icons, and crosses is common, but different authorities give different times as to when this should be done. Some suggest that it is done on the First Sunday in Lent; others suggest Passion Sunday. Of course, with the transference of Passion Sunday to Palm Sunday, a decision must be made whether Passiontide is retained as a two-week period or, following the prayer book, is reduced to Holy Week itself.

The hymns of Lent range from the informative to the introspective. Some teach the Church's theology of the season. Claudia Hernaman's "Lord, who throughout these forty days" (*The Hymnal 1982*, 142) connects the Lenten experience with the fast of Jesus in the wilderness and neatly frames the point of the season. The Latin Office hymn, "The glory of these forty days" (143), unites our Lenten experience with the fasting, penitence, and prayer of central figures from both the Old and New Testament, inviting us to see ourselves in the company of saints and to follow their good examples. Some hymns call us to penitence, frequently by suggesting themes and directions that our penitence should take. Gregory the Great's "Kind Maker of the world" (152) as well as George Smyttan's "Forty days and forty nights" (150) do this, occupying a place between the more didactic hymns and the hymns that model penitential prayer. The introspective hymns come in individual forms—like John Donne's prayer in "Wilt thou forgive that sin" (140, 141) or Martin Luther's paraphrase of Psalm 130 in "From deepest woe I cry to thee" (151)—but also model corporate confession for social sin like

David Hughes's "Creator of the earth and skies" (148). Last, it's worth noting that even in the Lenten hymnody, the goal toward which the season moves is not overlooked. Classic Office hymns like "Lord Jesus, Sun of Righteousness" (144) and Percy Dearmer's "Now quit your care and anxious fear" (145) alike point us toward love and Easter as the true end of the Lenten experience.

Holy Week

Holy Week constitutes the space of our deepest yearly meditation on the passion of Christ and ushers in the three great days that are the highlight of the Church Year. It is also in the space of a single week, and, if a family follows typical American churchgoing habits, they could miss all but one day (Palm/Passion Sunday) or even the whole season altogether! It can be said without exaggeration that this is the season where faithful attendance at—or at least attention to—the public liturgies of the Church matters the most and renders the most. Both the prayer book and the Revised Common Lectionary provide material for every day of the week, with the Sunday of the Passion: Palm Sunday, Maundy Thursday, Good Friday, and Holy Saturday receiving their own distinct liturgies in the block between pages 270 and 285 of the prayer book.

Palm Sunday was conflated with Passion Sunday in the mid-twentieth century by the Roman Catholic Church; this move worked toward the process of leveling the grades of Lent, but also recognized through the title what was actually going on in the service. That is, Passion Sunday didn't have a passion reading—Palm Sunday did. Indeed, there was little in the liturgy of Passion Sunday to signal a further shift toward the cross and passion than other Lenten Sundays: neither the Gospel (John 8:46-59) nor the other propers seemed more passional than normal. By contrast, the celebration of Palm

Sunday had included the reading of the entirety of Matthew's Passion (chapters 26-27) from at least the seventh century.

For most Episcopalians, this change makes no difference—the 1928 prayer book was the first American or English book to identify the Fifth Sunday in Lent as "Passion Sunday," and it directed no liturgical changes at the time. Only those who followed old traditions or Roman Catholic customs of the timing for veiling images and crosses, dropping the *Gloria Patri* from the end of the psalms, and singing different hymns at the Office noticed, and they had to decide whether to keep doing it following the Fifth Sunday in Lent or whether to shift these practices to Holy Week.

The combination of Palm and Passion Sunday may feel a bit odd. After all, we are used to a Sunday orienting itself around one Gospel and focusing on one theme. Palm Sunday isn't like this. There are three collects and a blessing—and two Gospels. Throw in a procession as well, and it's easy to get confused. Two things are happening here. First, we have to get Jesus into Jerusalem for the last week of his life. This is the Palm part. Second, in case the congregation doesn't make it to Holy Week services, we make sure that they at least hear the Passion reading—even if they miss the full experience of them. How do we work this so that the rest of Holy Week isn't just repeating the same stuff we just heard? This is where the logic of the three-year lectionary cycle is leveraged: at the Passion part of the Palm Sunday service, we hear the passion story from the Gospel appointed for the year (Matthew, Mark, or Luke). Then, during the last days of Holy Week, we always read from the Gospel of John. This offers us the same basic story, yet two different perspectives, one on Sunday, the other at the end of the week.

Out of the Palm Sunday material, my favorite part is the very first collect of the service. It sets the whole tone for the rest of the week to come:

> Assist us mercifully with your help, O Lord God of our salvation, that we may enter with joy upon the contemplation of those mighty acts, whereby you have given us life and immortality; through Jesus Christ our Lord. *Amen.*[13]

There you have it: "the contemplation of those mighty acts, whereby you have given us life and immortality." That's the perfect introduction for all that follows.

The days of Holy Week have been prayer book service days since the very first prayer book. It used to be that the passions from the four Gospels were read through the week: Most of Matthew's passion was read on Palm Sunday. Monday and Tuesday recounted Mark's passion, Wednesday and Thursday read through Luke's passion, and John's passion was read on Friday. Saturday finished off the end of Matthew's passion with the burial of Jesus. Our current Holy Week service moves in a chronological direction rather than a comprehensive one: The Passion Gospel of Passion Sunday comes from the Gospel appointed for the year, the days of Holy Week read from John's narrative beginning at chapter 12, which begins "Six days before the Passover..." The Daily Office Lectionary of Year One also prescribes similar but not identical readings from John 12 for Monday through Wednesday.

Holy Week is fundamentally about the journey to the cross. We accompany Jesus, his apostles, and the disciples on the last walk into Jerusalem and through the days that follow. The services of Maundy Thursday, Good Friday, and the Easter Vigil are best seen as a single liturgical unit with long pauses between its movements. For me, I can't help but hear strains of Renaissance settings of the Book of Lamentations floating all through Holy Week—as Lamentations was the heart of the Daily Office services and some amazing settings were composed for *Tenebrae*, the Office of Shadows that occurred in the early mornings at Matins and Lauds. We can take our cue from them: Holy Week has a restrained grandeur in order to communicate the horror of human hatred that we unleashed upon the Lord of Life.

Recognizing that, it's important to take a moment and consider our perspective: how we interpret these moments and where we find ourselves within the events of the passion. Some of the greatest devotions of the Passion—like the Stations of the Cross—come from the imaginative-affectional tradition of devotion. In these sorts of devotions, we use images, readings, hymns, and prayers to give ourselves the sense of being there, to imagine exactly what we would have seen and heard, and then to feel the emotions that witnessing these things would bring upon us. Certain traditions are better at this than others. For instance, I suggest that the African-American spiritual, "Were you there?" (*The Hymnal 1982*, 172) from the African-American experience stands strongly in this tradition. And, while we may not normally think of the English as emotional people, many of the passion devotions from late Sarum England, just before the Reformation, emphasize this imaginative-affectional spirituality. However, as I have spent time working with and reading through these devotions, I have identified what I believe to be a fundamental flaw in their imaginative construction.

These materials tend to identify heavily with the disciples and with the women who accompanied Mary. That is, we have images or texts that describe vignettes with graphic depictions of what is suffered by both Jesus and Mary in the events of the capture, judgment, torment, crucifixion, and death. The *Fifteen Oes* of Saint Brigit are a classic example of this as is the medieval hymn "At the cross her vigil keeping" (*The Hymnal 1982*, 159). The problem is that the identification of us is consistently and relentlessly with the disciples. We gain a clear sense of us and them. We are those who follow Jesus; they are those who slay Jesus. The devotions themselves, with this stark contrast, lead us to experience the crucifixion of Jesus not as humanity's inhumanity to the Son of Man but as the experience of what the Jews did to Jesus. Given the emphases of these devotions, it's no surprise that medieval and renaissance pogroms sometimes coincided with Palm Sunday and Good Friday. This Christian anti-Semitism and anti-Judaism is absolutely deplorable and has no place in our faith.

This kind of devotion creates and fosters an us-and-them perspective on Holy Week, missing one of the big patterns of scripture and undermining a proper understanding of the season and its liturgies. We misconstrue the basic teachings of the Church and the scripture on sin if we fail to account for the fact that we are them. This is not a new insight. Indeed, in the period of the Reformation and in a lot of Counter-Reformation Roman Catholic spirituality, this point is made, sometimes to excess. A good example of the proper reversal is in the hymn, "Ah, holy Jesus" (*The Hymnal 1982*, 158). The second verse in particular makes the turn that the Sarum materials lack: "Who was the guilty? Who brought this upon thee? Alas, my treason, Jesus, hath undone thee. 'Twas I, Lord Jesus, I it was denied thee: I crucified thee." We stand both as the disciples and as the crucifiers. The impact of Palm Sunday is muted if we fail to make the connection that the crowd that shouted "Hosanna" was the same crowd that shouted "Crucify him!" We need to be able to locate ourselves within both crowds. It is only with this perspective that we can hear the Good Friday Reproaches properly as words directed at us rather than condemnations of "the Jews."

It is a shame that more people don't come to the Maundy Thursday and Good Friday services. I realize these services are not on Sunday and fall outside the usual pattern. However, patterns lie at the heart of this whole liturgical spiritual project. We say that God is love. We say that Jesus is God incarnate and therefore the most perfect exemplar of love. But love is a very broad word. Consider all of the things that the word love is used for in American culture these days! Surely we as lovers of Christ mean something more significant, something more meaningful. Maundy Thursday and Good Friday are about a life patterned by love and therefore about the nature of love and the consequences of love. Christ came to preach love. Had the content of love been some feel-good message of self-satisfaction, no one would have demanded his death. That is not the love that Christ preached incarnate. He preached a love—and enacted a love—that made people deeply uncomfortable, that challenged the status quo, and that was not afraid to speak openly against sin, hypocrisy, and pride—particularly among those who saw themselves as most religious. Holy Week warns us of the consequences of preaching true love.

Maundy Thursday lays bare the strength and power of humble service. The *maundy*—the commandment from which the day gets its name—is the Gospel exhortation to love one another as Christ has loved us. All three of the great liturgical actions of the evening offer a powerful—and disturbing— example of what this love and service looks like. The Last Supper is an intimate gathering of friends, yet its elemental symbols and pregnant words reveal a host of deep meanings. The washing of the feet offers a vision of a leader who is strong enough in humility to perform the role of a menial servant in the midst of his friends. The stripping of the altar portrays in symbolic terms the stripping away, the falling away, of all supports, defenses, and shields. Jesus could have run. But he didn't. Therefore it is only fitting that we give John the last word: "No one has greater love than this, to lay down one's life for one's friends" (John 15:13).

Good Friday is our great festival of paradox: We celebrate the day that mortals slay the immortal, the day the Lord of Life gives himself up to death. And we call it good, firm in the conviction that in his dying, the power of death will be destroyed. Most of our acts this day involve paradox in one form or another. We lift high and venerate a very simple yet effective instrument of torture. We address a long series of collects to the One who did not respond to his own son's cry from the cross. We receive from the reserved Sacrament in the absence of a consecration a meal that proclaims his presence and power.

If not many make it to Maundy Thursday or Good Friday, fewer still appear for Holy Saturday, and yet we have a service for it. It is a simple Service of the Word that occupies a single page of the prayer book (p. 283). It is a service of marking time—an experience of liturgical waiting. We gather together and then—we don't really do a whole lot. The thing that speaks volumes here is all of the things left undone: It is basically a collect, the readings, a homily, and an anthem. There is no Eucharist; there are no greetings; there are no Prayers of the People. It is a shell of a gathering—as the Church is a shell without Jesus. It is the last service of Holy Week for as the sun sets, we prepare to turn the corner and head into Easter.

The Easter Season

Perhaps the greatest achievement of the twentieth-century Liturgical Renewal Movement is the restoration of the Easter Vigil. The dual emphases on Baptism and Easter come together in full flower in the splendor of a well-celebrated

Easter Vigil. Hearing the singing of the *Exultet* before a newly lit Paschal candle in the midst of a darkened nave at the end of a long Lent is one of the most spiritual moments of my year. The Vigil sets the tone for the rest of the Great Fifty Days as the Church celebrates the coming of Easter and the ongoing power of the Resurrection. Another related thrill comes the next morning as Morning Prayer kicks off with the Alleluia-laden "Christ our Passover" (*Pascha Nostrum*). Likely the oldest season of the Church year, the Easter Season follows Gospel chronology effortlessly, celebrating the bodily Ascension of Christ forty days after the Resurrection and ending with Pentecost, the gift of the Holy Spirit and the birth of the Church on the fiftieth day after the Resurrection.

The first week after Easter, from the Sunday of the Resurrection to the Second Sunday of Easter, is another special octave; every day is a prayer book holy day with special readings assigned for Eucharist and the Office, and no other feasts are allowed to fall within this week. If March 25 (the Annunciation) or a feast of the apostles falls within its span, they are transferred out to the days after the Second Sunday.

Easter is the season when we meditate on Christ's Resurrection and acquaint ourselves with the affection of joy. As I said of the affections earlier, this is not an emotion or an expression—it is a pattern of being. It is not about feigning a feeling or attempting to put on a happy face. It is more subtle, deeper, richer than that. This is simply the joy of living, the joy of resting in the presence of God, and in being in the presence of those you love. It takes its cue from the Resurrection, the triumph of life, the ultimate sign that love is stronger than death.

Part of the celebration for the prayer book is to add "Alleluias!" There are a number of places where alleluias are properly added in during the Easter season, notably at the fraction anthem at the Eucharist and also at the Eucharist's dismissal.

The hymns of Easter likewise add alleluias throughout. The hymns of Venantius Fortunatus connect the Resurrection with the return of spring in "Welcome, happy morning!" (*The Hymnal 1982*, 179) and "Hail thee, festival day!" (175). The theological link between the Exodus from Egypt and the crossing of the Red Sea with the Resurrection of Jesus that pervades the Easter Vigil is celebrated in many Easter hymns, including William Hammond's "Awake and sing the song of Moses and the Lamb" (181), Ronald Knox's "Through the Red Sea brought at last" (187), John of Damascus's "Come, ye faithful, raise the strain" (199, 200), and the Office hymn "The Lamb's high banquet called to share" (202). Jubilation and rejoicing are the hallmark of the season's praises.

The Church does not follow its usual pattern of fasting during Easter because of the celebratory nature of the season. Some churches also exercise the permission to occasionally omit the Confession of Sin during the Sundays of Easter.[14] Likewise, in some churches, it is the custom not to kneel during Easter for the same reason. This prohibition of kneeling is sometimes connected to a canon from the Council of Nicaea—the church council in 325 CE that agreed on the wording of what would become the Nicene Creed. A canon from that council prohibits kneeling on Sundays and throughout the Easter season. However, it comes from a liturgical environment where kneeling and multiple prostrations was the regular rule. It was a liturgical culture entirely unlike ours. Thus, it seems odd to impose one part of its practice during Easter (standing) and ignore the more regular and consistent part throughout the rest of the year (kneeling and prostrations). Contemporary accounts continue to show differences of practice from one region to another; whatever uniformity the council was attempting to impose, it did not achieve.

The Season after Pentecost

The Season after Pentecost is referred to in some Calendars as Ordinary Time. This is not intended to suggest that it is ordinary in the sense of being normal and not important, but rather that the Sundays are counted in an ordinal fashion (i.e., first, second, third). Unfortunately, this fine distinction is often easily and quickly lost. This is the long, green season that occupies somewhere between twenty-three and twenty-eight weeks out of the year, depending on when Easter falls. As far as I'm concerned, it is most closely connected with the affection of faithful endurance.

The beginning of this season can be a little tricky, particularly for those who are diligent in their use of the Daily Office. Sundays in this period are counted, as the table on page 32 of the prayer book shows, as Sundays after Pentecost. However, the collect and the readings are established by reference to a numbered Proper that is anchored around a calendar date. Thus, an ordinary Sunday like Proper 15 will be whatever Sunday falls closest to the date of August 17 (and we can find this out by looking through the Season after Pentecost either in the collects, the Eucharistic Lectionary, or the Daily Office Lectionary). The logic is that the fixing of Propers to calendar days minimizes the effects of a constantly moving Easter season. Thus, we can always count on the same readings showing up in the summer and fall. The difficulty comes at the very start. The season after Pentecost begins on the Monday after Pentecost. The problem is that the collect for the week is typically that of the preceding Sunday—but not in this case. Instead, we locate the Proper that falls closest to the date of Pentecost, use its collect, and begin lectionary readings from this point. The first Sunday of the season itself is the Feast of the Holy Trinity, one of our principal feasts. The week following the feast continues with the collect of the Sunday that would have been and continues the lectionary readings in course. Thus, due to the placement of Pentecost and the Feast of the Holy Trinity, the two earliest possible Propers—Proper 1 and Proper 2—will never actually be celebrated on a Sunday, although their collects and weekday readings may be used when Easter falls at its earliest dates.

As noted above, the Sundays of the Season after Pentecost hold the lowest order of precedence, and it is permissible to celebrate a holy day in place of the Sunday if it should happen to fall on a Sunday. Note, however, that it is not proper to move a feast that falls in the week onto a Sunday unless it is the feast of the parish's title (i.e., the saint or mystery that it is named for) or its patron (i.e., any saints whose relics might be enshrined in the church). And even those transfers are not permissible during the seasons of Advent, Lent, and Easter. The only other feast that may be transferred to a Sunday is the Feast of All Saints because of its status as a principal feast. Anything else requires the bishop's permission, as well as "urgent and sufficient reason." [15] There can be a temptation to shake things up a little bit as the green Sundays wear long. How could it hurt to transfer a feast now and then or to devote a Sunday to a special cause rather than using the appointed texts? Three reasons: First, the temptation can be strong to create cause Sundays. But once the practice starts, it can be a hard habit to break, and the weekly feast of the Resurrection can be subverted and obscured. The early Anglican fathers had to rescue Sundays from encroaching saints' days in their time, and there's no need to create a similar situation now with causes. Second, transferring the feasts or cause Sundays interferes with the notion of common prayer. One of the beauties of a lectionary system is that you can know what the readings will be next Sunday at your church or anybody else's church that follows the system. You can read, mark, and inwardly digest the readings ahead of time. If someone is changing these on a whim, though, it makes light of the commitment to read and pray in common with others. Third, there is a discipline in following the cycle.

The Last Sunday after Pentecost is officially titled in the prayer book, "The Last Sunday after Pentecost," and is "Proper 29, the Sunday closest to November 23." Just as the Revised Common Lectionary placed Transfiguration Sunday at the end of its Season of Epiphany, the Lectionary and the Roman Catholic Calendar appoint the final Sunday after Pentecost as the Feast of Christ the King. Again—as with the end of Epiphany—the prayer book has not adopted the title but has taken the concept: The collect and the readings celebrate the reign of Christ.

The Days of Optional Observance

Beyond the Principal Feasts, Sundays, Holy Days, and the Days of Special Devotion, only one category of days is left: the Days of Optional Observance. These are the ferial days or *ferias,* which means any day that isn't a Sunday or a feast. If you add together the seven principal feasts, forty-nine Sundays (as three are principal feasts), and the thirty-two holy days, that is a total of eighty-eight prayer book feast days, leaving 277 ferial days in a regular year.

The monthly listing of days between the Calendar rubrics and the list of titles of feasts gives us a potential set of people to be celebrated as lesser feasts on these days.

When lesser feasts were first introduced in 1963, there were 115 recommended lesser feasts on the list; the latest set of recommendations from 2015 offers 288 potential occasions. One of the issues over the latest list is the sheer volume of names brought forward; as you can see, even accounting for some of these falling on Sundays in any given year, it doesn't leave a lot of open days. The thing to remember, though, is this: They are all optional. You can choose to celebrate as many or as few as you would like.

Because of the cyclical nature of the Daily Office, Days of Optional Observance don't impact it much—the only impact is whether you choose to change the Collect of the Day. If a Eucharist is being celebrated on a ferial day, the prayer book provides a range of possible options. Here are six of them:

1. To celebrate a major feast that has fallen elsewhere in the week as provided in the prayer book.
2. To celebrate a lesser feast as a Day of Optional Observance appointed in the Church's Calendar.
3. To celebrate a lesser feast as a Day of Optional Observance not appointed in the Church's Calendar by using the Commons of Saints.
4. To celebrate the season by using the propers of the preceding Sunday.
5. To celebrate the season by using the propers appointed for a day in the given week of the season.
6. To celebrate an occasion provided for in the propers for Various Occasions.

In the prayer book system, Sundays are, for the most part, weekly feasts of the Resurrection. Weekdays are the place where more freedom is offered to depart from a fixed schedule and engage with the particular charisms and concerns of the local community. The option always exists to celebrate whatever season the Church happens to be moving through. But these days can be opportunities to celebrate saints, whether local or universal or to lift up a particular doctrine or intention through the use of the Propers for Various Occasions.

CHAPTER 4
THE COLLECTS

THE LITURGICAL MANIFESTATIONS OF THE CHURCH YEAR

The Church Year establishes fundamental organizing principles that direct our common liturgical life. The Daily Office and the Eucharist both exist within and are guided by it. When we look back to the liturgies of the medieval period, quite a lot of material used to mark the liturgical year and its passage. Remember, before the mid-twentieth century and the reforms of Vatican II, there was no three-year cycle—only a one-year cycle that repeated in an unchanging fashion. In medieval books—taking those of tenth-century England as an example—each Sunday Eucharist had its own particular set of liturgically proper materials: four prayers (the opening collect, a prayer over the gifts at the offertory, a proper preface, and a post-communion prayer), two readings (an Epistle and a Gospel), and four or five minor propers (usually one or two-line biblical texts sung by the choir at the entrance, after the

Epistle, before the Gospel, during the offertory, and during the communion).

That's a lot of stuff. And it doesn't stop there either.

Turning to the Daily Office, parts of the Eucharistic propers—especially the biblical readings—would be interwoven among the various elements. The Gospel in full would be read in the Sunday Night Office, and a line from it would usually appear before and after the *Song of Mary* (that is, an antiphon) at the Evening Office. The Epistle too might appear in Gospel canticle antiphons through the week and was frequently found tucked into the suffrages of the mid-day Offices. Of course, the opening collect of the Eucharist would reappear as the closing collect of each Office.

In Archbishop Cranmer's simplification of the liturgy and construction of the first *Book of Common Prayer*, most of these proper elements were swept away. In his 1549 book, he retained only four of the Eucharistic propers: the opening collect, the Epistle, the Gospel, and the psalm sung at the entrance (otherwise known as the *introit*). In the even more radical revision of 1552, the psalm at the entrance was dropped as well. With the stripping of the Gospel canticle antiphons, psalm antiphons, and variable suffrages from the reformed Daily Offices, Cranmer eliminated the possibility of retaining the delicate tissue of interactions between the Sunday Eucharist and the Office throughout the following week.

The only unifying element from the Church Year cycle that held the liturgical experience of the Eucharist and the Office together was the collect.

Cranmer could easily have done away with this too—but he didn't. Instead, he worked his way through the Sarum Missal, translating and retaining many of its collects where they were in accord with his understanding of the faith, crafting new collects where they were not. The English-speaking Church owes him a great debt of gratitude for this, because his work of translation and adaptation was masterfully done. Through him, we have access to ancient prayers that have sustained the Church over centuries, drawn into luminous models of prayer and praise.

Since Cranmer's day, prayer book people the world over have embraced the collect. Hundreds of collects have been translated, adapted, and composed to fill our prayer books and resources. Collects are not unique to Anglican churches, but they are a definitive aspect of our spiritual heritage.

While our last few prayer books have begun recovering seasonal elements in the Eucharist and the Office, the collect remains the single point of calendrical continuity that has the potential to unite the two liturgical services. Particularly as the one-year cycle has been replaced by a two-year Office lectionary and a three-year Eucharistic Lectionary, the collect remains the sole consistent element. The consistent practice of Anglican prayer books up to the present is the use of the Sunday (or prior festal) collect at the end of Morning and Evening Prayer. However, our current prayer book has made the use of the Collect of the Day optional in the Offices. I believe this is a mistake. The use and repetition of the Eucharistic collect within the Daily Office is the last common element that connects these two liturgical movements under the overarching aegis of the Church Year. Without this element, they become disconnected; we will have lost the intrinsic link, and the two services can be seen as two entirely different and unrelated devotions rather than the complementary pair that they were designed to be.

Collects can seem like just another bit of text—a sentence said by the priest as part of the opening stuff before we get to the real business of worship. On the contrary, I suggest that these brief prayers have a particular importance and impact that far outweigh their brevity. Indeed, their very brevity helps pull together threads of scripture, doctrine, and the seasons in concise, memorable, and powerful little packages.

I'd like to explore collects from two different directions. First, we'll examine what a collect is. Second, we'll look at how the collects function within the liturgical year and serve as key unifying units.

WHAT IS A COLLECT?

The original meaning of the term collect is lost in the mists of liturgical prehistory. The earliest Roman books refer to these prayers simply as *oratio* or *orationes*; the Gallican books produced in Gaul (modern France) in the seventh and eighth centuries used the term *collecta*. The Latin word is closely related to the English word—something has been collected— but what? There seem to be three possible answers: One suggestion is that the term refers to the prayer that should be prayed after all of the people have collected together. Another is that the collect brings together in one succinct statement the principal themes of the service being celebrated. The third is that, after a bit of silent prayer at the beginning of the service, the celebrant prays this prayer aloud as a means of collecting together all of the prayers that have been prayed silently and individually. This last possibly reflects the practice of bidding prayers, which is of great antiquity. I favor the last, but we will probably never know for sure.

One current liturgist, Fr. Bosco Peters, emphasizes the third option in his description of the four parts of a proper collect when it appears as the opening prayer of the Eucharist:

THE BIDDING: The presider invites the community to prayer—
"Let us pray"…

THE SILENCE: This is the heart of the collect. This deep silent praying of the community is what the collect is collecting. No silent prayer and it is not a collect, there is nothing to collect. Without this silence the "collect" is reduced to merely another little prayer cluttering the vestibule at the start of our service.

THE COLLECT: After sufficient silent prayer the presider proclaims the collect, gathering the prayers of the community, and articulating the prayer of the Church—the Body of Christ. As Christ's Body the collect is addressed in Christ's name, on Christ's behalf, to God the Source of all Being, in the power and unity of the Holy Spirit.

AMEN: The community makes the collect its own by a strong "Amen"—"so be it." [16]

His notion of a four-part scheme refocuses the collect as a summation of the whole community at prayer.

This is why congregational attempts to pray either the Collect for Purity or the Collect of the Day in unison fail. First, this is not an accurate reflection of how the congregation and the priest function in relation to one another. The collect is prayed by everyone even if only one voice is heard. Second, the beauty of collects often is in their alliteration and assonance—charming the ear by putting similar sounds close to one another—and through the rhythms and cadences—how syllables come together to form phrases and lines. Collects are intended to be chanted. You may not hear them sung very often, but the chant of the Church is their true vehicle. As a result, the rhythm is structured around the sounds and syllables that make them singable. This delicate aural aesthetic is undermined when a whole group attempts to move through it together.

As for the nature of a collect's essential character, Anglican writers have fallen over themselves for years singing its praises in extravagant ways. I find that one of the clearest and most helpful introductions to the collect comes from the radical theologian of the English Sarum Revival at the end of the nineteenth and beginning of the twentieth century, Percy Dearmer. In his usual acerbic tone, Dearmer writes:

> The collect is a definite literary form, a prose form with something of the character that a sonnet has in verse, but with a far more loosely defined structure; so that, though it is easier to make a poor collect than a poor sonnet, it is perhaps more difficult to make a good one. A collect is not merely a short prayer: many prayers are short—some, like the *Kyrie eleison* [Lord, have mercy], extremely short—but they are not collects; on the other hand, it would not be difficult, though the result would be unpleasing, to write a prayer of some length that kept strictly to the collect form.
>
> Unity is the essential characteristic of the collect. To be good, it must have color, rhythm, finality, a certain conciseness as well as vigour of thought; but it must be a unified petition, or it becomes something else than a collect. We might indeed say that it must be one complete sentence, an epigram softened by feeling; it must be compact, expressing one thought, and enriching that thought so delicately that a word misplaced may destroy its whole beauty. We cannot safeguard this balance, which is so easily upset, by setting down any definite rules, such as that a collect must consist of four parts. There is a real danger of a notion like that obtaining currency, and of everyone who tries to write a collect fitting his material into a Procrustean bed, and finding fault with every example that does not conform to his imaginary rule. As a matter of fact, many if not most of the finest collects do not consist of those four divisions.[17]

After airily dismissing the four-part structure of the collect, Dearmer goes on to explain it and clarify its importance (but doesn't number the final element giving him four where we will speak of five). Dearmer makes some excellent points here; in particular, I'd like to take up two in the form of comparisons. One is obvious and explicit; the other is less so, but one that Dearmer would approve.

First, the collect is like a sonnet; second, the collect is like a haiku. Dearmer's comparison of the collect to the sonnet is quite apt. Sonnets are poems defined by a certain structure, rhythm, rhyme scheme, and topic. Certain poets have defined these parameters through particularly notable examples of the genre—namely Renaissance poet Francesco Petrarch and Elizabethan playwright William Shakespeare—and their work shapes the convention. Skilled poets are able to work within the form and experience the rules and structures as canvasses to define an area of play rather than rigid guidelines. Truly remarkable poets are able to bend or break the rules, subverting the form and their readers' expectations in order to achieve something sublime. And yet, this subversion works because the poets have grasped a deeper structure to which they are adhering beyond the basic guidelines.

The same is true of collects; there are rules and guidelines. The rules guide the process of understanding and crafting the collect. A collect generally consists of a single sentence. It may be a quite long sentence with several relative clauses thrown in, but it is a single sentence. As a result of being a single sentence, it has one main point—Dearmer calls it the "unified petition." Then there are usually five components:

1. The Invocation. This is the naming of the Person of the Trinity to whom the prayer is addressed.
2. The Relative Clause/Acknowledgement. This clause often begins with a "who" and usually says something about the identity of God that will relate to the rest of the prayer; it often ends with a colon.
3. The Petition. This is what is being asked for.

Sometimes there may be a second petition that is related to the first. Classically this may start with "Grant" or "Grant, we pray…"

4. The Statement of Purpose/Result. This clause explains why we're asking for what we're asking for or describes what we hope will be the result of the request. This often starts with "that."

5. The Ending/Doxology. We end by bringing in the rest of the Trinity (or, at the very least, Jesus).

Here's an example of how these five parts break down on a common and well-known text, the Collect for Purity that appears in the early part of the Eucharist on page 355 of *The Book of Common Prayer*:

The Invocation	Almighty God,
The Relative Clause/ Acknowledgement	to you all hearts are open, all desires known, and from you no secrets are hid:
The Petition	Cleanse the thoughts of our hearts by the inspiration of your Holy Spirit,
The Statement of Purpose/ Result	that we may perfectly love you, and worthily magnify your holy Name;
The Ending/Doxology	through Christ our Lord. *Amen.*

The unifying concept here is that we are requesting the God who knows our secret thoughts to cleanse them for the proper worship of him.

Another example is the collect for the Fifth Sunday of Easter (p. 225):

The Invocation	Almighty God,
The Relative Clause/ Acknowledgement	whom truly to know is everlasting life:

The Petition	Grant us so perfectly to know your Son Jesus Christ to be the way, the truth, and the life,
The Statement of Purpose/ Result	that we may steadfastly follow his steps in the way that leads to eternal life;
The Ending/Doxology	through Jesus Christ your Son our Lord, who lives and reigns with you, in the unity of the Holy Spirit, one God, for ever and ever. *Amen.*

The unifying concept here is John 14:6, asking that we might know the truth in order to follow that way to share in life.

Dearmer throws in an example of a short prayer that is not a collect but could be confused with one. It was composed and distributed in England during World War I:

> O Lord God Almighty, look down with pity upon those who are suffering the miseries of war. Have compassion on the wounded and dying; comfort the broken-hearted; make wars to cease; and give peace in our time; for the sake of him who is the Prince of Peace, even thy Son, Jesus Christ our Lord.

Now, this is a perfectly fine prayer—it's just not a collect; there's nothing wrong with it; it's simply another sort of prayer following different guidelines that could be mistaken for a collect because it might appear on the surface to share some characteristics.

Let's take a look at why it's not a collect. It looks collect-shaped because it's short, it starts with an invocation, and ends with a standard collect ending. However, what follows the Invocation isn't a Relative Clause or an

Acknowledgement—it's a petition. And four more petitions follow on after that. After the first sentence and where each semicolon falls you could easily insert "Lord, in your mercy/ *Hear our prayer.*" This is a brief, private intercession rather than being a collect. Its unity is difficult to assess; generally speaking, the prayer is about the miseries of war, but the content of the petitions is more wide-ranging than what we would expect to find in a collect.

This five-fold form is another example of how the prayer book teaches us to pray. When you have spent a sufficient amount of time with collects and memorized the structure, it is easier to produce an extemporaneous prayer that follows these guidelines.

However, as Dearmer mentions, there is more to it than simply following the rules. Some collects don't follow this structure, like the collect for Proper 3 (p. 229):

The Petition	Grant,
The Invocation	O Lord,
The Petition, continued	that the course of this world may be peaceably governed by your providence;
Secondary petition	and that your Church may joyfully serve you in confidence and serenity;
The Ending/Doxology	through Jesus Christ Lord, who lives and reigns with you and the Holy Spirit, one God, for ever and ever. *Amen.*

While this is similar to the prayer Dearmer cites from World War I, the collect for Proper 3 has fewer petitions (two instead of five), and the thought is more unified.

Another differing structure is that of the collect for Monday in Easter Week (pp. 222-223):

The Petition	Grant, we pray,
The Invocation	Almighty God,
The Petition, continued	that we who celebrate with awe the Paschal feast may be found worthy to attain to everlasting joys;
The Ending/Doxology	through Jesus Christ Lord, who lives and reigns with you and the Holy Spirit, one God, for ever and ever. *Amen.*

This is probably the shortest a collect can be in terms of components and still be considered a collect.

The point here is that the not every collect of the prayer book fits the rules—nor needs to fit the rules—but they all share in the same fundamental concept and approach. The five-part structure is normal and typical, but it's not uncommon to see some variations. If we choose to compose our own collects, it's good to stick close to the rules, but they need not be considered straight-jackets either.

Just as a collect has rules regarding its form, elements, and content as a sonnet does, there's something about its character that is also like a haiku. While the classical Japanese poetic form has rules, the central experience of a haiku is that it is very short—only eighteen *on* (which are roughly comparable to syllables). A haiku is unified and has a seasonal reference. A good haiku evokes an effect. The use of language is intentional and particular. Because it is so short, every word matters; the placement of every word matters. While the seasonal reference is an important part, many Westerners miss them because specific words or turns of phrase have seasonal resonance within Japanese culture. The master Bashō demonstrates these elements (in William J. Higginson's translation):

old pond…
a frog leaps in
water's sound

It deftly creates a single experience, the translator's first
line setting a scene, the second providing a glimpse of action.
Rainy springtime is evoked by the frog—but the frog itself is
part of what makes the poem what it is. Classical Japanese
poetry often uses this kind of a frog for its haunting call
particular to springtime; Bashō keeps this musical frog silent
but gives the water a voice instead!

A good collect should be like a haiku in that it gives a
unified experience, communicating a single, self-contained
thought. Furthermore, this thought may be allusive, using
loaded language to point outside of itself to references that a
culturally literate interpreter should pick up. Finally, a good
collect should leave us with a feeling, an intention, or a resolve
to enact that for which we have just prayed. Let's return again
to Cranmer's collect for the First Sunday of Advent (*The Book
of Common Prayer*, p. 211):

> Almighty God, give us grace to cast away the works of darkness,
> and put on the armor of light, now in the time of this mortal life in
> which your Son Jesus Christ came to visit us in great humility; that
> in the last day, when he shall come again in his glorious majesty
> to judge both the living and the dead, we may rise to the life
> immortal; through him who lives and reigns with you and the Holy
> Spirit, one God, now and for ever. *Amen.*

The unified concept here is about receiving the grace to
turn from darkness to light and to live according to the light
in the presence of Christ, teacher and judge. The language
of light and dark connects to key Advent themes where the
coming of Christ is often spoken of as the coming of light
and the dawn (…a people who have walked in darkness

have seen a great light...; ...more than watchmen for the morning...; sleepers, awake!; ...be watchful...; etc.). Cranmer also is making a very specific biblical allusion. In the one-year lectionary cycle that he knew, the Epistle for Eucharist on Advent 1 was invariably Romans 13:8-14, which includes these verses:

> Besides this, you know what time it is, how it is now the moment for you to wake from sleep. For salvation is nearer to us now than when we became believers; the night is far gone, the day is near. Let us then lay aside the works of darkness and put on the armor of light; let us live honorably as in the day...(13:11-13a).

The collect's phrase foreshadows the Epistle, and, when the collect was repeated throughout the week after hearing that Epistle, the connection would have been remembered. (In our current three-year cycle, this Epistle only appears on Advent 1 in Year A.) The season, the scripture, and the practice of the moral life are united in the collect.[18]

Note, too, that the structure is altered a bit from the usual. There is no Acknowledgement following the Invocation; however there is a relative clause in the petition that could easily be one. This is what would happen if we attempted to "fix" the collect:

> Almighty God, whose Son Jesus Christ came to visit us in great humility; Give us grace to cast away the works of darkness, and put on the armor of light, now in the time of this mortal life that in the last day, when he shall come again in his glorious majesty to judge both the living and the dead, we may rise to the life immortal; through him who lives and reigns with you and the Holy Spirit, one God, now and for ever. *Amen.*

What gets lost here is the effect of the multiple comings of Advent. Cranmer's collect creates a balanced structure by evoking an advent at the end of the petition clause with another advent in the result clause; they mirror each other. Moving the Acknowledgement to the Acknowledgement position obscures the parallelism and weakens the collect. By separating the coming of Christ "in great humility" by a greater space of words and phrases from the coming "in glorious majesty" the juxtaposition between the two and the sense of paradox is diminished.

Furthermore, the "now" gets buried. In Cranmer's collect, the "now" occupies a prominent position at the start of a phrase. Putting it here both reminds the hearers that we are moving into a new movement of the Church's year, a chance to start over, and a chance to seize the salvation that the Coming King offers. This resonates even more with the Epistle where Paul likewise urges his hearers that now is the proper time to wake from sleep and take up salvation.[19] Where the words and phrases go matters in terms of the overall effect.

When we encounter collects, therefore, we want to be attentive to these factors. What is the theological and spiritual center of gravity of the collect? What does the collect inspire in us and lead us toward? Is it leading us deeper into the season or a particular mystery of life-in-Christ by using allusions or references?

Holli Powell, one of the hosts of "The Collect Call" podcast, created a word cloud with all of the words of the Rite II collects.[20] A word cloud is a means of analyzing a set of texts. The software calculates the relative frequency of various words in the text, then produces an image. In the image, the most frequently used words appear larger, those used less often are smaller or don't appear at all. When Holli plugged in the complete collects, the resulting word cloud was dominated by doxology. That is, the consistent ending in praise of the Trinity came to the fore, and the biggest, most obvious words were God, Jesus, Holy, Spirit, ever, lives, reigns, and Amen.

It is worth sitting with this for a moment. When the collects are taken together as a mass, praise of the Living Triune God dominates. This is a big-picture pattern into which the prayer book is forming us.

Curious about the inner content of the collects, Holli tried it again, this time without the doxologies. The top words here were Jesus, Christ, things, grace, life, love, faith, and glory. Commenting on this word cloud, she says, "I love that the largest 'non-God' words here…are glory, grace, love, and faith—if this doesn't say something about our spiritual journey, I don't know what does!"[21]

In the collects we ask most persistently for grace. Yes, we want grace to help us to do a variety of things, but the primary—perhaps primal—request here is for God's help and assistance as we go about the work that we have been given to do. It is interesting to note in the word cloud the size of the word "things"—stuff matters! It would probably require another study to analyze the specific ways in which the word things is used throughout the collects, but I see this as a basic reminder of the spiritual importance of incarnate reality. In the prayer book's language, we are not just spirits that think ideas; we are bodies, passing through the created world into which God entered in frail flesh.

The final point to note about collects is that, just as particular poems take on a life of their own and shape the cultural vocabulary, the same is true of collects. The collects of the prayer book span an enormous amount of Christian history. When Cranmer prepared the first *Book of Common Prayer*, he took most of the collects directly from the Sarum Missal and Breviary. Many of these, in turn, went back to the Gregorian and Gallican liturgies that spread throughout the Christian West in the seventh and eighth centuries. Those that Cranmer found objectionable he either adapted or replaced entirely with compositions of his own. As time went on, more collects were added by significant figures in Anglican history like Bishop John Cosin who played an influential role in the construction of the 1662 English prayer book that is foundational for many colonial prayer books and is still England's official text. More recent collects have been added from around the world. Other collects go back to the earliest Western sources in the Leonine sacramentary, which scholars date to the sixth century.

Many of the collects that we read have been forming Christian theology and spirituality for well over a thousand years. It's one thing to claim continuity with the Christian tradition of the ages; it's another to demonstrate it—and our collects do. They provide a direct connection with the oldest streams of the tradition enriched by fertilizations from later ages.

COLLECTS AND THE LITURGICAL YEAR

Having taken some time to explore the collect form, let's turn to how the collects function to give a more concrete sense of shape to the liturgical year.

While the prayer book is filled with a variety of collects, the most influential are those appointed for Sundays and the principal feasts. This is because they get repeated so often in practice. A collect appointed for a regular Sunday can be prayed at least fifteen times over the course of the week: In addition to the Sunday Eucharist, it can be repeated every day of the week at Morning and Evening Prayer. The repetition is both intentional and important. The Anglican tradition is not confessional in a technical sense; that is, our beliefs are not established by a confessional document in the same sense that the Lutheran and Reformed churches are.[22] The center of our unity is the prayer book, and the collects as bite-sized crystallizations of doctrine, interpretation, and practice are a primary source of our theology. Repeating them day after day, week after week, year after year, instills a shared theological vocabulary within the praying community.

As a result, maintaining the weekly repetition of collects is a significant part of how we acquire and recall our theological heritage. In recent years, there has been a tendency to multiply collects. With the introduction of a more complete sanctoral calendar in the current prayer book and in *Lesser Feasts & Fasts*, more and more Days of Optional Observance are receiving their own proper collects. Collects have also been provided for every day of Lent and many of the days of Easter. Incorporating these new collects alongside a commitment to the faithful use of the Sunday collects—particularly in the Daily Office—is a challenge. There are two main options: The first is to retain the Sunday collects to the exclusion of the supplementary material. The second is to use both: The supplementary Collect of the Day would be used first, the weekly collect would then follow.

Short yet substantial, the collects are ideal candidates for memorization. As each Sunday rolls around, I try to take a few minutes to memorize the collect. As I move through the week, I can stop and reflect on it, rolling its words around in my mind. Instead of passively receiving the piety and theology of the prayer book, I can actively engage it in my life of prayer and daily experience.

THE SEASONAL COLLECTS

There is another way that the collects reinforce the liturgical year. Starting with the English prayer book of 1662, several collects were appointed to serve as seasonal collects. A note with the Collect for the First Sunday of Advent designated that it should be read after the Collect of the Day throughout Advent:

> Almighty God, give us grace to cast away the works of darkness, and put on the armor of light, now in the time of this mortal life in which your Son Jesus Christ came to visit us in great humility; that in the last day, when he shall come again in his glorious majesty to judge both the living and the dead, we may rise to the life immortal; through him who lives and reigns with you and the Holy Spirit, one God, now and for ever. *Amen* (*The Book of Common Prayer*, p. 211).

A similar note with the Collect for Ash Wednesday required that this collect be read after the Collect of the Day through Lent:

> Almighty and everlasting God, you hate nothing you have made and forgive the sins of all who are penitent: Create and make in us

new and contrite hearts, that we, worthily lamenting our sins and acknowledging our wretchedness, may obtain of you, the God of all mercy, perfect remission and forgiveness; through Jesus Christ our Lord, who lives and reigns with you and the Holy Spirit, one God, for ever and ever. *Amen (The Book of Common Prayer*, p. 217).

The Collect for Christmas, given its own octave, was appointed to be read every day after the Collect of the Day until the Feast of the Circumcision:

Almighty God, you have given your only-begotten Son to take our nature upon him, and to be born [this day] of a pure virgin: Grant that we, who have been born again and made your children by adoption and grace, may daily be renewed by your Holy Spirit; through our Lord Jesus Christ, to whom with you and the same Spirit be honor and glory, now and for ever. *Amen (The Book of Common Prayer*, p. 213).

This concept greatly expanded in the American 1928 prayer book: The collects for Palm Sunday, Easter Sunday, the Ascension, Pentecost, and All Saints Day were all given octaves—for the whole week following the feast, these collects were read after any other appointed collect falling in this time. Thus, on the Sunday after All Saints, the congregation would hear first the collect appointed for the Sunday, then the collect appointed for All Saints Day. This accomplished two things: First, it emphasized the importance of these feasts; second, as more collects were introduced—as in Holy Week—the repetition of the octave collect helped give a better defined shape to the period. The current prayer book no longer requires these seasonal or octave collects, but they remain an effective practice for reinforcing the seasons and feasts.

CALENDAR CONCLUSIONS

The prayer book offers the Calendar as a means of giving deliberate structure to the Christian experience of time. By shaping our common life around major festivals—Easter preeminent among them—we give festal expression to core truths about the God with whom we are in relationship. Key elements of the creeds are underscored and unpacked in the liturgies and the seasons supporting them: the Incarnation of Jesus in Christmas; his suffering, death, and burial in Lent and Holy Week; his Resurrection at Easter; his ascension with the Ascension; the Holy Spirit in Pentecost and the time following; the return of Jesus as Lord of Time in Advent.

The seasons train us in the central religious affections—ways of being that are composed of emotions, thoughts, understandings, and deliberate choices about how we lead our lives and pattern them after Jesus and the saints. These seasons of focus are not meant to be emotional straightjackets but more intensive times of examination and discovery.

The sanctoral aspect of the Calendar invites us to reflect on the person and virtues of Jesus as they have been incarnated in his followers and friends. This great cloud of witnesses who share in our Baptism continue in the risen life of Jesus Christ and remain as fellow witnesses and ministers with us. They support us with their examples and prayers as we join in one great company around the throne of God.

Lastly, the collects remain a central point of connection. In addition to providing a prayed point of continuity between our Eucharists and the Daily Offices, they communicate the themes and doctrines of the seasons. Through their allusions, they draw us deeper into meditation on the scriptures and the teachings of the Church. Tight, compact, luminous objects of devotion, they are the perfect size for memorization and rumination as we seek to live a life attentive to God.

NOTES

1   Modern Christians are often surprised to learn that the Jewish and Roman opponents of early Christianity did not dispute that Jesus was a wonder-worker; rather, they believed that the wonders he accomplished were attributable to either demons or sorcery (or both). See, for instance, Origen's *Against Celsus*, Book 1.68 and 71, Tertullian's *Apology* ch. 22, as well as the charges recorded in the Gospels themselves (Matthew 9:34; 12:24; Mark 3:22; Luke 11:15; John 10:20-21; etc.).

2   This antiphon is appointed in some old breviaries for use in the Lauds (morning) Office on Epiphany. It also appears in *Saint Augustine's Prayer Book*, pp. 219-220.

3   Don Saliers, *The Soul in Paraphrase: Prayer and the Religious Affections* (Cleveland: OSL Publications, 1980).

4   There are forty uses of the term holy one(s) (*hagioi* in Greek) in this sense of saints within the Pauline letters. Examples are Romans 1:7; 12:13; 15:25; 1 Corinthians 6:1,2; 14:33; 16:1, 15; etc.

5   This is why we have the tables. It's a lot easier to just use the tables rather than to try to calculate these things yourself. The bottom line is that the Gold Number identifies when the first full moon after the Spring Equinox falls. Easter then is the first Sunday after the full moon. The directions for how to use the Golden Number in combination with the Sunday Letter appear on pages 880-881 in *The Book of Common Prayer*.

6   One notion in Late Antiquity suggested that a person's life was somehow more complete or perfect if the date of their death fell on the day of their birth or conception. As a result, some church thinkers have argued that the first Good Friday therefore *had* to fall on the date of the Annunciation. I don't think that's necessarily the case but considering the two feasts/events in relation to one another is quite poignant, especially considering that Mary herself was present and privy to both events. One classic Anglican reflection on this conjunction is the poem, "Upon the Annunciation and Passion falling upon one day. 1608," by the famous poet and Anglican priest, John Donne. (When this conjunction does happen, the prayer book tells us to transfer the Annunciation out of Holy Week to the first free day after the second Sunday of Easter.)

7   While the liturgy in the West had generally been fairly uniform, the emerging technology of printing allowed the Roman Catholic Church to formalize liturgical texts in a way never before possible. While they allowed exemptions for liturgical traditions that had been around for a very long time, everyone else was required to use the new, officially printed editions.

8   We talk about the Collect for the First Sunday in Advent in the section on collects.

9   See above on the relationship between the lectionary first published in the 1979 prayer book and the Revised Common Lectionary. Many of the more Protestant Church bodies that participated in the construction of the RCL don't recognize or celebrate seasons in the same way as The Episcopal Church and the prayer book; as a result, the RCL doesn't observe the seasons in exactly the same way that the prayer book does.

10   To make things more complicated, General Convention passed a resolution in 2012 allowing parishes to use the lectionary compiled for the prayer book as long as they received permission from their bishop.

11   You may wonder where love of neighbor shows up in this list: It's tucked into the call to "prayer, fasting, and self-denial" (*The Book of Common Prayer*, p. 265). Fasting is not just going without food as some sort of holy diet. The intention is that you reduce the amount of food that you eat so that these resources can be given to those who do not have it; we abstain from food so that we can take the food or money we would have spent on food and offer it to charity. Furthermore, in the time that we save from not eating, we engage in prayer for ourselves and for the world, loving our neighbors in the passive act of intercession as well as in the active act of giving alms.

12   There's a hymn that is specifically about the putting away or burying of the alleluia during Lent—"Alleluia, song of gladness" (*The Hymnal 1989*, pp. 122, 123). In its original form it was sung on the evening before Septuagesima, the start of the now-suppressed pre-Lenten period. Because it's tucked away in the middle of the Epiphany hymns, though, its significance is easy to overlook. It is a great choice for either the Last Sunday of Epiphany, for a midweek service before Ash Wednesday, or simply for meditating upon in the days leading up to Lent.

13   *The Book of Common Prayer*, p. 270.

14   The permission to "[o]n occasion…omit" the Confession is found on *The Book of Common Prayer*, p. 359.

15   The permission to move a feast of title to Sunday in a green season or during Christmas is found in the third paragraph on page 17 in the Calendar directions.

16   Bosco Peters, "collect—four parts," n.p. [cited 8 March 2016]. Online: http://liturgy.co.nz/collect.

17   Percy Dearmer, *The Art of Public Worship* (London: Mowbray & Co., 1919), 149-50.

18   Unfortunately, due to two different factors, the collects and scriptural allusions that might be contained rarely link up with the Gospel of the Day. First, the change from the one-year Eucharistic Lectionary to a three-year cycle means that, even when an attempt has been made to keep the traditional reading, it only appears one year out of three. Second, in the composition of

the 1979 prayer book, many of the collects were moved from their original location to a new place in the Church Year if a strong seasonal reference did not locate them. One clear example is the collect currently appointed for Proper 28; it had been the collect for the Second Sunday of Advent since the sixteenth century!

19 Romans 13:11.

20 The episode where Holli (and her co-host Brendan O'Sullivan-Hale) discuss the word cloud is the episode for the Third Sunday after Epiphany, released on January 21, 2015 (http://www.acts8moment.org/the-collect-call-for-the-third-sunday-after-epiphany/). The discussion of the word cloud can be found between 4:00-7:40 minutes.

21 *Ibid.*

22 The 39 Articles were intended to be an English parallel to some of the continental Confessions, and the Church of England still requires priests to swear to them at their ordination. But they do not have the same character throughout the rest of the Anglican Communion as similar documents in other churches. For example, there is no mention of them in the ordination services in the current prayer book or the current Canadian book.

SECTION 2
THE DAILY OFFICE

CHAPTER 5
THE ESSENCE OF THE DAILY OFFICE

The Calendar gives us the big picture—the year is the grand cycle. The Daily Office, on the other hand, is the smallest liturgical cycle, giving shape to our hours and days. If the Calendar and collects help us see the full arc of salvation history, the Daily Office helps us see the life of faith as a daily activity that must be consistently chosen from among a hundred other things all clamoring for our time and attention. This is devotion as the constant daily practice of the faith.

Just as a runner is someone who gets out there every day— or at least several times a week—and pours some sweat on the pavement, so too someone who is formed by the liturgy and the Daily Office has to consistently choose it day after day, not just once in a while as the mood strikes. The Office is a discipline. To be formed by it requires constancy and dedication—but it is well worth the effort.

The essence of the Daily Office must be found on one hand in Paul's exhortation for Christians "with gratitude in your hearts [to] sing psalms, hymns, and spiritual songs to God" (Colossians 3:16), and, on the other hand, to "pray without ceasing" (1 Thessalonians 5:17). The two central themes here are the use of songs and poetic praises offered to God and that continuous prayer springs from deliberate acts of prayer. As we consider the Daily Office and its various parts and acts, we will return time and time again to these two basic principles that form its foundation.

PSALMS, HYMNS, AND SPIRITUAL SONGS

In her book, *Worship*, Evelyn Underhill, an Anglican mystic of the twentieth century, reinforces the poetic character of the Daily Office and the significance of that quality:

> Liturgical worship shares with all ritual action the character of a work of art. Entering upon it, we leave the lower realism of daily life for the higher realism of a successive action which expresses and interprets eternal truth by the deliberate use of poetic and symbolic material. A liturgical service should therefore possess a structural unity; its general form and movement, and each of its parts, being determined by the significance of the whole. By its successive presentation of all the phases of the soul's response to the Holy, its alternative use of history and oratory, drama and rhythm, its appeals to feeling, thought, and will, the individual is educated and gathered into the great movement of the Church. . . . Nevertheless since its main function is to suggest the supernatural and lead men out to communion with the supernatural, it is by the methods of poetry that its chief work will be done. . . . [P]oetry still remains a chief element at least in the Daily Office, which is mainly an arrangement of psalms, canticles, and scripture readings.[1]

She goes on to remind us of the interpretive errors that occur when we attempt to read poetry literally and miss its deeper sense and direction. As she sees it, poetry in the liturgy has three main purposes:

(1) It is the carrying-medium of something which otherwise wholly eludes representation: the soul's deep and awestruck apprehension of the numinous....

(2) It can universalize particulars; giving an eternal reference to those things of time in and through which God speaks to men....

(3) It is a powerful stimulant of the transcendental sense....

All these characters of poetry are active in good liturgy, and indeed constitute an important part of its religious value. Moreover, poetry both enchants and informs, addressing its rhythmic and symbolic speech to regions of the mind which are inaccessible to argument, and evoking movements of awe and love which no exhortation can obtain. It has meaning at many levels, and welds together all those who use it; overriding their personal moods and subduing them with a grave loveliness.[2]

Great art—great poetry—captures our minds and hearts and suffuses reality with a new light, a new perspective. It helps us see our ordinary, everyday world as not so ordinary and cracks open everyday reality to help us see the beauty, glory, and wonder that is concealed within it. It helps us see new possibilities; it helps us see grander movements.

Like great poetry, scripture invites us into a different way of seeing the world and our relationships within it. It invites us to experience the whole cosmos arrayed around the throne of God as portrayed in the heavenly throne-room of Revelation 4-6 and leads us to speculate about what it means to live in a world where justice, mercy, and loving-kindness are fundamental guiding principles. We are invited to recognize our own world transformed and suffused with the light of God. We function as mirrors, lenses, and crystals, reflecting—focusing—diffusing—the divine light, casting it through our facets upon the world and the people around us.

With its language of poetry, the Daily Office reminds us
of and orients us to this understanding and reflection. It also
can help us move beyond a literalism and dogmatism that
can either frustrate or limit our sense of the holy and the
divine. The Athanasian Creed can be a hard pill for many
to swallow. On the one hand, it is chock full of complicated
and philosophical technical terms. On the other, it ends with
a declaration of damnation with a certainty that seems to
arrogate to itself a judgment properly left with God alone. The
Episcopal Church has never been comfortable with it. Bishop
Samuel Seabury, the first American Episcopal bishop, wrote
that he was never convinced of the propriety of reading it in
church, yet he did want to include it along the same lines as
the Articles of Faith to show that we hold the common faith
of the West. Indeed, the 1979 revision is the only American
prayer book to include it. Especially as modern people, we
don't know what to do with it—but the monks did. They
sang it as a canticle complete with antiphons at the Morning
Prayer service of Prime on Sundays, the poetic and musical
setting potentially subverting its dogmatism and softening its
philosophical formality in song.

After speaking of the eight individual Hours that formed
the classical Daily Office in the West, Underhill draws them
together and unites them with their purpose:

> The complete Divine Office, then,…is best understood when
> regarded as a spiritual and artistic unity; so devised, that
> the various elements of praise, prayer, and reading, and the
> predominantly poetic and historic material from which it is built up,
> contribute to one single movement of the corporate soul, and form
> together one single act of solemn yet exultant worship. This act of
> worship is designed to give enduring and impersonal expression
> to eternal truths; and unite the here and now earthly action of
> the Church with the eternal response of creation to its origin. It

is her "Sacred Chant," and loses some of its quality and meaning when its choral character is suppressed: for in it, the demands of a superficial realism are set aside, in favour of those deeper realities which can only be expressed under poetic and musical forms.[3]

The more we sing the Office, the more in touch we are with these melodies, harmonies, and rhythms. Yet, even if we are reading the Office alone in our rooms, we can still find the cadences.

On a purely literary level, we can go through the Office step by step and note the presence of poetry and music. The psalms form the heart of the Office. We respond to the scripture readings with canticles, most of which are infused and inspired by the psalms—or songs like them. The suffrages themselves are verses of psalms recombined and related to one another in new ways. The collects and prayers speak in the language of the psalms and scriptures.

As we pray the Office and sing it—whether aloud or in our hearts—we are incarnating the Pauline injunction to sing psalms, hymns, and spiritual songs to God and to one another. As its poetry becomes more deeply a part of us, as these songs become implanted within our hearts, they lead us to a more beautiful lens for locating God at work in our world.

TO PRAY WITHOUT CEASING

This notion of having the songs and psalms implanted in our hearts and consciousness leads us to the second principle, to pray without ceasing. To learn the meaning of this phrase, we turn our eyes to the Desert Fathers and Mothers, who devoted their entire lives to its meaning.

The legalization of Christianity in Rome during the fourth century brought a flood of converts and triggered a crisis of spirituality. For decades, Christian authenticity had been bound up with martyrdom; fidelity to the way of the cross was identified with the willingness to die a martyr's death at the hands of a hostile state. With martyrdom waning, where was an earnest Christian to turn?

The answer came in the form of the desert. Christians who sought to embody the commands of scripture sold their possessions, renounced family life, and sought lives of prayer and austerity in the deserts, either on their own or in the company of like-minded souls. This way of life was popularized by bishops and theologians who wrote inspiring accounts of the lives of simple men and women and the spiritual riches they uncovered. Bishops and teachers like Athanasius, Jerome, and John Cassian wrote in detail about the lives and the rigorous spiritual practices of these early monks and the practice flowered into monasticism and has fed the Church spiritually for centuries.

As we sift through the literature of the early monastic movement and the desert saints who founded it, we come back repeatedly to this injunction to pray without ceasing, to pray some form of the Daily Office and the fundamental belief that the use of the Office was the key to praying without ceasing. The characteristic pattern of desert life is captured in Athanasius's brief description of how Saint Antony lived:

> The money he earned from his work he gave to the poor, apart from what he needed to buy bread, and he prayed often, for he learned that one should pray to the Lord without ceasing. He also listened attentively to the scriptures so that nothing should slip from his mind. He preserved all the Lord's commandments, keeping them safe in his memory rather than in books.[4]

Note the way that work, prayer, and memorization of the scriptures are interconnected here. This way of life is further clarified by an episode where a desert hermit was arguing with a group of pietists called the Euchites or Messalians:

> Some of the monks who are called Euchites went to Enaton to see Abba Lucius. The old man asked them, "What is your manual work?" They said, "We do not touch manual work but as the Apostle says, we pray without ceasing." The old man asked them if they did not eat and they replied they did. So he said to them, "When you are eating, who prays for you then?" Again he asked them if they did not sleep and they replied they did. And he said to them, "When you are asleep, who prays for you then?" They could not find any answer to give him. He said to them, "Forgive me, but you do not act as you speak. I will show you how, while doing my manual work, I pray without interruption. I sit down with God, soaking my reeds and plaiting my ropes, and I say, 'God have mercy on me; according to your great goodness and according to the multitude of your mercies, save me from my sins [Psalm 51:1,2].'" So he asked them if this were not prayer and they replied it was. Then he said to them, "So when I have spent the whole day working and praying, making thirteen pieces of money more or less, I put two pieces of money outside the door and I pay for my food with the rest of the money. He who takes the two pieces of money prays for me when I am eating and sleeping; so, by the grace of God, I fulfill the precept to pray without ceasing."[5]

This blend of piety and practicality is found throughout this early literature. The life described is filled with basic manual labor—weaving ropes or baskets made from the leaves of the desert palms or scratching out subsistence gardens from rocky soil—suffused with constant prayer. Indeed, the Egyptian monks in particular were famous for prayers that were brief but frequent.

The prayer recited by Abba Lucius is an adaptation of the start of Psalm 51. Reading through the *Life of Antony* and the description that Athanasius gives of Antony's struggles in spiritual travail, a pattern emerges. At a great turning point in Antony's life, during a struggle with demons that left him both physically and spiritually battered, he retained his faith and focus by ceaselessly chanting, "If they place an encampment against me, yet my heart shall not be afraid" (Psalm 27:3). When people came from the cities, hoping to find him dead, he would pray verses from Psalms 68 and 118. Throughout the literature, the words of the psalms constantly appear in prayers and discussions. In truth, the conversations are full of scripture, but consistently the psalms predominate. The Egyptian brief but frequent prayers that appear in the corpus are almost always drawn from scripture and the psalms. One of the works of Evagrius of Pontus (345-399 CE) consists entirely of one-liners from scripture to be used for prayer in situations organized by the eight vices identified by the desert monks.

For these monks—many of whom were illiterate—scripture came through hearing. Scripture was heard and memorized in the Daily Offices. The foundation of the Office gave them the words they needed to meditate on in the midst of their work and to truly pray without ceasing no matter what they were doing.

Perhaps the preeminent connection between the scriptures, the psalms, and praying without ceasing comes from the second conference on prayer recorded by John Cassian. Abba Isaac says that the whole goal of the monastic way of life can be summed up like this: "This, I say, is the end [goal] of all perfection—that the mind purged of every carnal desire may daily be elevated to spiritual things, until one's whole way of life and all the yearnings of one's heart become a single and continuous prayer." [6] Cassian's companion, Germanus, asks how this sort of focus can be achieved. The reply from Abba

Isaac is that there is one particular formula for meditation that can secure this result:

> The formula for this discipline and prayer that you are seeking, then, shall be presented to you. Every monk who longs for the continual awareness of God should be in the habit of meditating on it ceaselessly in his heart, after having driven out every kind of thought, because he will be unable to hold fast to it in any other way than by being freed from all bodily cares and concerns. Just as this was handed down to us by a few of the oldest fathers who were left, so also we pass it on to none but the most exceptional, who truly desire it. This, then, is the devotional formula proposed to you as absolutely necessary for possessing the perpetual awareness of God: "O God, make speed to save me; O Lord, make haste to help me" [Psalm 70:1].[7]

Yes, this is the line that is used as a verse and response to open each of the prayer Offices. No, that's not an accident.

Cassian makes the explicit connection between the Daily Office and the continuous prayer of the Egyptian monks in his other book, *Institutes*, but he does so by framing it in the midst of one of the disputes about monastic practice. By the end of the fourth century, there were two major centers of monastic practice—the deserts of Egypt and the deserts of Palestine. They had different ways of praying the Daily Office. The Egyptian model was the same format as what appears to have been done in many of the early cathedrals of the period—one public service in the morning and another in the evening. Twelve psalms were sung, then there was a reading from the Old Testament, then one from the New Testament. That was it for the day. The Palestinian model was to gather more frequently. Jerome, writing from his monastery in Bethlehem, advises this:

Farther, although the apostle bids us to "pray without ceasing," and although to the saints their very sleep is a supplication, we ought to have fixed hours of prayer, that if we are detained by work, the time may remind us of our duty. Prayers, as everyone knows, ought to be said at the third, sixth, and ninth hours, at dawn and at evening....We should rise two or three times in the night and go over the parts of scripture which we know by heart.[8]

He instructs the parents of a young woman dedicated to the Church to train her in the same way: "She ought to rise at night to recite prayers and psalms; to sing hymns in the morning; at the third, sixth, and ninth hours to take her place in the line to do battle for Christ; and lastly to kindle her lamp and to offer her evening sacrifice."[9]

The Egyptians responded to these alternate prayer practices rather harshly. One characteristic response comes from the Egyptian-trained Epiphanius:

The Blessed Epiphanius, Bishop of Cyprus, was told this by the abbot of a monastery he had in Palestine, "By your prayers we do not neglect our appointed round of psalmody, but we are very careful to recite [the prayer Offices of] Terce, Sext and None." Then Epiphanius corrected them with the following comment, "It is clear you do not trouble about the other hours of the day, if you cease from prayer. The true monk should have prayer and psalmody continuously in his heart."[10]

Epiphanius suggested that by having more set hours of the day, the monks were neglecting this continual prayer of the heart and instead were satisfied only to pray when the clock told them it was time to do so. Frankly, this is kind of a cheap shot. An argument could equally be made that since the Palestinian monks were hearing the psalms more, they had better opportunity to memorize them and keep them always in their hearts—but the (Egyptian) sayings don't give us the Palestinian abbot's response!

In light of this argument between the two parties, Cassian tries to take a middle path. After explaining the Egyptian system and before talking about how to pray the day hours, he says:

> For, among [the Egyptians as opposed to the monasteries of Palestine and Mesopotamia] the Offices that we are obliged to render to the Lord at different hours and at intervals of time [i.e., the day Offices of Terce, Sext, and None] to the call of the summoner, are celebrated continuously and spontaneously throughout the course of the whole day, in tandem with their work. For they are constantly doing manual labor alone in their cells in such a way that they almost never omit meditating on the psalms and on other parts of scripture, and to this they add entreaties and prayers at every moment, taking up the whole day in Offices that we celebrate at fixed times. Hence, apart from the evening and [morning] gatherings, they celebrate no public service during the day except on Saturday and Sunday, when they gather at the third hour for Holy Communion. For what is offered [freely] is greater than what is rendered at particular moments, and a voluntary service is more pleasing than functions that are carried out by canonical obligation. This is why David himself rejoices somewhat boastfully when he says: "Willingly shall I sacrifice to you." And: "May the free offerings of my mouth be pleasing to you, Lord."[11]

Cassian is, in essence, admitting that the Egyptians have a more perfect practice: the two Offices of Morning and Evening Prayer give the stern Egyptian monks all they need to pray without ceasing for the rest of the day. But then he goes right ahead and tells his monks to pray the additional hours in the middle of the day in Palestinian fashion. The Egyptian way may be better, but the Palestinian is easier—and is likely better training for those still needing to learn their psalms.

These two groups show us two different ways of using the Daily Office to learn how to pray without ceasing. The Egyptian model is to have only two long Offices with psalms and readings at both. The Palestinian model is to have shorter and more frequent Offices with psalmody, leaving the reading of scripture for the long Office at night. The Palestinian model wins decisively in the West; Benedict expresses in his rule what has become normative in the West: eight liturgical services of prayer with an additional monastic business meeting—Chapter—that itself acquires liturgical material. Indeed, this pattern of frequency in corporate recitation of the Offices gets taken to its extreme in the monasteries of Cluny in France. At one point, the monks spent a full eight hours of the day singing liturgies!

With the creation of *The Book of Common Prayer* at the Reformation, Archbishop Cranmer put the Anglican churches onto the other path. Whereas for centuries the Western Church had followed the Palestinian model, Cranmer turned us back to the Egyptian model. Up until our present book, our Offices had consisted of the same elements as the Egyptian Office: psalms, a reading from the Old Testament, a reading from the New Testament, and prayers, all done twice a day. (The 1979 book gives a "Palestinian" nod with the introduction of Noon Prayer and Compline.)

If prayer without ceasing is our goal (and why shouldn't it be?), we must recall that the Egyptian model is the harder path. In order to fulfill the call, we would be wise to follow that model. Pray the long Offices as they're appointed, but then—throughout the day—make our private prayers "brief but frequent." Take a verse that strikes you in the morning. Ponder it through the day; make it your prayer. Repeat it to yourself as you sit in silence. Whisper it to yourself as you work. Roll it around in your mind while you eat. Make it part of your prayer without ceasing.

This, then, is the essence of the Office—to make our spiritual sacrifice of praise and thanksgiving. By speaking in "psalms, hymns, and spiritual songs to God," our hearts are lifted and our minds expanded to see a world imbued with God. As we take the words of the psalms and the scriptures into ourselves, we provide ourselves with the basic resources to pray without ceasing. The practice of the Office—whether together or alone—builds up in us the pattern of praise and points us in the way of the habitual recollection of God.

THE SACRIFICE OF PRAISE
AND THANKSGIVING

When the Church Fathers spoke of the chief morning and evening services of the Daily Office—Lauds and Vespers in the Western Church—they often did so with reference to the temple sacrifices. A classic example is Isidore of Seville (c. 560-636) whose encyclopedic writings formed the basis for most Western treatments of the liturgy for almost a thousand years. In describing Vespers, he writes:

> Vespers is the end of the Daily Office and the setting of another daylight. Its solemn celebration is from the Old Testament. It was the custom of the ancients to offer sacrifices and to have aromatic substances and incense burnt on the altar at that time. [David], that hymn-singing witness, performed a royal and priestly Office saying: "Let my prayer be counted as incense before you, and the lifting up of my hands as an evening sacrifice" (Ps 141:2). (De Eccl. Off., 1.20.1).

Isidore asserts a few things that we need to look at more carefully. First, he finds Vespers in the Old Testament. Second, he clarifies this remark by talking about sacrifices, particularly around the offering of incense. Third, he mentions David, citing a psalm in support of his statements. What is he talking about, and in what sense do we take this?

Looking through the legislation in the Torah, the first five books of the Hebrew scriptures, we find a double reference to what Isidore was describing. Numbers 28:1-8 gives a summary:

> The LORD spoke to Moses, saying: Command the Israelites, and say to them: My offering, the food for my offerings by fire, my pleasing odor, you shall take care to offer to me at its appointed time. And you shall say to them, This is the offering by fire that you shall offer to the LORD: two male lambs a year old without blemish, daily, as a regular offering. One lamb you shall offer in the morning, and the other lamb you shall offer at twilight also one-tenth of an ephah of choice flour for a grain offering, mixed with one-fourth of a hin of beaten oil. It is a regular burnt offering, ordained at Mount Sinai for a pleasing odor, an offering by fire to the LORD. Its drink offering shall be one-fourth of a hin for each lamb; in the sanctuary you shall pour out a drink offering of strong drink to the LORD. The other lamb you shall offer at twilight with a grain offering and a drink offering like the one in the morning; you shall offer it as an offering by fire, a pleasing odor to the LORD.

So—lambs, bread, and wine. This legislation is described again at the end of Exodus 29; Exodus 30 then gives directions for the incense altar right before the Holy of Holies in the inmost part of the temple and states: "Aaron shall offer fragrant incense on it; every morning when he dresses the lamps he shall offer it, and when Aaron sets up the lamps in the evening, he shall offer it, a regular incense offering before the Lord throughout your generations" (Exodus 30:7-8).

Although these twice daily offerings are described separately, we find them joined together in some of the standard summary statements of priestly activity in the temple. Thus, when King Abijah tries to persuade the people of Israel to join the kingdom of Judah, he argues, "We have priests ministering to the LORD who are descendants of Aaron, and Levites for their service. They offer to the LORD every morning and every evening burnt offerings and fragrant incense, set out the rows of bread on the table of pure gold, and care for the golden lampstand so that its lamps may burn every evening" (2 Chronicles 13:10b-11a). When we think about services in the temple, then, this was a big piece of the daily activity: the twice daily burnt offerings of food and incense. The best description that we have from the time of the temple is in Ecclesiasticus 50:12-21 where the service is described while praising Simon, son of Onias, high priest from around 219-196 BCE. While interesting in its own right, the only point that we need to observe from this description is that it includes a description of the Levites singing a psalm at the time of the sacrifice. This agrees with the much later—and much more comprehensive—description of this ceremony in the *Mishnah* (the third-century, written collection of Jewish oral teaching) where set psalms are appointed for the sacrifices for each day of the week.

To recap: there were daily temple sacrifices at morning and evening where prayers were prayed, psalms sung, and sacrifices performed—both food and incense. This is the Old Testament precedent that Isidore is referring to. I am not suggesting that there is any direct liturgical link between the sacrifices and the Offices, only that the pattern is similar and that common elements are likely due to a Christian appropriation of an Old Testament practice.

These offerings of food, drink, and incense are the type that anthropologists refer to as alimentary offerings. That is, in these sacrifices, the community is feeding the deity. In traditions that include images or statues of the gods, they may be clothed during this time as well. While it is easy to dismiss these offerings as primitive and pointless, to do so misses their deeper meaning. Even in those societies, only the very young or unsophisticated believed that the gods needed these feedings and would perish without them. Indeed, Psalm 50 explicitly mocks this shallow understanding: "If I [the Lord] were hungry, I would not tell you, for the whole world is mine and all that is in it. Do you think I eat the flesh of bulls, or drink the blood of goats? Offer to God a sacrifice of thanksgiving and make good your vows to the Most High" (50:12-4). Rather, the community is taking some of its common supplies—food, drink, things that people use—and choosing to give them up. The fact that useful (and sometimes even scarce) resources are being exclusively devoted to the deity is a symbol of the community's dedication to their god. That's what's really behind this: These sacrifices are an act of self-dedication showing the material loss the community is willing to incur for the sake of faithfulness to their deity. This kind of sacrifice (and there are other kinds that we'll talk about later) demonstrates dedication because a limited good is being directed toward the god rather than the well-being of the community (or individual).

Psalm 141, with its spiritualization of the sacrifice, is pointing to something important when the psalmist asks that the prayer itself be considered a substitute for or an act of worship united—though at a distance—with the act of sacrifice: "Let my prayer be set forth in your sight as incense, the lifting up of my hands as the evening sacrifice" (141:2). Even though the psalmist isn't actually burning lambs, the act of prayer itself reflects an act of sacrifice. A good that is inherently limited—time itself—is being voluntarily dedicated to God.

Thus, if the morning and evening sacrifices of the temple are seen as acts of communal self-dedication to God, the Morning and Evening Prayers of the Church mirroring these sacrificial acts are also acts of self-dedication. We are voluntarily giving up twenty to thirty minutes to God—time that could be spent doing a hundred, a thousand, other things but instead we choose to spend this most precious resource in the praise of God.

There are two direct links that the Church has appropriated from the Old Testament practice that connect us with the spirit of these sacrifices: the use of psalms and the presence of incense. When we sing the psalms at morning and evening prayer, we are uniting our voices across time not just with the early Anglicans of Cranmer's day, not just with Isidore's Spanish monks, but also with the Levites serving God in the Jerusalem temple. We are separated by centuries, yet united in song.

Likewise, when we use incense—and this usually occurs either at formal expressions of public worship or, on the other end of the spectrum, as the act of an individual worshiper praying alone—we use it in direct remembrance of the incense offered to God in the temple ceremonies. We are not trying to recreate the temple sacrifices or to put ourselves under Old Testament ceremonial legislation, of course, but—like the psalms—we offer the incense in spiritual unison with the offerings of God's people through time. Thus, when incense is used at the Offices, it should be used to cense the altar alone and not the people around it. At this point, we are not using incense as a holy purifier but rather offering it directly to God as a sacrifice in and of itself and as a visual representation of the prayers ascending to God's throne.

By putting substantial prayer Offices at the hinges of the day—morning and evening—the Church joins its worship spiritually and symbolically with the twice daily sacrifices God commanded the Israelites to perform in scripture. As they did in worship, we too are sacrificing something of value—our time—to God as an act of dedication. When we pray the psalms, say the prayers, and lift up our hands with or without incense, we unite ourselves with the people of God across time and offer our own sacrifice of praise and thanksgiving.

CHAPTER 6
THE ANATOMY OF THE DAILY OFFICE

THE SERVICES

When we consider the Daily Office—the regular prayer services of the Church and our official public services on all days of the year that aren't holy days—we see that a number of items fall under this heading. They are grouped together at the front of the prayer book:

Rite I (Traditional language)

Rite II (Contemporary language)

Daily Devotions for Individuals and Families

Additional Directions

Let me make a few observations here.

First, a distinction is drawn in the title of some services as "Daily" and others as "An Order." Four services earn the term Daily: Morning and Evening Prayer in Rites I and II. (The brief devotions receive the term, Daily, as a class rather than individually.) This title reinforces their importance and their place in the Church's understanding of the liturgical round. The others beginning with "An Order…" are recommended but do not have quite the same stamp of authority or necessity as those identified as Daily.

Second, you can't actually pray either Morning or Evening Prayer with just the contents of this section. You need at least three other pieces to complete the service. They are:

The Collects for the Church Year

Collects: Traditional

Collects: Contemporary

The Psalter (pp. 581-808)

Daily Office Lectionary

Third, instructions on how to do the services are scattered throughout the book. This can be confusing. The majority of what you need to know can be found in the service itself. However, directions on who should do the service are found in the brief "Concerning the Service" notice found just before the service instructions. Some possible points of confusion are addressed in the "Additional Directions" at the end of the section. Items specific to the psalms and the readings may be found in the notes prefacing the Psalter and the Daily Office Lectionary; clarifications on the Calendar are tucked away among the collects.

Fourth, the Rite II services and the Daily Devotions agree in dividing the day into four chief liturgical sections: Morning, Noon, Evening, and Night. The patristic and medieval churches had their own counts for daily liturgical divisions (6 and 7+1 respectively); we have one as well. The fact that we have one at all hearkens back to the patristic and medieval models, but the fact that the count is less than both of the earlier models reflects our intention that these hours not be burdensome; they ought to be possible for the regular working person—not just a monk or hermit. Four sets of prayer a day may seem like a lot, but they are actually more doable than the alternatives, especially as two of those are recommended rather than required.

When it comes to services that you might experience in churches, Morning and Evening Prayer are the big ones. In my years as an Episcopalian, I've seen Morning and Evening Prayer done in a number of ways in a number of places. Noonday Prayer is less common. I've only experienced it in churches that have a special vocation to keeping the full liturgical round like St. Mary the Virgin, Times Square. It tends to be a small group or individual Office. Compline too tends to be individual or small group due to its nature as a bedtime Office. I have seen it done regularly and publicly only in intentional communities like monasteries or seminaries. It is not uncommon to use Compline to conclude evening church meetings or during multi-day retreats, though. Additionally, there seems to be a growing interest in the use of Compline as a choral experience: Both St. Mark's Cathedral in Seattle and Christ Church, New Haven, have well-known Compline services that create a place of chant, candles, and beauty, inviting Christians, seekers, and non-Christians alike to experience Christian liturgy as a place of holiness.

I don't recall ever experiencing an "Order of Worship for Evening." It was an interesting idea with classic roots new to this prayer book, but it has never generated the interest that its framers hoped.

The Daily Devotions are, by their very nature, not intended to be public church services—these are individual or household liturgies. I honestly can't say how much they are used; I don't hear very much about them around the church. I think that may be a missed opportunity for us. As a father of young children, I am fond of them; they instill the concept of regular prayer but are not too long or burdensome for even young children. Early on, our family adopted the devotion "At the Close of Day" as bedtime prayers for our girls. Since it is short and sweet, both of them had (quite unconsciously) memorized it even before they were able to read. I have frequently thought that a colorful laminated placemat with the text of the devotions "In the Morning" and "In the Early Evening" on either side might be a way to get these devotions into the kitchens and consciousness of families with children.

THE STRUCTURE OF THE OFFICES

The structures of Morning and Evening Prayer closely mirror one another. These twin Offices are meant to complement and reinforce one another. Noonday Prayer and Compline share in the same overall movement as the main Offices, but the elements do not fit together in the same way. Compline, in particular, cleaves closer to models of older liturgies and therefore follows a slightly different logic than the other three. An Order of Worship for the Evening has its own internal structure and possibilities, some of which mirror the Offices, others of which do not—it is doing a different thing and should be considered apart from the other liturgies in this section.

If we put the elements of the four prayer Offices in parallel with one another, common elements emerge. Optional elements are in italics; common elements are in bold:

	Morning Prayer	Noonday Prayer	Evening Prayer	Compline
[Fore-Office]	*Opening Sentence*		*Opening Sentence*	Versicles[12]
	Confession & Absolution		*Confession & Absolution*	*Confession & Absolution*
Invitatory & Psalms	Opening Versicles	Opening Versicles	Opening Versicles	Opening Versicles
	Invitatory	*Hymn*	Invitatory	
	Appointed Psalms	Appointed Psalms	Appointed Psalms	Appointed Psalms
Lessons	OT *Scripture Reading*		OT *Scripture Reading*	
	Canticle		Canticle	
	NT Scripture Reading	Scripture [Sentence]	NT Scripture Reading	Scripture [Sentence]
	Canticle		Canticle	*Hymn*
	Apostles' Creed		Apostles' Creed	
The Prayers				Brief Suffrages
	The Lord's Prayer	The Lord's Prayer	The Lord's Prayer	The Lord's Prayer
	Suffrages		Suffrages	
	Collects	Collects	Collects	Collects
	Hymn		*Hymn*	Canticle
	Concluding Prayers		Concluding Prayers	
	Blessing	Blessing	Blessing	Blessing

Notice the arc we have here. We start with scripture and move to prayer. One way to make sense of this pattern is that we start with edification and then we move to praise—but that's not the best way to think about it. This is the Office; it's **all** praise! It would be better to say that we begin with praise that reveals and reminds us who God is (and, specifically, who God is for his people through time), then we continue with praise that offers our response to who God is.

The large headings printed in Morning and Evening Prayer divide the Offices into four natural parts that can also be applied to Noonday Prayer and somewhat to Compline. There is no initial heading, which is why I've supplied one, Fore-Office, in the chart. The headings reinforce the character of the arc. The pattern starts with the psalms highlighting their crucial function in the Office ecosystem. Notice that the presence of psalms is never optional. This book of divine praises is the scriptural centerpiece of the Office. Then we move to the scripture readings. I think that the heading, "The Lessons," in Morning and Evening Prayer is an unfortunate choice of words. It reflects a holdover mentality from the early Reformation era that locates worship's purpose in its instructional value. Even "The Readings" would be a better way to label what is about to occur that doesn't prejudice the purpose of these scriptures in the same way that the term lessons does. Then we move to the prayers. We get several different kinds of prayer in these sections but many cut across the four Offices: the Lord's Prayer, suffrages, collects, and blessings. Our prayer is not all of one type, and our Offices lead us through a variety as they school us in the arts of praise.

THE ELEMENTS OF MORNING AND EVENING PRAYER

The Fore-Office

These are the elements of the Fore-Office:

Element	Required?	Variation (if any)
Opening Sentences	Optional	Seasonal/ Occasional
Confession of Sin	Optional	

The Fore-Office elements are, as a group, optional. Their use represents our first theological choice as we begin the Office each day. These initial bits date back to our most Puritan point—the 1552 English prayer book—when we as a Church were wrestling with the great Reformation questions. One of these revolved around the issue of sin and grace, and an answer is framed by way of the Fore-Office. In short, this section originally suggested that due to human sin, we can't even worship God properly without a healthy dose of grace and therefore without confessing our lack of it and need for it.

On the other hand, the ancient opening of Morning Prayer—"O Lord, open our lips" (taken from Psalm 51:16)—was meant literally back in the monastic days; silence would be kept in the monasteries from the end of Compline, the last liturgical words of the day, until the beginning of Morning Prayer. Those ancient opening words were literally the first words spoken each day. To use that opening after a page and a half of talk blunts its force a bit. (As does chatty conversation before Morning Prayer or breakfast table dialogue. I find it harder to apply the lip-opening rationale seriously when I pray the Office at 9 in the morning rather than 6 a.m.)

In any case, the prayer book gives us the freedom to go either way: either begin with confession or begin with lip-opening. It certainly makes sense to use the Confession of Sin on the penitential days, those identified in section 4 of the Calendar as "Days of Special Devotion," but other than that, it's up to you and how much penitence you need that day.

The Opening Sentences

While these used to be a scriptural introduction to penitence (and were all penitential in character), our Opening Sentences now serve to set the mood. Morning Prayer offers a much more extensive selection that allows us to invoke either the liturgical season that we're in or the character of the day; Evening Prayer offers a more limited set (but also allows us to use the Morning options if we prefer).

At Morning Prayer, you'll note that each liturgical season is offered a couple of choices. The idea is that you start from the top and work your way through the sentences as the season progresses. If you choose to use the provided sentences at Evening Prayer, you will see there are eight, which gives us a set to rotate on a weekly basis. Of course, you can always just pick what you like.

The Confession of Sin

When it comes to the Confession of Sin, I have to confess that I'm a fan of the longer exhortation to confession in Morning Prayer in Rite I. The opening lines ground our common purpose in praying the Office together:

Dearly beloved, we have come together in the presence of Almighty God our heavenly Father,

- to render thanks for the great benefits that we have received at his hands,

- to set forth his most worthy praise,

- to hear his holy Word, and

- to ask, for ourselves and on behalf of others, those things that are necessary for our life and salvation (*The Book of Common Prayer*, p. 41).

The Rite II version drops the first of these points, not because we have ceased "to render thanks" but to underscore that the primary purpose of the Office is praise—the direct worship of God not tied to obligations or to a transactional model. That is, while we do need to thank God for his gifts to us, we also want to avoid the implication that we are somehow paying God for miracles with prayer either in advance or after the fact.

Rite I offers the traditional version of the confession while Rite II presents the wording that appears in the Rite II Eucharist. The former confession contains more vibrant imagery concerning our wrongdoing; the image of the lost sheep, in particular, provides a nice resonance with the invitatory psalms in Morning Prayer that compare the congregation to sheep under God's pastoral guidance. The latter confession is more clearly structured to reflect our twofold duty to love God and neighbor, and to acknowledge our failures in doing so.

The Invitatory and Psalter

These are the elements of the Invitatory and Psalter:

Element	Required?	Variation (if any)
Opening Versicles	Yes	A little
Invitatory Antiphon	Optional	Seasonal
Invitatory	Morning: Yes Evening: Optional	Morning: Seasonal
Appointed Psalms	Yes	Choice of Pattern

This section gives us a great big block of musical material, chiefly psalms, after a short dialogue that gets things going. Most of this material is not optional as it forms one of the great theological centers of the Office. If the Office is a "sacrifice of praise," then this is a big part of where that offering actually happens.

Opening Versicles

As mentioned above, the Opening Versicles of Morning Prayer ("O Lord, open our lips…") come from Psalm 51 and as discussed, were literally true in a monastic environment; most orders observed a Great Silence from the end of Compline to the beginning of Matins where no talking was allowed. These words would be the first words spoken in the morning. The Opening Versicles of Evening Prayer ("O God, make speed to save us…") are from Psalm 70:1 and reflect the breath prayer taught by John Cassian and the Desert Fathers. These are the normal opening versicles of the Offices from before the Reformation. In the English prayer books, they were included at Morning Prayer as well, right after the morning versicles.

The only variation is that the "Alleluia" gets dropped in Lent and Holy Week.

Invitatory Antiphons

The invitatory antiphons are sentences used with the invitatory to communicate a sense of the season or occasion. Morning Prayer has them; Evening Prayer does not. Options are given for seasons and for holy days. (Lesser feasts do not receive their own antiphon and use the appropriate seasonal option.) The first part of the antiphon establishes a sense of the season or event; the second is an invariable call to praise,

"O come, let us adore him," from Psalm 95:6 (although our present prayer book rendering of this phrase is: "O come, let us worship/bow down"). And, yes, the Christmas hymn, "O Come All Ye Faithful," is a deliberate riff on the structure of the invitatory antiphon.

We are not given any clear direction as to exactly how the antiphon is to be used with the *Venite* or other Invitatory Psalm. (It is not used with the Christ our Passover as it has its own internal Alleluia antiphon.) There are two common ways to use it. The easiest is simply to use it before and after the psalm. The other and more traditional method is to include it several times within the psalm; the musical settings in the hymnal confirm that this should be done at each section break.

Invitatory

The invitatory is an opening song or psalm that literally invites the worship of God. The prayer book contains five different options for Morning Prayer and a single one for Evening Prayer. Three of the morning options are all shades of the same text, Psalm 95. It is customary to refer to the psalms by the first couple of words in Latin. The monks didn't memorize the numbers, so they simply referred to the opening words. This custom was continued by Cranmer at the Reformation and has stuck. In our case, it's particularly useful because our *Venite*, the first word of Psalm 95, is actually not identical with the psalm. The Rite I *Venite* contains the first seven verses of Psalm 95, then substitutes verses 9 and 13 of Psalm 96 for the condemnatory verses at the end of Psalm 95. The Rite II *Venite* simply omits these verses. However, at points (particularly Fridays in Lent and Friday and Saturday in Holy Week), all of Psalm 95 is appointed. Psalm 100, the *Jubilate*, is also an option and was historically used when Psalm 95 appeared among the Morning Prayer psalms.[13] For Easter, the Christ our Passover (*Pascha Nostrum*) is provided. It must be used during Easter Week and may be used for the rest of the Easter season. I prefer to use it throughout the season, as it is a good daily reminder that Easter is fifty days long. The Evening Prayer invitatory is an ancient hymn from the Greek Church, O Gracious Light (*Phos hilaron*). It doesn't need antiphons nor are any provided.

At the heart of the invitatory is an invitation. The appointed texts urge those praying them to worship. Psalm 95 holds such a privileged place because it issues the invitation three times in rapid succession. It opens with a repeated call to worship in verses 1 and 2: "Come let us sing...let us shout for joy...Let us come...and raise a loud shout to him with psalms." The call repeats in verse 6: "Come, let us bow down." The other element of Psalm 95 that makes it so attractive is found at the end of verse 7: "Oh, that today you would hearken to his voice!" Although this passage logically goes with the next section of the psalm—which gives the rebellion of the people under Moses as an example of what not to do— the Rite II *Venite* ends here. In addition to the call to come and worship, we are reminded to also listen and take heed of what God is telling us. The Rite I *Venite* does not include any of the condemnatory section but includes additional encouragement for praise from Psalm 96 and retains the notion that God is also coming to meet us in our worship.

The *Jubilate* contains these elements as well. It opens with an exhortation to worship: "come before his presence with a song" (Psalm 100:1), and repeats it, "Enter his gates with thanksgiving; go into his courts with praise; give thanks to him and call upon his Name" (Psalm 100:3).

During Easter time, Christ our Passover is Cranmer's compilation of Sarum antiphons drawn from the writings of Paul. The repeated "Alleluia" is its own internal antiphon, so it doesn't need an invitatory antiphon to accompany it. As appropriate for the resurrection season, this text focuses on the passage from death to life and Christ's victory over the grave. The repetition at the beginning of the second and third sections, "Christ...raised from the dead," and the conclusion with its triumphant, "all shall be made alive," is one of my favorite pieces of the Easter experience.

The Evening Prayer invitatory, O Gracious Light, served as the Eastern Church's lamp-lighting hymn for centuries. In an electric-lit culture, we usually miss the symbolic moment when the day moves from light to dark; this hymn helps remind us. At its heart, this is a simple hymn of praise to Christ as the light of the world that praises the Trinity at the hinge of the day.

The Psalm or Psalms

The appointed psalms come next. As I have said, this is the historical and theological center of the Office, and the next chapter is devoted to exploring the psalms within this context. The main decision is which psalm scheme to adopt. The book gives a choice of two; the first appears in the Daily Office Lectionary while the second is found in the section of the prayer book containing the psalms.

The first option is the lectionary cycle. This cycle spreads out the 150 psalms across seven weeks. The cycle begins on the first week of Advent, the first week after Epiphany, the eighth week after Epiphany (if there should be one), the second week of Easter, with Trinity Sunday and Proper 2, Proper 9, Proper 16, and Proper 23. The earlier iterations of the cycle often are not complete because of a number of proper psalms around Christmas, the length of the Epiphany season, proper psalms for Holy Week and Easter, and on what

Proper the season after Pentecost begins. The last three cycles, though, are only interrupted by occasional holy days.

If you look at the layout of this particular lectionary, a pattern emerges. Psalms were specifically picked for Saturday evening, Sunday morning, and Sunday evening. Next, the many parts of the lengthy Psalm 119 were assigned to Wednesdays, alternating between evening and morning. Then, the remaining psalms were distributed to each week, trying to balance out the number of verses and placing some penitential or passion psalms on Fridays (i.e., Psalms 22, 51, 69, and 88). Psalm 95 falls in the evening—so you don't need to worry about it appearing right after you have used it as the invitatory at Morning Prayer. (Psalm 100, though, falls on Tuesday morning of week six.) The pattern shows that the emphasis is on having appropriate psalms for public worship on Saturday nights and Sundays. In addition to this, provisions are made for dropping verses of psalms or whole psalms that might be deemed offensive or problematic to congregations. On balance, each Office prays just under thirty psalm verses.

The second option is the monthly cycle found within the Psalter itself. Turning to page 585 in *The Book of Common Prayer*, the first page of the Psalter, you'll see a note in italics above the title of Psalm 1: "First Day: Morning Prayer." On page 589 before the start of Psalm 6 is another note: "First Day: Evening Prayer." These notes are given for thirty days, morning and evening. If a month has a thirty-first day, the psalms given for the thirtieth are repeated. On average, this cycle provides about forty-five verses of psalms for each Office. (The longest is the evening of the fifteenth with seventy-three verses; the shortest is the evening of the second with twenty-four. Most counts fall between the high thirties and low fifties, though.)

The monthly cycle highlights the catechetical role of the Office. That is, it emphasizes the continuous repetition of the psalms for the purpose of learning them. It presents a less flexible cycle that is not particularly responsive to seasonal awareness. Most of the people I know who use this cycle (myself among them) only deviate from it for the Principal Feasts. This can lead to unusual combinations when a particular angry psalm might show up on a happy festival or a joyous one occur where it doesn't seem to fit. Often it is in these moments that I learn something important—either about the psalm or the occasion—that had always been present; I just hadn't noticed it before. The odd combination casts the new insight in relief and makes it stand out.

In contrast, the seven-week lectionary covers the psalms but over a longer period. Its strength is that it lends itself to occasional use. That is, the monthly cycle is used best and works best when it is prayed daily. The seven-week cycle neither assumes nor requires a previous discipline. Similarly, using proper psalms for holy days is the better option if a parish that doesn't normally pray the Office together decides to hold an Evensong.

THE LESSONS

These are the elements of the Lessons:

Element	Required?	Variation (if any)
Old Testament Lesson	Morning: Yes Evening: Optional[14]	Daily
Canticle	Yes, if reading	Variable
New Testament Lesson	Yes	Daily
Canticle	Yes	Variable
Apostles' Creed	Yes	None

This section contains the biblical readings and the sung canticles. It concludes with the Apostles' Creed, which reminds us of the Church's interpretive lens for the scriptures.

The Lessons and the Office Lectionary

The Daily Office Lectionary provides for three readings per day over a two-year cycle: an Old Testament reading, an Epistle reading, and a Gospel reading. Both Morning and Evening Prayer can accommodate—and have traditionally had—two biblical readings each for a total of four per day. As a result, you have a choice: You can use the three readings as appointed and distribute them through the Offices (usually two at Morning Prayer and the third at Evening Prayer) or you can find another reading. The normal way to do this is to use the Old Testament reading from the off-year and place it as the first reading for Evening Prayer.

In terms of completeness, the lectionary does a good job with the New Testament. Of the Gospels, all of Matthew and Mark are read each year. Luke is missing about fifty verses (4 percent of its length), but these are the genealogy and the iconic birth story and his appearance in the temple at age twelve, which are included in the Eucharistic Lectionary. John is missing about eighty verses (9 percent of its length), and these are all sections from the passion and resurrection narratives, which, again, are well represented in the Eucharistic Lectionary.

Of the New Testament apart from the Gospels, the large stand-alone books of Acts, Hebrews, and Revelation are read in their entirety each year. We read 97 percent of both the Pauline Epistles and the general Epistles. Missing from the general Epistles is one section from 1 Peter 3 dealing with wives being submissive to their husbands; most of the material missing from the Pauline Letters, primarily from 1 Corinthians and 1 Timothy, similarly deals with the social roles of women and slaves. Two verses missing from Romans loom large in many current discussions of human sexuality.[15]

When we come to the Old Testament, the percentage drops. Overall, across both years—or in one year if you read two readings—we read just under half of the Old Testament. When you look at it by category, we read more percentage-wise of the minor prophets than any other grouping (72 percent as opposed to the others at about 40 percent). This is due mostly to the brief length of these books. Year One reads through about 22 percent of the Old Testament and contains more of the histories and the major prophets. Year Two reads about 25 percent and contains more of the minor prophets, the law, and the wisdom literature. There is some overlap in which certain passages are read in both years (apart from the holy day readings). This occurs mostly in Isaiah, the histories, and Genesis and Exodus, but it accounts for under 10 percent of what is read each year.

Why so little of the Old Testament by percentage? It's pretty simple: math. The Gospel readings and other New Testament readings average about eight and seven verses long respectively. The Old Testament readings currently average a little under ten verses in length. If you were going to move through the entire Old Testament, you would have to more than double that amount. If you want to keep the length of the three readings balanced, this is the problem you're going to have to face.

The original Daily Office Lectionary scheme that Cranmer came up with when he compiled the first *Book of Common Prayer* included most (but not all) of the Old Testament each year. Readings were typically assigned by chapter not verse; thus, on January 4, for example, you would read Genesis 5 in the morning and Genesis 6 in the evening. The corresponding New Testament and Gospel readings that were of an equal length went through the full cycle three times in a year. That is a lot more reading than what we have now. In fact, looking over the past 500 years, we have seen the length of the readings steadily drop over time. The goal is to get people to pray the Office and read their scriptures. The trend has been to reduce the time it takes by reducing the amount of scripture required.

Like the seven-week psalm cycle, the Daily Office Lectionary has two different options for the sake of occasional use. For the most part, biblical books are read through continuously. That is, a reading will generally stick with a book and read straight through it, or, when it does skip material, it usually does so sequentially. However, this sequence is interrupted for Sundays. A different cycle of readings appears on Sunday for the benefit of those who only experience the Offices once a week—or less—and who may have occasion to experience a Sunday reading and not any of the others. Thus, the Daily Office Lectionary will jump on Sundays to a different place and pick up a different story than what has been read through the rest of the week.

The Canticles

Following each biblical reading is a canticle. When I first experienced Episcopal Morning Prayer as a Lutheran seminarian, I was completely baffled by the canticles. The priest leading the group would call out a number; she never had any hesitation about what to pick. Some canticles were often said, but others were never said. Furthermore, other people in the group seemed to know in advance what she was going to say. I had a hard enough time finding the right number, since the first canticle that I saw was numbered 8! Eventually, I got it all figured out, but I have never forgotten my initial confusion.

What I didn't know was that the canticles numbered 1 through 7 are located in Morning Prayer: Rite I. Canticles 8 through 21 are in Morning Prayer: Rite II. All of the canticles in Rite I appear in contemporary language in Rite II, but not vice-versa. Furthermore, there is no inherent or logical connection between the Rite I numbers and their Rite II counterparts. So your first challenge in negotiating the canticles is navigating through them. Some canticles are also usually used for Morning Prayer, while others are customarily used at Evening Prayer (which is why I never heard them).

There is a basic principle at work here. In both the Rite I and Rite II blocks, the canticles appear in canonical/chronological order. Thus, the Rite I block starts with material from the Apocrypha, goes through the canticles from Luke in canonical order, then moves to the two compositions from the Early Church. In a corresponding fashion, the Rite II block starts with material from Exodus, then goes to the canticles from Isaiah before moving to the Apocrypha but adds an additional one before moving to the Luke material and items from Revelation, then ending with the Early Church compositions.

As with the invitatory psalms, the names of the canticles are given both in English and in a classical language, usually Latin. People and reference works may use either name, so it never hurts to be familiar with both.

Canticles 1 and 12 are "A Song of Creation" (*Benedicite, omnia opera Domini*). The *Benedicite* comes from one of the additions to the book of Daniel that is found in the Greek Old Testament but not in the Hebrew version. It's best understood as an expansion of the content and theme of Psalm 148 where all creation is called upon to worship and give glory to God. In the narrative, this is a song put into the mouth of Daniel's three companions in the midst of the fiery furnace. As a result, sometimes this will be referred to as "the song of the three young men." In the former prayer books, this canticle was used as the first canticle during penitential seasons when the *Te Deum* was suppressed. That's not because there's anything penitential about it—it's one of the most joyful canticles around! Rather it is because this was the second canticle found in the pre-Reformation prymers (medieval prayer books) and Books of Hours; if the *Te Deum*—which was the first canticle in them—was dropped, this one was next in line. Hence, the tradition grew that the *Benedicite* should replace the *Te Deum*, and this tradition subsequently formed the prayer book practice.

Canticles 2 and 13 are "A Song of Praise" (*Benedictus es, Domine*). This song comes from the same place as the previous canticle and comes right before it in the text. While the first one calls all creation to bless God, this is an example of such a blessing. It praises God, envisioning him enthroned within a grand temple having aspects of the temple in Jerusalem but being located "in the firmament of heaven." Dwelling "between the Cherubim" is a reference to the mercy seat on the Ark of the Covenant, which was kept in the Holy of Holies, the inmost part of the Jerusalem temple.

Canticles 3 and 15 are "The Song of Mary" (*Magnificat*). This is one of the most beautiful songs in all of scripture and is Mary's response to the dual greeting from her cousin Elizabeth and the yet-unborn John the Baptist. Based in part on the Song of Hannah (1 Samuel 2:1-10) and with echoes of Psalm 138 and 146, it admirably anticipates Luke's Beatitudes (Luke 6:20-26)—and, indeed, they are well worth studying together. In the pre-Reformation system, Evening Prayer (their Vespers) only had one canticle—and this was it. As a result, it became the standard third canticle, the one after the first reading of Evening Prayer. It still holds this place in both Rite I and Rite II services of Evening Prayer.

Canticles 4 and 16 are "The Song of Zechariah" (*Benedictus Dominus Deus*). This song was sung by Zechariah, the husband of Elizabeth and father of John the Baptist, at his son's birth. This was the standard second canticle of Morning Prayer and was the chief canticle of the pre-Reformation version. I have always found the second part of this song especially meaningful. Through the voice of Zechariah, we who pray this canticle are commissioned and reminded of our duty to spread the Gospel—and are given a convenient summary of it, focusing on forgiveness, mercy, light, and walking in the paths of peace.

Canticles 5 and 17 are "The Song of Simeon" (*Nunc dimittis*). Simeon, having waited all his life to see the Messiah, holds the infant Jesus in his arms at the end of his days and sings this song. With its themes of ending and new beginning, a growing light and a coming peace, it was used in the pre-Reformation system at Compline just before sleep. Adapted into the prayer book system, it became the fixed fourth canticle, following the second reading of Evening Prayer.

Canticles 6 and 20 are the "Glory (be) to God" (*Gloria in excelsis*). While it begins with the song of the angels at the birth of Christ, the rest of the canticle is a composition from the Early Church. Familiar to most of the Western Church from its use at the beginning of the Eucharist, its appearance here is an eastern element; this was the standard morning canticle for the Eastern Churches.

Canticles 7 and 21 are the "We Praise Thee/You" (*Te Deum laudamus*). Another composition of the Early Church, the *Te Deum* was sung at Matins on Sundays and festivals. At the Reformation, the prayer book appointed this as the first canticle of Morning Prayer every day of the year except for the forty days of Lent. Its connection with festivals was strong enough that, by the early medieval period, the *Te Deum* was sometimes used with some additional suffrages as a celebratory liturgy.

Canticle 8—the first of the canticles only found in Rite II's contemporary language—is "The Song of Moses" (*Cantemus Domino*). It is "especially suitable for use in Easter Season" because this is the song sung by Moses and the Israelites after their deliverance from Egypt through the Red Sea. The Red Sea passage has long been understood as a symbol of Baptism and Resurrection, and this connection is stated explicitly in the Easter Vigil's own victory song, the *Exultet*.

Canticle 9 is "The First Song of Isaiah" (*Ecce, Deus*). Coming from the prophet Isaiah, this song concludes his vision of the messianic age to come. This song is to be sung in celebration of what God has accomplished and the salvation wrought through his messiah. For us, it is a reminder that we stand in the midst of the "already/not yet;" God's promises have been fulfilled in the person of Jesus, yet we do not always perceive the fulfilment of these promises. The use of this canticle is a sign of hope.

Canticle 10 is "The Second Song of Isaiah" (*Quaerite Dominum*). This song comes from the latter part of Isaiah. It closes out a section that encourages the people, exiled in Babylon, to return and rebuild Jerusalem to its former glory. It urges them to seek the Lord and to trust in the fulfillment of the divine word at a point when many doubted that the city would ever be rebuilt and the land reclaimed. The language of repentance makes it particularly suitable in penitential seasons.

Canticle 11 is "The Third Song of Isaiah" (*Surge, Illuminare*). This song from the end of Isaiah, also from the time at the end of the exile (around 520 BCE), exhorts the people with a vision of the rebuilt Jerusalem. This vision of a preternaturally brilliant city that calls the nations to it influenced Revelation's vision of the New Jerusalem as the

Bride of the Lamb and, subsequently, the theology of the Church as a New Jerusalem. The images of light connect it strongly to the themes of both Advent and Epiphany.

Canticle 14 is "A Song of Penitence" (*Kyrie Pantokrator*). This canticle comes from the brief apocryphal book, *The Prayer of Manasseh*. Manasseh was crowned as king of Judah at the age of twelve around 700 BCE and reigned for fifty-five years. He has the dubious honor of being the most evil king to hold the throne of Judah. The narrative of his reign in 2 Kings 21 is a catalog of idolatry and slaughter. The retelling of it in 2 Chronicles 33, however, includes a scene of Manasseh's repentance and makes mention of a prayer where he humbled himself before God and received forgiveness of his sin. Although our composition is likely not this prayer itself, it certainly represents what the prayer could have been.[16] It is, as the prayer book note suggests, the perfect canticle for Lent and for other penitential circumstances.

Canticle 18 is "A Song to the Lamb" (*Dignus es*). While the Book of Revelation is known for its apocalyptic imagery and its abuse by those who would read modern political events through it, it should be better known as the book of the New Testament that contains the most songs! This canticle comes from the description of the heavenly throne room. We are treated in Revelation 4-6 to a vision of the throne room of God, where a set of concentric circles of worshipers arrays the whole created order in a ceaseless song of praise to God and to the Lamb. This is the celebration of the saints and angels and all creation in thanksgiving for creation and redemption.

Canticle 19 is "The Song of the Redeemed" (*Magna et mirabilia*). In an interlude between acts of judgment and the seven last plagues, the seer John has a vision of the martyrs singing a song described as "the song of Moses, the servant of God and the song of the Lamb" (Revelation 15:3). This canticle is that song. From the introduction, then, the author of Revelation intended this song to be in conscious continuity with our Canticle 8, the Song of Moses.

Now that we've gotten through all of these, how do we go about using them and what's the best way to arrange them? What canticle should you use when—and why?

There are several ways of answering this question. Like so much about the prayer book, it depends on your tradition—and that, in turn, gives us the simplest answer. Does your parish pray the Office together? If so, it's best to find out what pattern they go with and use it.

If not, there are a variety of choices. I'll talk you through three of them.

The simplest is a traditional pattern that has the least amount of variation. As I mentioned in discussing the canticles, the prayer books up until the present one had a fairly fixed order. There were four readings, two at each Office, and a canticle after each reading. The first canticle was either the *Te Deum* or the *Benedicite*—depending on the season. The three Gospel canticles, the *Benedictus*, the *Magnificat*, and the *Nunc Dimittis* were the second, third, and fourth canticles respectively. The reason why these canticles appear in these positions is based on how Cranmer consolidated the eight hours of prayer into two: Morning Prayer received the *Te Deum* from Matins and the *Benedictus* from Lauds; Evening Prayer received the *Magnificat* from Vespers and the *Nunc Dimittis* from Compline. Thus, the simplest way to arrange the canticles is to use this basic pattern.

One of the more complex options is the way that the prayer book recommends. After the Offices themselves, a means of deploying all of the canticles appears on pages 144 and 145. We'll start with the suggestions for Morning Prayer on page 144. The basic idea is that the Old Testament Lesson receives an Old Testament canticle and the New Testament

Lesson receives a New Testament/Early Church canticle. Sundays and feast days retain the traditional canticles, though not in the traditional order; Wednesday and Friday—the traditional fasting days—receive the more penitential materials, especially in Lent. Additionally, in Lent and Advent the *Te Deum* and *Gloria* are replaced by other options. The easiest way to use this chart is to write it in where you intend to use it. As a result, in several of my prayer books, I have copied it into the blank space at the bottom of page 84 and have also written the appropriate days and seasons at the top of the canticles themselves.

The suggestions for Evening Prayer on page 145 assume the use of two lessons at Evening Prayer. If you are only using one lesson, use the second column and alternate between the *Magnificat* and *Nunc dimittis*. Otherwise, it alternates between the *Magnificat* and the *Nunc dimittis* for the second canticle except on Sundays and feast days when both are used. On weekdays the first canticle rotates through a set of Old Testament options.

A third way to proceed is by a blend of these two. For those who want to retain the classical use of the *Benedictus* and the *Magnificat* but also experience the variety of new canticles that this prayer book offers, the Old Testament option for Morning Prayer can be followed with the *Benedictus* after the second lesson; the New Testament option for Morning Prayer can be used to follow the first lesson at Evening Prayer and use the *Magnificat* after the second lesson.

The truth is, it doesn't matter which pattern you use—only that you use one. The canticles serve as constant reminders that a most proper response to God is bursting out into song. The advantage of a pattern is that, like the lectionary, we intentionally move through several options—not just picking our favorite parts. And, in the act of being paired up, the canticles and the readings invite us to regard them together as a set. What does the reading say to us in light of the canticle's praise? Conversely, what light does the reading shed on the canticle as it informs us about the nature of God and our relationships with him and his creation?

The Apostles' Creed

Finally, after all of this biblical material, the Lessons finish up with the Apostles' Creed. As we discussed in the Calendar section, the creed is the Church's guideline for interpreting scripture. In this position, the Apostles' Creed stands both as a summary of our faith and a reminder of our key interpretive principles: all readings, all canticles, are read in light of the life, death, and resurrection of Jesus and the revelation of the Triune God.

THE PRAYERS

These are the elements of the prayers:

Element	Required?	Variation (if any)
Lord's Prayer	Yes	None
Suffrages	Yes	Choice of 2
Collects	Yes	Variable
Prayer for Mission	Yes	Choice of 3
General Thanksgiving	No	None
A Prayer of St. Chrysostom	No	None
Blessing	No	None
Closing Benediction	No	Choice of 3

After having frontloaded the Office with adoration, praise, and thanksgiving in the psalms and the scripture lessons, we move toward intercession and petition.

The Lord's Prayer

Since the second century, Church writers have urged that the Lord's Prayer be prayed three times a day.[17] Incorporating it within Morning and Evening Prayer is one of the simplest ways to accomplish this. In this central prayer, we remind ourselves to align our wills with God's, we ask for our daily sustenance, and we commit ourselves to forgiving that we might be forgiven. Taking Christ's words upon our lips, we properly start our prayers by grounding ourselves in his prayer.

The Suffrages

The world that birthed the Church had a great respect for canonical works. The deep study of Homer's works and Virgil's *Aeneid* gave birth to a new art form, the *cento*, or, as we now call it, the mashup. As a means of demonstrating their mastery of canonical texts, authors would compose new works created entirely by taking snippets, phrases, and lines from these epics and using them to construct a new story. The rules for this kind of poetic composition were first written out by Ausonius in the fourth century. Needless to say, Church writers took part. One of the first great compositions by a Christian woman writer was Proba's life of Jesus constructed entirely from pieces of the *Aeneid*.

Since we see this kind of play at work with the epics of the time, it is not surprising to find it in the liturgies that were being constructed around this time as well. Our suffrages are composed in just this style. Rather than taking pieces out of Virgil, though, the suffrages are put together with pieces from different psalms. Suffrages A are a version adapted from the Sarum Breviary for the first prayer book and used thereafter with some modifications. The Morning Prayer Suffrages B are a very old set that historically traveled along with the

Te Deum. As a result, my preference is to use this set whenever the *Te Deum* is used as a canticle. The Evening Prayer Suffrages B are not related to the cento form and are standard intercessions.

The Collects

The officiant is then directed to say "one or more of the following Collects." The Collect of the Day is listed first along with seven other collects. According to the rubric, we may choose to use the Collect of the Day and another collect, to simply pray the Collect of the Day, or to skip it and to pray only one of the printed collects. As I have argued in the chapter on the Collects, the Collect of the Day is an important link that binds us to the Church Year and connects our Office cycles with our weekly Eucharists. We don't have to pray the Collect of the Day—but it's definitely a good idea.

Of the next seven collects, the first three are identified as pertaining to specific days of the week. Although the remaining four have titles related to various other purposes, it takes no great stretch of the imagination to create from them a weekly cycle. Indeed, it is probably not accidental that the collect that would fall on Thursday evening contains such strong Eucharistic resonances given that the Eucharist was established on a Thursday evening.

The Prayers for Mission

The final required element in the Office is the inclusion of one of the three prayers for mission or a form of general intercession. The prayers for mission are, at root, prayers for the whole Church, asking that it be strengthened to fulfill its fundamental mission of manifesting the good news with which we have been entrusted. The third prayer in the morning has a particularly rich image of Christ's arms extended on the cross embracing the world; the second prayer in the evening is based on a prayer by Saint Augustine and paints a lovely picture of the compassionate presence of God.

The option for a general intercession has two main referents. At Morning Prayer, this is the point where the Great Litany may be inserted. Classically, it was prayed on Wednesday, Friday, and Sunday at the conclusion of Morning Prayer because it served as the transition to the Eucharist that was appointed on those days. The regulation to insert it on those days remained in the American prayer books until the 1928 revision, and it still appears in the English *Book of Common Prayer*. Alternatively, two prayers were written to be used together at the end of the service on days when the Litany was not being used: the Prayer for All Sorts and Conditions, which served as a general intercession, and the General Thanksgiving. While the General Thanksgiving is still included here, the Prayer for All Sorts and Conditions has been relegated to the back of our prayer book on pages 814-815.

The Final Prayers

A set of optional prayers then follows. The General Thanksgiving is a much-loved prayer for its stately cadences and its even-tempered joy. The echo of the *Benedictus* in the passage that speaks of "walking before you in holiness and righteousness all our days" is surely not accidental. The Prayer of Saint Chrysostom likewise puts beautiful poetry to our request that God hear our prayers and grant them as may be best for us. Just as this section opened with the Lord's Prayer asking that "your will be done," this final prayer comes full circle, requesting that we be reconciled to the answering of our prayers— whether we receive the answer that we wish or not. The final optional act is to bless God and for us, in turn, to receive a blessing as well.

CHAPTER 7
THE PSALMS

THE SOURCE OF THE PSALMS

At the heart of the historic discipline of the Office are the psalms. The recitation of the psalms has always been a central part of the Office, and many of the other elements in the Office are either borrowed from or directly inspired by the psalms. As a result, it's worth taking a closer look at them.

Psalms (capitalized) refers to a book of the Old Testament containing 150 chapters. These chapters are, for the most part, discrete poems or songs known as psalms (not capitalized) that involve the relationship between God and his people, whether individually or corporately. What makes the psalms unusual, given our typical perspective on the Bible, is their direction. That is, we ordinarily consider the Bible to be God's self-revelation to humanity—God's Word, revealing himself to us. The psalms, though, are prayers from humanity to God, noteworthy for their emotional vulnerability and self-disclosure—feeling often more like humanity's self-revelation to God! Thus, the psalms are a paradox of sorts: divine revelation laying bare the soul of humanity.

Recalling our metaphor of running and training, verses from the psalms, some of the most beloved and well-known, can serve as a kind of mantra—similar to what some people use for exercise. The psalms also can be seen as similar to the war stories that runners tell one another—both the triumphs and the struggles. The psalms give us the companionship of knowing that others have trained before us, and they, like us, have had both good and bad days. The psalms lay bare the reality that this training can be unbelievably joyful but also incredibly painful.

Having noted this unusual state of affairs, let's turn to the question of authorship. Who composed the psalms, and how and why does that matter in our reading of them? One view, deriving from modern biblical scholarship, asserts that we don't know who wrote the psalms—they are largely an anonymous collection. Another view, the traditional view handed down by the Early and Medieval Church, asserts that King David was the author of the psalms. Yet a third view, given by the psalms themselves, helps us nuance and appreciate the importance of both perspectives.

By looking at language in relation to dialect shift over centuries, the possible original settings of the psalms, relationship to other scriptural texts, and parallel material from the Ancient Near East, modern academic scholarship of the Bible sees the book of Psalms as a collection of material spanning several centuries from a diverse set of sources. Some psalms give a pretty clear indication that they were connected with worship in the temple; others don't have a temple anywhere near them. Some are connected to court life; others are written in the voice of the poor pleading for justice against rich oppressors. Some connect the king and temple worship in ways that require a setting in Solomon's Temple before its destruction by Babylonian armies in 587 BCE; others reflect on that act of destruction and one famously records the lament of those taken into exile to Babylon and taunted to sing the songs of their homeland for their captors. Some are gems of theological complexity and subtlety; others reflect a more simplistic conception of God and the human-divine relationship. Some are placed in the voice of the king, yet others (like Psalm 131) are heard more easily in the voice of a young mother.

So what meaning do we take from this? For me, this breadth of the collection, the diversity of the voices and the anonymity of the writers gives me the sense of being in contact with a whole people of God at prayer. This anonymous collective is part of the great cloud of witnesses, just as I am—just as I will be when twenty-five centuries have covered my own tomb with dust. From this perspective, the authors who wrote the psalms may be nameless and faceless but are by no means either voiceless or soul-less. Indeed, what gaps the chasms of time between then and now is their earnest cry—whether it be joy, devotion, or fear—a cry I recognize within my own breast as well. Thus, the diversity of the collection and the anonymity of its myriad authors and editors bind us to our heritage as the sons and daughters of God moving through time.

On the other hand, the tradition has insisted upon the person of King David as a centerpoint around whom the psalms are hung. While modern scholarship agrees that at least a few of the psalms contain linguistic and conceptual markers consistent with David's time and place—and that therefore could conceivably have been written by him—it rejects the notion of Davidic authorship of the full Psalter, saying that would be inconsistent with internal evidence from the psalms themselves. Whether it's historical or not, there is some spiritual value for us in seeing the psalms in relation to David, so it's worth looking more closely at why this attribution was so important to the Church through the ages.

The first reason is because the biblical narratives about David frequently connect him with music. According to 1 Samuel 16:14-23, even before the episode with Goliath, David was taken into Saul's service precisely because his music soothed the king. Even after rising to a high rank and commanding the king's armies, David still played music daily for Saul—indeed these music sessions twice became opportunities for the increasingly deranged Saul to attempt to kill David lest he usurp the throne (1 Samuel 18:5-12; 19:9-10). Three songs ostensibly from the hand of David appear in 2 Samuel: the first his lament at the death of Jonathan and Saul (2 Samuel 1:17-27), then an adaptation of Psalm 18 (2 Samuel 22), and finally a song before his death (2 Samuel 23:2-7) that names him "the sweet psalmist of Israel."

Later biblical materials build on this aspect of David's legacy. 1 and 2 Chronicles portray David as setting up all of the details of the temple's worship even though the structure wouldn't be built until the reign of his son, Solomon. Even later still, the apocryphal book of Ecclesiasticus honors David's musical achievements as much as his military ones saying,

> In all that [David] did he gave thanks to the Holy One, the Most High, proclaiming his glory; he sang praise with all his heart, and he loved his Maker. He placed singers before the altar, to make sweet melody with their voices. He gave beauty to the festivals, and arranged their times throughout the year, while they praised God's holy name, and the sanctuary resounded from early morning (Ecclesiasticus 47:8-10).

A more profound connection of David to the psalms is the fuller picture that we get of him in the Samuel-Kings material. While the pages of scripture are filled with memorable people,

few are drawn with great emotional depth. Two characters of
the Old Testament stand out as fleshed-out emotional beings:
Job and David. The view we get of Job is one-sided, though.
Due to the purpose of the book, we see Job in various stages
of lament and despair. In David, however, we see a man at
full-stretch: the passionate lover, the exuberant warrior, the
reverent monarch, the penitential father. We see him at his
best and worst, in his highs and in his lows; he experiences the
complete emotional range that the Psalter explores. In him we
can make this anonymous collection personal and individual.
We can see how events in his life might have prompted the
cries of despair or the calls of joy—and find the parallels in
our own lives.

A final reason why the Early and Medieval Church
strongly emphasized the Davidic authorship of the psalms
is because they saw the psalms as deeply prophetic. They
understood David to be uttering divinely inspired praises. But,
more particularly, they saw him engaging in an act of divinely
facilitated clairaudience reaching across the centuries: he was
writing in the tenth century BCE what his descendant Jesus—
Son of David—would be feeling in the first century CE. In
insisting upon the Davidic authorship of Psalms, the Church
could assert that they gave a unique perspective into the
interior life of Jesus. The Gospels tell of his deeds and allude
to how he felt; having established the genetic connection, the
psalms lay bare Jesus' own prayers and tribulations.

As modern people, it is harder for us to embrace this
perspective wholeheartedly than it was for our ancestors.
Nevertheless, the Christological reading of the psalms has an
important place in our spirituality. Granted, it requires some
rather creative interpretive gymnastics to explain how some
psalms show the psychology of Jesus. However, despite these
problematic areas, the Church is saying something profound
in attributing the emotional range and depth of the psalms

to Jesus. It is another way to explore and ponder the full humanity of Jesus. Only a Jesus who feels deeply, passionately, fully, is a completely human (while completely divine) Redeemer. Indeed, this perspective brings us full circle to the paradox of revelation with which we began: How are human prayers to God part of God's self-revelation to us? Seeing them in and through Jesus' own self-communication to the Father clarifies how the revelation of the depths of our own humanity connects to divine self-revelation.

Having looked at the modern idea of corporate, anonymous authorship alongside the early and medieval understanding of Davidic authorship, I would like to add in a body of scriptural material that can serve as a mediating, uniting term. The psalms in the prayer book lack one contextualizing piece that you find when you read the psalms in a Bible: the superscriptions. These are brief headers that appear at the start of most of the psalms—only twenty-four lack them in the Hebrew text of the Old Testament. These headers aren't original to the psalms but have been added in the process of compiling and editing. They likely tell us less about history and more about interpretation. Often, these superscriptions give instructions to the choirmaster or give a tune name. (The tunes themselves have been long since lost.) Some superscriptions, however, attribute the psalm to either individuals or groups.

Predictably, seventy-three of the psalms are attributed directly to David, fourteen of which are connected with specific incidents in his life. However, several other names also appear: One is attributed to Moses, two to Solomon, three to Jeduthun (this one is unclear—this could be a person's name or an instrument), then groups identified in Kings and Chronicles with Temple Levites, eleven to Asaph, and twelve to the Sons of Korah, with Heman and Ethan named explicitly.

Religious traditions hate a vacuum, though. In the Septuagint, the translation of the Old Testament into Greek that occurred in Alexandria sometime around the second century, superscriptions were added to twenty-two of the psalms, leaving only Psalms 1 and 2 without them. Significantly, Psalms 146 to 148 are attributed to Haggai and Zechariah, writers and leaders of the post-exilic period.

In essence, the interpretative tradition reflected in the superscriptions enable us to have it both ways. On one hand, the superscriptions explicitly refer to a wide range of people all of whom were involved in the creation, editing, and compiling of the Psalter. They give enough names to confirm our sense of Psalms as a communal document in process over a long period of time. Also, they forestall simplistic attempts to pigeonhole the psalms as strictly Davidic. On the other hand, they solidly connect the psalms to a significant, emblematic figure of history—David—who stands forth not only as a heroic figure, an anointed leader, and a cultic pioneer, but also as a thoroughly flawed human being who, nevertheless, was "a man after God's own heart."

THE FORMATIVE QUALITY OF THE PSALMS

One of the reasons why Psalms was selected for our daily meditation rather than Proverbs or Isaiah is because it was seen as uniquely formative. That is, there is something about the psalms that shape Christian character in a particular way. In order to properly understand the focus of the Daily Office on the psalms, we need to take a closer look at this.

Psalms has been recognized from the time of the Early Church as unique among the books of the Bible. One of the clearest expositions of this comes from Athanasius in his letter on Psalms to Marcellinus where he pulls out two characteristics in particular. The first special characteristic of the psalms is that they are a microcosm of the rest of scripture. Athanasius writes; "Each book of the Bible has, of course, its own particular message." He goes on to list what some of those are:

> "Each of these books, you see, is like a garden which grows one kind of special fruit; by contrast, the Psalter is a garden which, besides its special fruit, grows also some of those of all the rest." [Then Athanasius connects a wide variety of psalms to events in the historical books of the Old Testament]: "You see then, that all the subjects mentioned in the historical books are mentioned also in one psalm or another; but when we come to the matters of which the Prophets speak we find that these occur in almost all." [18]

Athanasius is talking about witnesses to Christ, and he offers another section where he connects the psalms to a long list of items from the birth, life, death, resurrection, and ascension of Jesus. Of course, these days, we not only recognize that the psalms contain messianic passages that the Church properly associated with Jesus, but also that the evangelists themselves used both passages and themes from the psalms in their own constructions of the Gospel narratives. So the psalms really do act as a microcosm. They contain all of the major genres of Old Testament writing, from histories, wisdom, legal material, prophetic curses, and destruction oracles, as well as promises of hope and salvation. The psalms also both represent and prefigure a host of New Testament themes—recalling that the New Testament quotes more from Psalms than any other book of the Old Testament.

If the psalms are a microcosm of scripture, if they represent a summary of scripture, a condensation of scripture, then they have to be profoundly interpretive. When you summarize something, it means that you are pulling out the key points.

There is not space for everything, so central themes and actions get selected for summarizing. Thus, the psalms don't just summarize things; they put their own particular spin on them, they infuse them with their own particular angle such that when we encounter these situations elsewhere in the Bible, our perspective has already been shaped by the approach the psalms have taken in highlighting what's of primary importance.

The second special characteristic of the psalms is their focus on interiority—they speak to the inner life of the individual and the community more consistently than any other set of texts. Athanasius says it this way:

> Among all the books, the Psalter has certainly a very special grace, a choiceness of quality well worthy to be pondered; for, besides the characteristics which it shares with others, it has this peculiar marvel of its own, that within it are represented and portrayed in all their great variety the movements of the human soul. It is like a picture, in which you see yourself portrayed and, seeing, may understand and consequently form yourself upon the pattern given. Elsewhere in the Bible you read only that the Law commands this or that be done, you listen to the prophets to learn about the Saviour's coming or you turn to the historical books to learn the doings of the kings and holy men; but in the Psalter, besides all of these things, you learn about yourself.
>
> You find depicted in it all the movements of your soul, all its changes, its ups and downs, its failures and recoveries. Moreover, whatever your particular need or trouble, from this same book you can select a form of words to fit it, so that you do not merely hear and then pass on, but learn the way to remedy your ill. Prohibitions of evil-doing are plentiful in scripture, but only the Psalter tells you how to obey these orders and refrain from sin. Repentance, for example, is enjoined repeatedly; but to repent

means to leave off sinning, and it is the Psalms that show you how to set about repenting and with what words your penitence may be expressed.[19]

Athanasius points to the personal and interior quality of Psalms. No other book of scripture—with the sole exception of Job—contains such intimate expressions of personal feeling—not only intimate but also uncensored in ways that sometimes both shock and offend us. Of course, as Athanasius reminds us, what shocks and offends may be a reflection of what we do not wish to see in ourselves.

The emphasis upon interiority is one of the ways that the psalms place their own interpretive spin on the other biblical material. Sometimes the psalms give a flat account of something: In the beginning, God created stuff. But far more often, the psalms embed their summary of other biblical events into personal or communal pleas: *God, we're having a really hard time right now. Hey—remember that time in creation, when you created all of that stuff? We could really use you to do something like that for us now.* The psalms don't just recall the mighty acts of God; through prayer, they remind us and God of the mighty acts done on behalf of our ancestors, and they give us the courage and the boldness to beseech God's mercy for mighty acts here and now.

Through attentive practice of the Daily Office, the psalms and canticles give us an interpretive lens through which we experience the rest of scripture. Three fundamental concepts within the Psalter are crucial and inescapable elements of a Christian social conscience. First, the psalms and canticles show us the center—that is, they define a reality where all creation is oriented toward God and participates together in the mutual worship of God. Second, they emphasize the rule of law—that is, they emphasize that justice is a key attribute of God and that justice, righteousness, and equity must be central values for us because they flow directly from the identity of God. Third, they form us in the habit of empathy because they place in our mouths the words of the poor, the marginalized, the oppressed, and they invite us to see the world through those eyes, to recognize the injustices seen through those eyes.

First, the psalms center us, orienting all of creation toward God. We see this most clearly in the lauds psalms—147 to 150—and in the *Te Deum* and the Song of the Three Young Men. The Song of the Three Young Men, the *Benedicite*, is a second-century BCE expansion of Psalm 148 that calls sequentially upon all parts of the created order to praise God: "O all ye works of the Lord, bless ye the Lord; praise him and magnify him for ever." Then we proceed from the Cosmic Order with the angels, the heavens, the sun, moon, showers and dews, frost and cold, nights and days to the earth and its creatures with the mountains and hills, the whales and all that move in the waters, the fowls of the air, the beasts and cattle and finally proceed to the people of God, the priests of the Lord, the servants of the Lord, the spirits and souls of the righteous. This is nothing less than a doxological ontology: Things exist and persist to the degree that they recognize and praise the Creator who created them. There is a center, there is a source, there is a stable point around which everything else is anchored. And it is God. God has made us and not we ourselves.

This is a crucial point in establishing a social conscience of any kind. There is something greater. There is something beyond us and beyond our desires to which we are accountable. Our desires and appetites, the desires and appetites of those who currently hold political, economic, or social power, stand accountable to something greater, to something more permanent, more stable, and more real than they are—than we are. It is from this place and in orientation to this reality that we are able to offer a critique of existing systems—even existing systems within which we find ourselves ensnared. We renew this orientation in our acts of worship and praise. As Evelyn Underhill reminds us, the heart of true worship is adoration. She writes, "For worship is an acknowledgement of Transcendence; that is to say, of a Reality independent of the worshiper, which is always more or less deeply coloured by mystery, and which is there first." This adoration, this acknowledgement of transcendence, this reality independent of ourselves of which Underhill speaks is the pure and unadulterated praise that we find ourselves called to in the psalms: "Kings of the earth and all peoples, princes and all rulers of the world; Young men and maidens, old and young together. Let them praise the Name of the Lord, for his name only is exalted, his splendor is over earth and heaven." Notice that the political powers here get put on notice. But the psalms are happy to get even more explicit than that:

> Praise the LORD, O my Soul! I will praise the Lord as long as I live; I will sing praises to my God while I have my being. Put not your trust in rulers, nor in any child of earth, for there is no help in them. When they breathe their last, they return to earth, and in that day their thoughts perish. Happy are those who have the God of Jacob for their help! Whose hope is in the LORD their God; Who made heaven and earth, the seas, and all that is in them; who keeps his promise for ever (Psalm 146:1-5).

The very strong message here is that all political powers and systems are transitory and ephemeral in the face of God and in the face of the reality that endures beyond even the full span of creation. There is a standard—and we aren't it.

Furthermore, as all creation persists in and through its ceaseless praise of God, all of creation stands as fellow witnesses with us to the creating Word. When we despoil and disdain the created order and fail in stewardship of it, we cease that which is not ours to silence. As we diminish creation, the universal song of praise to God is likewise diminished.

The first concept in the psalms and canticles for our formation is that they show us the center—that is, as previously stated, the psalms and canticles define a reality where all creation is oriented toward God and participates together in the mutual worship of God. We stand rightly within this order when we join in acknowledging God as the center and ground of all being and when we offer the respect due to our fellow witnesses to the glory of God.

The second fundamental concept in the psalms and canticles is that the emphasis is on the law. They regard justice as a key attribute of God and thus justice, righteousness, and equity must be central values for us. One of the things that's so fascinating about this is how often we see it in direct relation to the first concept—the worship of God flows directly into praise for justice:

Worship the Lord in the beauty of holiness; let the whole earth stand in awe of him. For he cometh, for he cometh to judge the earth, and with righteousness to judge the world and the peoples with his truth (*The Book of Common Prayer*, p. 45).

For those of us who pray the Morning Office in Rite I, we hear these words almost every day. It is composed of two snippets from Psalm 96 that have been grafted onto the end of Psalm 95. And that's entirely appropriate because these two psalms form part of a block from 93 to 99 that celebrate God as king and that underscore this tight connection between the universal praise of God and the universal justice of God. Thus we get the end of 96:

Tell it out among the nations: "The LORD is King! He has made the world so firm that it cannot be moved; he will judge the peoples with equity." Let the heavens rejoice and let the earth be glad; let the sea thunder and all that is in it; let the field be joyful and all that is therein. Then shall all the trees of the wood shout for joy before the LORD when he comes, when he comes to judge the earth. He will judge the world with righteousness and the peoples with his truth.

The end of Psalm 98 resounds with the same theme:

Shout with joy to the LORD, all you lands; lift up your voice, rejoice, and sing. Sing to the LORD with the harp, with the harp and the voice of song. With trumpets and the sound of the horn shout with joy before the King, the LORD. Let the sea make a noise and all that is in it, the lands and those who dwell therein. Let the rivers clap their hands, and let the hills ring out with joy before the LORD, when he comes to judge the earth. In righteousness shall he judge the world and the peoples with equity.

One word on this judgment language: We Christians can sometimes hear this with the wrong ears and take this the wrong way. In so many of our traditions, judgment is about sin. You're always going to come out on the short end of the stick, and the judgment of God is something to be feared rather than rejoiced over. (Why are the hills so darned happy about this? Do they really hate me that much?) C. S. Lewis in his writings on the psalms gives us a very helpful frame of reference to better hear this as good news. He says that too often we hear judgment and think of it as a criminal proceeding where God is going to put us in the dock and convict us. The judgment here in the Psalter, however, is best thought of as a civil case—it's a property matter. The world is not as it should be. Things are not the way that God intended.

The resources of the land and seas, the bounty of the earth are not distributed as they ought to be. The good news, the reason why the trees and woods and floods rejoice, is that God is going to set things right. The goods that God intends for us will be apportioned as he designed. This judgment is good news because of the justice and equity of God.

Implicit in this judgment, however, is that there are those who are taking more than their appointed share. There are individuals and cliques and powers and systems that accrue benefits to themselves that were intended for others. Remember Psalm 146 that we mentioned above, the one that said, "put not your trust in rulers, nor in any child of earth"? The first half of the psalm is a call to the praise of God; the second half hammers this point home:

> Happy are they who have the God of Jacob for their help! whose hope is in the LORD their God; Who made heaven and earth, the seas and all that is in them; who keeps his promise for ever; who gives justice to the oppressed and food to those who hunger. The LORD sets the prisoners free, the LORD opens the eyes of the blind; the LORD lifts up those who are bowed down; the LORD loves the righteous; the LORD cares for the stranger; he sustains the orphan and widow, but frustrates the way of the wicked. The Lord shall reign for ever, your God, O Zion, throughout all generations. Hallelujah!

From here, of course, it's a clear and easy jump to the Song of Our Lady that has grounded Evening Prayer for lo these many centuries:

> He hath showed strength with his arm; he hath scattered the proud in the imagination of their hearts. He hath put down the mighty from their seat, and hath exalted the humble and meek. He hath filled the hungry with good things and the rich he hath sent empty away (*The Book of Common Prayer*, p. 65).

The justice and equity that stand as primary characteristics of God must be plumb lines for us as well. The justice and equity of God demand that we insist on and advocate for the just rule of law. Rule of law is a very simple concept: It's the notion that there is a system of standards that apply equally to everybody. The rules are the same for everybody, no matter your power or your prestige. That's equity. I am a privileged twenty-first century American. This culture is all I know, and every once in a while I need to be reminded that the way I live and the justice system I take for granted is an anomaly in the long stretch of human history. This way of life is the exception—not the norm. When I taught preaching at Emory's Candler School of Theology, one of the best sermons that I heard was from a Nigerian Anglican priest working through a passage from Deuteronomy. It was a celebration of and a stirring call for the rule of law that is tenuous at best in his homeland. It opened my eyes. I can assume rule of law. We can assume it. But when we start assuming it, we stop safeguarding it. The justice of God and the equity of God demand that we open our eyes to ensure that the rule of law is being carried out even in remarkably well-run systems such as in America and Canada. The psalms insist on God's concern for the widow, the orphan, the stranger, the blind, and disabled—in short, those who had no voice or power and thus no recourse to justice in the patriarchal and often capricious justice of the first millennium BCE. Our own social conscience is formed and aligned with the scriptural witness when we ensure that the poor and marginalized in our communities are receiving their just due under law—that the justice modeled by God is being practiced by our courts and systems. In the grand scheme of human history, it's only fair to say that our systems of justice are doing a good job, and yet they still fall short of God's vision for justice.

The scriptures speak of sin, and our own lives can attest to its reality and power. Thanks to the enduring power of sin, we must be watchful lest those in positions of power and privilege use their prerogatives for oppression. Vested systems of power, whether in governments or corporations or the Church itself, need to be held accountable to the rule of law and the demands of both justice and equity. This attention, this attentiveness, is part of the preferential option for the poor that has driven much of Roman Catholic social teaching in the twentieth century.

The psalms and canticles emphasize the rule of law: That is, they emphasize that justice is a key attribute of God and that justice, righteousness, and equity must be central values for us because they flow directly from the identity of God.

The third key concept for our formation from the psalms is that they create a habit of empathy as we speak the words of the poor, the marginalized, the oppressed. We see the world through those eyes and recognize the injustice.

I am an educated, straight, white male from the American middle class, meaning that I am in the upper class globally, with a steady paying job and a house. I have it good. And that's who I am. I can't be anyone other than who I am. These combined conditions can create a perspective that assumes everyone has had and will have the same advantages that I have. But how do I get a clearer picture of the world as it really is and as it is experienced by the millions and billions who have not had the same advantages? How do I transcend myself? How do I raise myself out of my cultural ghetto for a broader and more informed view of the realities of the world? Certainly travel, seeking out and listening to the experiences of others, helps as does directly serving the poor, the homeless, and addicted at the South Baltimore Station with my parish. But these experiences are magnified and aided by the daily reminders tucked into the psalms about life in a situation far, far different from mine.

Old Testament scholar John Day calls the individual lament psalms the "backbone of the Psalter."[20] Depending on how you classify them, forty-six of the psalms—almost a third—fall into this category. Add in another thirteen or so communal laments, and we see that many of the individual and communal thanksgiving psalms start from a situation of need and desperation. When we pray these psalms, we take into our mouths the pleas, complaints, and cries of those who are oppressed, who have experienced loss and injustice. Sometimes the laments are familiar to us. Sometimes they offer us comfort because we recognize in a voice almost three thousand years old a shared experience of betrayal or attack. At other times they imaginatively invite us into these experiences and challenge us to relate to them. They engage our empathy and require us to exercise and stretch it, to understand the world in a different way. They invite us to see life through other sets of eyes, eyes that have seen things that we have not seen and, honestly, that I earnestly pray we never see.

One of the hardest types of psalms to wrestle with are those we refer to as the imprecatory psalms, the cursing psalms. And there are even parts that pop up in some other, nicer, psalms that make us recoil. If you're curious which ones these might be, look at the Daily Office Lectionary in the back of the prayer book. The imprecatory psalms are marked as optional; they are the verses that have parentheses around them to let you know that you don't really have to read them.

But I want to take a look at one. I invite us to consider this psalm from an empathetic point of view. Psalm 137 starts out beautifully. In fact, the whole first section is a favorite of many people, and there was a popular folk song based on it:

By the waters of Babylon we sat down and wept, when we remembered you, O Zion. As for our harps we hung them up on the trees in the midst of that land. For those who led us away captive asked us for a song, and our oppressors called for mirth: "Sing us one of the songs of Zion." How shall we sing the LORD's song upon an alien soil? If I forget you, O Jerusalem, let my right hand forget its skill. Let my tongue cleave to the roof of my mouth if I do not remember you, if I do not set Jerusalem above my highest joy.

There you go—beautiful, plaintive, a true cry from the heart. Then we get these verses:

Remember the day of Jerusalem, O LORD, against the people of Edom, who said, "Down with it! down with it! even to the ground!" O Daughter of Babylon, doomed to destruction, happy the one who pays you back for what you have done to us! Happy shall he be who takes your little ones and dashes them against the rock!

We are shocked and offended. Is that seriously in the Bible? Certain atheists take joy at pointing out the horrible sentiment expressed at the joy of baby killing and offer it up as an example of the warped mentalities of religion.

A little context is helpful here. This psalm dates shortly after 587 BCE when the Babylonian armies sacked Jerusalem for a second time. They had already been there ten years earlier when Judah rebelled against their Babylonian overlords. The first time, many of the leaders (including the prophet Ezekiel) were taken into exile in Babylon as a warning against further revolts. The rulers of Judah didn't listen, and they didn't learn. They revolted again, and the second time the Babylonian retribution was unrelenting. The city was entirely leveled to the ground, the temple was utterly destroyed. The vast majority of the population was put to the sword and those who survived were taken to Babylon in chains. The Babylonian client-states in the region were welcome to whatever was left behind, and Edom in particular savaged the refugees. The book of Lamentations gives a more sustained sense of the devastation and despair while the oft-overlooked book of Obadiah explains in detail Edom's betrayal of Jerusalem and calls an oracle of wrath upon them for their actions.

That's the background of Psalm 137, the experience of these singers who refuse to sing a song of joy in their captors' land. In short, they are wishing Edom and Babylon the horrors already visited upon their own homes, their families and children. Does that experience make these lines okay, this sentiment justified? No, of course not. If you are offended by these lines, then congratulations: Your moral sense is intact. But these verses should cause us not to question the morality of God or the psalmist but to try and wrap our heads around the kind of horrific experiences that spurred these pleas. I have never experienced the brutal sack of my homeland, and I pray I never will. I do not want to be able to understand this psalm. And yet the stark reality of the situation is that multitudes of people around the world, both victims and veterans—some of whom are in our congregations— understand this only too well.

When I take these words into my mouth, I am forced to consider what kind of experience that must be, what depths of pain cause otherwise rational and faithful people to make this kind of plea to God. The Psalter places this experience of oppression before my eyes, my heart, and my imagination. In praying these alien lines, I am forced into an exercise of empathy that will broaden my soul. Likewise I can say: "Hear my prayer, O God; give ear to the words of my mouth. For the arrogant have risen up against me, and the ruthless have sought my life, those who have no regard for God" (Psalm 54:2-3). Or "My enemies are saying wicked things about me: 'When will he die, and his name perish?' Even if they come to see me, they speak empty words; their heart collects false rumors; they go outside and spread them. All my enemies whisper together about me and devise evil against me" (Psalm 41:5-7). Or even verse 21 from Psalm 109: "I am poor and needy, and my heart is wounded within me." While I cannot honestly claim these words as my own, I can imaginatively extend my own experiences of betrayal and trouble to better understand them. And I can use these psalms as a point of reference in my conversations with those who have shared this type of experience. Regular praying of the psalms in the Office is not a substitute for engaging the people in your communities in these situations. But I believe your encounters with others may well be aided as a result of this sort of diligent, attentive, and empathetic exercise of reading the psalms.

This is the third fundamental concept from the psalms: They form us in the habit of empathy because they place in our mouths the words of the poor, the marginalized, and the oppressed, and they invite us to see the world through those eyes and to recognize the injustices seen through those eyes.

A regular discipline of praying the Daily Office nourishes the soul with the psalms and canticles that have the potential to shape the concerns within us and aid us in seeing them more clearly throughout the rest of scripture. When we allow the psalms to speak their wisdom to us, they will form in us the conviction that God is the center and the source by which all other systems and powers are critiqued; that the justice, righteousness, and equity that characterize God must be reflected in our societies and systems; that we can transcend ourselves and situations by exercising our empathy and broadening our souls to the experiences of others. But this doesn't happen on its own. Simply running through the words isn't enough. All of the catechetical and formational potential of the Daily Office, the Psalter and canticles, and scripture itself is for nought without the discipline of attentiveness.

Praying the Office every once in a while isn't enough. It has to become a discipline. That doesn't mean that if you miss a Morning or Evening Prayer cycle that you're lost, but power lies in the force of habits. Habits of mind, habits of devotion, habits of thought. That's what transforms us—patterns of life.

It is the same with the psalms. The benefits that we have talked about only occur with attentiveness. If you are not being attentive, then you might as well be reading the sports page. It is only while reading these words with our minds and our hearts engaged, with our souls open to the movements of the Spirit, that they can unleash their potential to melt our hearts of stone.

How do we go about doing this? What is the best way to read and pray the psalms to get the most out of them?

PRAYING THE PSALMS IN THE OFFICE

The traditional monastic practice of chanted psalmody— inherited by the Anglican tradition—is a form of breath meditation. That is, the psalms are read in such a way that the text corresponds to the breath, particularly deep, elongated breathing that assists the body with falling into a restful receptive state enabling deep contemplation of the texts. First, I will discuss the traditional technique for breathing the psalm used for congregational singing and speaking of the Psalter. Second, I will discuss how these breathing techniques may be adapted for solo use, either in reading the psalms aloud or silently.

There are two chief methods by which the psalms are sung in Anglican churches: the traditional Gregorian chant of the Western Church and Anglican chant. Originally, Anglican chant started as Gregorian chant harmonized, but it shifted, developed, and grew into its own particular style. While I have sung a certain amount of Anglican chant, I have spent a lot more time singing the psalms to Gregorian chant. I believe that it is through the tradition of chant that we encounter the psalms most deeply.

The typical psalm tone has six parts. The first part is called the incipit and typically contains two or three notes that move in an upward direction. When a psalm is being sung, the incipit is only used at the very beginning of the psalm or when psalm verses begin again after an antiphon. (Gospel canticles are different in that the incipit is sung at the beginning of each verse.)

The second part is the reciting tone. This is a note on which the majority of the psalm verse is sung. The psalm is recited on this note until it hits one of the next two parts.

The third part is the flex. This is a single note that drops either a second or a third. In the case of a psalm verse with a long first half, the flex is used as a brief break for the choir to catch a quick breath before returning again to the reciting tone. If, in *The Book of Common Prayer*'s printing, a psalm verse goes to a new full line before the asterisk, a flex would be used (e.g. Psalm 1:3; 2:2, but not Psalm 1:1,5; 2:8 because the line break does not start a full line).

The fourth part is the mediant. The mediant comes shortly before the asterisk that marks the middle of the psalm verse. The exact distance from the asterisk depends on the number of stressed syllables in the final words; the required number varies by psalm tone.

The fifth part is the reciting tone again. In the eight psalm tones that correspond with the eight modes, this reciting tone is exactly the same as the first reciting tone. The ninth tone, *Tonus peregrinus*, which means wandering tone, has a different reciting tone in the second half than in the first half.

Note that there is no equivalent to the flex in the second half of the psalm verse. For instance, you might expect the equivalent of a flex at the end of the second line in Psalm 1:1, but there is no such part.

The sixth part is the final cadence. Like the mediant, where it begins in the last line of the psalm is based on the number and placement of stressed syllables in relation to the psalm tone itself.

You can see for yourself what these look like in a work like *The Plainsong Psalter*. Alternatively, all of the canticles from the prayer book appear with chant tone settings in the service music portion of *The Hymnal 1982* starting at S177.

Chanting the psalms in the traditional manner attends to breath. One designated person—the cantor—begins the psalm and sings from the incipit to the first mediant alone. Then the rest of the congregation joins in on the last half of the verse. From that point, the two sides (facing each other in a traditional choir configuration) alternate verses.

As one side comes to the end of a verse, the other side inhales, preparing to take up the next verse. As the verse ends, the other side picks it up smoothly, leaving no break or gap between the two. If the verse does not directly follow an antiphon, the verse begins directly on the reciting tone. Singing clearly expends the breath that the side had taken before the verse started. If there is a flex, the side snatches a quick catch breath before continuing on.

By the time the side reaches the mediant, there is not much breath left. There is a significant pause at the mediant because at that point the side exhales the remaining breath, then inhales a full new breath. As a community or a new person begins singing the psalms in this way, the break—which may last five, six beats or even longer—will seem unnaturally long. Resist the temptation to rush; take the time to breathe.

With a full new breath in their lungs, the side then proceeds to the end of the verse and exhales the remaining breath after the final cadence. The other side then smoothly moves to the next verse.

Speaking the psalms in community follows essentially the same pattern as singing. The designated leader in the cantor's role speaks the first line from the incipit to the first median. After the asterisk, the whole group finishes the verse. Then they begin alternation by sides, usually starting with the leader's side. They begin right after the conclusion of the previous verse, read to the asterisk, exhale, breathe in again, and finish the verse as the next side smoothly takes it up.

The first few times you hear the psalms read this way, it will likely take you by surprise—it will sound like there's a big gap in the middle of the verse. Those unfamiliar with this practice, or unsure if they're doing it right, will have a tendency to rush the pause and to start speaking again as soon as possible. However, even in reciting, the mechanics of the breath work in exactly the same way as singing. Because speaking requires less breath control than singing, the urge to rush the breathing pause at the mediant is greater. Again, resist the urge.

If you chant the psalms by yourself, the pattern is basically the same as singing them communally. The difference is that at the end of every other verse, there is no alternate side to begin where you leave off. As a result, the end of each line must be treated in the same manner as the mediant. Exhale all of the breath left in your lungs and breathe in a new breath. Then continue on to the next verse.

If you are reading the psalms aloud by yourself, the pattern again follows that of singing. Take a full breath, read to the asterisk/mediant, exhale, breathe in a new breath, then read the second half of the verse. Exhale again, inhale, then start the next verse. If a flex occurs, grab a quick catch breath.

Reading silently is the only form of reading that is not fundamentally based on the communal singing pattern. Basically, the difference between reading silently and reading or singing aloud is that no breath is expended in the process. As a result, exhalations and inhalations must be balanced differently. The best way to proceed is to simply alternate half-verses. Inhale slowly as you silently read to the mediant; exhale slowly as you read to the end of the verse.

Following these directions for encountering the psalms will accomplish several things. First, tying the psalms to breath forces you to slow your reading pace and to pay more attention to what you are reading. It is easy to let the words flow beneath your eyes and for your attention to wander. Tying the text to the breath will make you read more slowly even if you are reading silently (when you are more prone to rush).

Second, tying the two together also slows down and regulates your breathing. Regulation of breathing is regulation of the whole body. The slower, deeper breaths will encourage a meditative state of mind that will enable you to relax and concentrate more completely on the text. The more you concentrate, the more your mind retains and passively memorizes.

Third, when read or sung in community, following the breath will tie the whole community together in closer harmony. Listening and being attentive to the breath patterns of those around you so that you begin and end the mediant pauses at the same time will yoke the community closer together in common prayer. There is an indescribable harmony that accompanies a nonanxious attention to the community's breath—a literal discerning of the Spirit that moves within the gathered people at prayer.

CONCLUSION OF THE DAILY OFFICE

The Daily Office is the recurring discipline of the liturgical life. Habits are powerful things, and the Church has established the eternal rhythms of the Office as the central pattern by which Anglican Christians are formed. A person is a runner if they run regularly; a person is a singer if they sing every day; a liturgical Christian is one who prays the Office. The heart of the Office is the psalms. In the prayers and praise of Israel, we find a summary of the scriptures, we hear honest wrestlings with the mysterious ways of God, and we catch glimpses of Christ who is the scripture's fullness and fruition. The twin Offices of Morning and Evening Prayer are our daily sacrifice of praise and thanksgiving. As we consecrate a period of time each morning and each evening to God, we join our voices with saints across the ages as we pattern ourselves in a continual turning toward God.

NOTES

1   Evelyn Underhill, *Worship* (London, Harper & Brothers, 1937), p. 119.

2   Ibid, p. 120.

3   Ibid, pp. 124-125.

4   Life of Antony 3, *Early Christian Lives*, p. 10.

5   *Sayings of the Desert Fathers*, pp. 120-121.

6   *Conferences* 10.7.3.

7   *Conferences* 10.10.2.

8   Letter 22. 37.

9   Letter 107.9.

10 *Sayings of the Desert Fathers*, p. 57.

11 *Institutes* 3.2.

12 Versicles are a set of one-liners that alternate between two groups— usually whoever is running things and the congregation. The lines usually come from scripture. They do in the case referred to here.

13 In the monthly system of reading the psalms, Psalm 95 appears on the morning of the nineteenth day of each month. Therefore, the *Jubilate* is used whenever this happens, if this course of reading the psalms is used.

14 The lectionary provides three readings, but there can be slots for four readings each day. Thus, an optional Old Testament Lesson can be included if you want to use all four slots. If you choose this route, you use the Old Testament reading from the other year of the Daily Office Lectionary as the first reading at Evening Prayer.

15 It should be noted that these verses from Romans were omitted in a revision of the Daily Office Lectionary completed in the 1940s.

16 Although we can't know for sure, it seems likely that this prayer was written at some point in the second century BCE and may have been composed in Greek rather than Hebrew or Aramaic.

17 The earliest reference is from *Didache* 8. We're not sure exactly when the *Didache* was written; some authorities suggest it may have been as early as the end of the first century CE (and thus around the same time as the later Gospels and Epistles). Certainly it existed by the first part of the second century. Later second and third century writers make the same point repeatedly. Clement of Alexandria refers to prayers three times a day (*Stromata* VII, 7, 40:3) as does Origen (*On Prayer* 12.2), Tertullian (*On Prayer* 25), and Cyprian (*On the Lord's Prayer* 34).

18 "The Letter of St. Athanasius to Marcellinus on the Interpretation of the Psalms," pp. 97-119 in Athanasius, *On the Incarnation*. Edited and translated by a Religious of C.S.M.V. (Crestwood, N.Y.: St. Vladimir's Seminary Press, 1996), pp. 97, 98, 99.

19 Ibid, p. 103.

20 John Day, *Psalms*. (Old Testament Guides; Sheffield: Sheffield Academic Press, 1992), p. 19.

SECTION 3
THE HOLY EUCHARIST

CHAPTER 8
SPIRITUALITY OF THE EUCHARIST

There are a lot of different approaches to talking about the
Holy Eucharist. Books, long books, multi-volume books have
been written on the Eucharist and on its spirituality. In these
pages, we can do no more than lightly scratch the surface.
I am not going to try to be comprehensive; rather, I hope
to give you some perspectives, some lenses, through which
to view the Eucharist in hopes that they can enrich your
understanding of what we do in this celebration and what it
means for our Christian life together. I will begin with a big
metaphorical step back and give the broadest possible, big-
picture view before we head back in and explore our prayer
book Eucharist.

STARTING WITH SACRIFICE

We are modern twenty-first-century people; we can't be
anything other than this. We know our world, and, for us,
Eucharist is a church ceremony that happens on Sundays. I
want to start by taking us out of our environment and putting
us in a completely different headspace. A new perspective

will help us get a different angle on something that we have witnessed and experienced over and over again. I would like to approach it from the perspective that the Eucharist, as religious practice, is deeply rooted in the sacrificial customs of Mediterranean antiquity.

So, the place to start is the ancient Mediterranean mindset; we need to have a sense of what those people were thinking in order to have a better sense of the environment of Jesus and the Early Church. One particular element to highlight: When we think about sacrifice, and animal sacrifice in particular, we tend to focus on one particular aspect of it—the death of the animal. But when we do so, we miss many other factors. We fixate on the moment and the concept of death, and we fail to see the other things that surround it.

To get into this alternate headspace, I would like us to start out in Homer's *Iliad*. One of the great epics of world literature, the *Iliad* is a long poem originally composed and handed down orally; it was written down in Greek probably at some point in the eighth century BCE. It tells the story of the great siege of Troy, a Greek city on the coast of modern-day Turkey, and the struggle of other Greeks—Achaeans— against the Trojans. As a result, the *Iliad* gives us a glance into Greek society at a time when it was closely aligned with its ancient neighbors in the Middle East.

In the midst of the drama, one of the leaders tries to resolve a god-sent plague in the Greek camp by returning a captive to her father, a priest of Apollo, and bringing along a hecatomb (100 cattle) as recompense.

Once they get there, a sacrifice happens. That's where we'll pick up:

[A] When prayers were said and grains of barley strewn,
they held the bullocks for the knife, and flayed them,
cutting out joints and wrapping these in fat,

two layers, folded, with raw strips of flesh,
for the old man to burn on cloven faggots,
wetting it all with wine.

[B] Around him stood
young men with five tined forks in hand, and when
the vitals had been tasted, joints consumed,
they sliced the chines and quarters for the spits,
roasted them evenly and drew them off.

[C] Their meal now prepared and all work done,
they feasted to their hearts' content and made
desire for meat and drink recede again,
then young men filled their winebowls to the brim,
ladling drops for the god in every cup.

[D] Propitiatory songs rose clear and strong
until day's end to praise the god, Apollo,
as One Who Keeps the Plague Afar; and listening
the god took joy. After the sun went down
and darkness came, at last Odysseus' men
lay down to rest under the stern hawsers.

(*Iliad*, I.526-46)

I have added in some letters to help us keep track of the
action. One of the ways to analyze what is happening in
this scene is to break it down into four pieces: [A] marks the
deaths of the animals; [B] is when the meat gets cooked; [C]
describes the meat being eaten together; and [D] is where the
god is praised.

I want to emphasize some points here. First, yes, a lot of
animals are dying here. But notice how little emphasis is given
to that fact. The animals die, but that does not seem to be the
central point of this operation. Second, if there is a central
point, it would be about the party and not the preparation.

The emphasis is placed on the meal. Third, we should not miss the act of social reconciliation that is occurring. The men of Odysseus are not random guests who stopped in; they are pirates who sacked this town a short time before. The last time these men saw each other, they were likely trying to kill each other! The fact that the priest and his young men sat and ate with Odysseus and his men must not be overlooked. Fourth, there is an act of divine reconciliation going on as well. The god, Apollo, looks with favor upon both the act (the restoration of the girl) and the sacrifice, and is present with them, listening.

Some church people love to argue about the basic nature of the Eucharist: Is it a sacrifice or is it a meal? The way we answer this question has broad implications. For example, it determines whether the thing in the front of the church is an altar or a table.

Well, what would Homer say?

Let me suggest three main takeaways from this description of a Homeric sacrifice. First, there is the fact of the hecatomb: That's a lot of cow! Consider all of the economic effort that goes into raising 100 head of cattle. This is a lot of property and wealth being dedicated to the god. It is given to the god, and the giving is motivated by the god, with the secondary result of the gift being that it is also shared with the community. Second, meal and sacrifice are intimately related. We cannot escape the way that these are inextricably bound to one another. It is not an either/or; it is definitely a both/and. The meal cannot happen without the deaths, and the deaths enable the meal. Now, did the Greeks ever have sacrifices where the meat was not eaten, when it was burnt entirely? The answer is yes, but typically that occurred when they were making sacrifices to the dark gods of the underworld, the gods they had no interest in eating with! And that leads to the third point. The meal is bidirectional: The humans are communing with one another and communing with the god to whom the sacrifice is being offered. Again, it's a both/and. Keeping Homer and his lessons in mind, I think the best way for us to consider the Eucharist is to see it as a sacrificial meal of reconciliation. All three of these words are important: There is a sacrifice; it enables a meal. And the meal both symbolizes and enacts reconciliation among those who gather around it.

Now, I am not suggesting that there is a direct line between Homeric sacrifice and the Christian Eucharist. Too much time and too many changes separate the two. However, there are broad, continuous themes in Homer that can be found in the Old Testament record as well as in the world of late antiquity that birthed the Church. If we take a look at the type of sacrificial events that show up in the Old Testament, we find three major categories. The first are the whole burnt offerings. As we discussed when talking about the Daily Office, you see this most in those alimentary offerings, when the point was to feed God in the temple. The second are the sin and guilt offerings. With these sacrifices, some of the meat was burned, the other portion was given to the priests to eat; you didn't get to party if you were paying for a sin. The third are the thanks and freewill offerings. These were the occasions of rejoicing in God's presence or thanking God for his benefits. These sacrifices were shared with the priests and the community. This is the kind of meal most closely related to what we see in the Homeric vision.

Furthermore, 1 Corinthians 10 reveals just how prevalent these understandings remained in the life of the Early Church. In this chapter, Paul wrestles with the issue of whether Christians are allowed to eat meat sacrificed to idols. The question is whether eating such meat is itself an act of communing with the god to whom it was sacrificed. On one hand, Paul wants to deny that the old gods have any power over the faithful; on the other hand, he understands how powerful the associations remain and does not want weaker Christians to be harmed by what they see more mature Christians doing. What makes this issue even more complicated is that most of the meat sold in a Greek market of his day would have come from a temple sacrifice.

So, how does this look into the past help us understand what we do today? Well, it gives us a bit of perspective when we say that the Eucharist is a sacrificial meal of reconciliation. No part of this phrase need stand in opposition to any other part of it. Sacrifice, meal, and reconciliation appropriately belong together. To argue otherwise stands in contradiction with the milieu from which this rite came.

EUCHARIST AS SACRIFICE

In what sense is the Eucharist a sacrifice? In a strictly literal sense, nothing dies. Your priest doesn't get up on Sunday morning and kill something in front of you. And yet, tradition emphasizes that the Eucharist is a sacrifice. Chronologically speaking, Paul's letters represent the earliest Christian writings that we have—and it is his words that we use at the fraction: "Christ our Passover is sacrificed for us, therefore let us keep the feast." 1 Corinthians 10 and the following chapter (after an aside regarding women's hair) speak of pagan sacrifices and the Eucharist as fundamentally analogous and competing rites:

> The cup of blessing that we bless, is it not a sharing in the blood of Christ? The bread that we break, is it not a sharing in the body of Christ? Because there is one bread, we who are many are one body, for we all partake of the one bread. Consider the people of Israel; are not those who eat the sacrifices partners in the altar? What do I imply then? That food sacrificed to idols is anything, or

that an idol is anything? No, I imply that what pagans sacrifice, they sacrifice to demons and not to God. I do not want you to be partners with demons. You cannot drink the cup of the Lord and the cup of demons. You cannot partake of the table of the Lord and the table of demons (10:16-21).

Rhetorically, Paul is insisting upon the continuity between pagan sacrifice, Jewish sacrifice, and the Eucharist: The same intrinsic mechanism occurs—the act of sacrifice and the subsequent sharing in the meal is a sharing in and with the spiritual being with whom the sacrifice is performed, whether divine or demonic.

Now, exactly how the Eucharist is a sacrifice, and what we mean by that, has been a major point of argument between Protestants and non-Protestants (Roman Catholic and Eastern Orthodox alike). To get at the heart of the prayer book spirituality of the Eucharist, it is sufficient to agree on this central point: We are participating in Christ's own self-offering at his own invitation.

We don't believe that anyone is re-sacrificing Jesus. Indeed, the book of Hebrews goes to some lengths to note that one of the ways in which the self-sacrifice of Jesus is greater than that of the temple sacrifices is because those sacrifices must be redone year after year; the act of Jesus was done once and accomplished for all time. Our repeated actions are joined to his single great action.

And that's where our attention focuses—the great action. In the Eucharist, the events of the Last Supper and the Crucifixion are superimposed upon one another through Christ's own words and promise. Our Eucharistic prayers in both Rite I and II do this:

All glory be to thee, Almighty God, our heavenly Father, for that thou, of thy tender mercy, didst [A] give thine only Son Jesus Christ to suffer death upon the cross for our redemption; [B] who made there, by his one oblation of himself once offered, a full, perfect, and sufficient sacrifice, oblation, and satisfaction, for the sins of the whole world; [C] and did institute, and in his holy Gospel command us to continue, a perpetual memory of that his precious death and sacrifice, until his coming again (*The Book of Common Prayer,* p. 334).

The prayer begins by specifically talking about the passion and death of Christ on the cross at [A]. Then, at [B], it moves into language that both identifies this action as an act of sacrifice but also goes to great lengths (clearly with Hebrews 7-10 in mind!) to establish several things: that this death was fundamentally a self-offering—not forced; that this one offering was sufficient for all times; and that this act in itself accomplished everything that needed to happen to reconcile God and humanity. Having established these points, the prayer comes back to the Eucharist itself and identifies it as a regular reminder of that sacrifice (using the word again to make sure we don't miss it) for the Church.

Or, to say the same thing with some slightly different emphases, we also pray this:

Holy and gracious Father: In your infinite love you made us for yourself; and, when we had fallen into sin and become subject to evil and death, [A] you, in your mercy, sent Jesus Christ, your only and eternal Son, to share our human nature, to live and die as one of us, [B] to reconcile us to you, the God and Father of all.

[C] He stretched out his arms upon the cross, and offered himself in obedience to your will, a perfect sacrifice for the whole world (*The Book of Common Prayer,* p. 362).

Here we see the same fundamental pattern. In [A] Jesus is sent to us. The mention of his death is balanced by mention of his life—a reminder of the redemptive action of the Incarnation—but his death is clearly in focus here. Then [B] identifies the goal of both his life and death: reconciliation between God and humanity. While this prayer doesn't use the same sort of legal language to proscribe the terms of the reconciliation as the Rite I prayer above, this section functions in the same way as the [B] part of the prayer, assuring us that the reconciliation promised was effected by the totality of Christ's life and death. Continuing, [C] specifically moves to the cross and picks up a few remaining points. Again, the prayer uses the word sacrifice and, in direct reference to it, emphasizes that this cruciform (cross-shaped) death was a self-offering. It was neither an accident nor was it compelled: It was a decision, freely given.

Sacrifice here is functioning as a central vehicle of reconciliation. In Antiquity, whom you ate with carried great significance, particularly social significance. To eat with someone said something publicly about who you were and what sort of company you kept. Remember, one of the chief charges against Jesus was that he ate with tax collectors and sinners, the wrong kind of people. Just as in the Homeric sacrifice, we saw former enemies sitting down together around a meal, the Eucharist likewise gathers together a broken humanity in an act of reconciliation. People are brought together over food.

But the bidirectional aspect we noted in the Homeric sacrifice is present here as well; this is also where we recognize that the Eucharist doesn't just focus on the Last Supper and the Passion. It also connects us with those odd meals on the foggy lakeshore and the journey to Emmaus where the disciples break bread with the Risen Christ. This memorial of his passion is also a remembrance of his resurrection and his resurrected communion with his disciples. This brings home one of the key points about a sacrificial meal. It wasn't just about sharing a meal at the temple with their family and the other people they brought to help celebrate, and it wasn't just about sharing with the priests. They were all sharing a meal together with the god as well. Our Eucharistic meal isn't just a remembrance of a dead Jesus; it is eaten in the presence of the Risen Christ. Both of these factors play an important part in what's going on in the Eucharist.

Recognizing and growing more deeply into the spirituality of the Eucharist is bound up with our ability to grasp the sacramental paradox: In the Eucharist, the Body of Christ is eating with Christ and is eating Christ in order to participate in Christ's work of the reconciling of all creation.

EUCHARIST AND OBLATION

There's one more point that I want to return to as we consider the relationship between the Homeric sacrifice and the Christian Eucharist. That's the notion of the hecatomb. As we said before, the hecatomb was a sacrifice of 100 cattle. It represented a huge amount of wealth dedicated to the god. It was precious and costly.

Where is that element in our rite?

We offer bread and wine. That's not terribly expensive— particularly given the sort of wine we normally offer!

One of the historical characteristics of Anglican Eucharistic prayers is what is sometimes referred to as the self-oblation; here are four examples from *The Book of Common Prayer*:

- Rite I, Prayer I: "And here we offer and present unto thee, O Lord, our selves, our souls and bodies, to be a reasonable, holy, and living sacrifice unto thee…" (p. 336).

- Rite I, Prayer II: "And we earnestly desire thy fatherly goodness to accept this our sacrifice of praise and thanksgiving, whereby we offer and present unto thee, O Lord, our selves, our souls and bodies" (pp. 342-343).

- Rite II, Prayer B: "Unite us to your Son in his sacrifice, that we may be acceptable through him, being sanctified by the Holy Spirit" (p. 369).

- Rite II, Prayer D: "Grant that all who share this bread and cup may become one body and one spirit, a living sacrifice in Christ, to the praise of your Name" (p. 375).

You see, if we take the language of our prayers seriously, we are offering something costly at the altar. We are not just offering Jesus—we are offering ourselves as well.

In this act of self-giving, we give ourselves over to God's great plan of redemption: "to restore all people to unity with God and each other in Christ" (p. 855). We take our own place in the sacrifice of reconciliation as we live this message.

CHAPTER 9
THE SHAPE OF THE EUCHARIST

Despite the variety of options available, any prayer book Eucharist still has a fundamental shape and character that defines it. Every Eucharist has two complementary halves, each of which celebrates the mystery of the presence of Christ. First, there is a celebration of Christ as the living Word of God who has been breathed by the Father and communicated through the Spirit. Second, there is the celebration of Christ as Incarnate Savior who offers himself in love to the Father through the Spirit. The highlight of the first half is the manifestation of Christ in the proclamation of the Gospel. The highlight of the second half is the manifestation of Christ in the celebration of the Eucharistic meal. These two highlights should be seen as parallel with one another.

It is easy for Episcopalians (and others) to see the Eucharistic meal as the Main Event of the morning and to regard everything else as prelude. To do this, though, is to misunderstand the fullness of the revelation that we are receiving. We say that we are a people of the book and in a sense that's true. However, Jesus is not a book—he's a person. Like all people we are able to learn about him by encountering him in a variety of ways. Scripture gives us one angle of access to Jesus. But it is incomplete if that knowledge isn't fleshed out with the Christ whom we meet in the sacraments. By the same token, we are in danger of misunderstanding the Living Jesus of our sacramental experience if our grasp of his identity and character is not deeply grounded in the words of scripture. The two major parts of the service both show us Christ.

THE SERVICES

The Eucharistic liturgies are collected together on pages 316-412.

[Traditional Language Preliminary Material]

> An Exhortation
>
> The Decalogue: Traditional
>
> A Penitential Order: Rite One

[The Traditional Language Service]

> Concerning the Celebration

The Holy Eucharist: Rite One

> The Word of God
>
> The Holy Communion

Eucharistic Prayer I

> Alternative Form of the Great Thanksgiving

Eucharistic Prayer II

> Offertory Sentences
>
> Proper Prefaces

[Contemporary Language Preliminary Material]

> The Decalogue: Contemporary
>
> A Penitential Order: Rite Two

Broadly speaking, there are four different ways of celebrating the Eucharist within this section: Rite I, Rite II, Communion under Special Circumstances, and An Order for Celebrating the Holy Eucharist. The first two (Rites I and II) are the normal liturgies for Sundays and holy days. The third, Communion under Special Circumstances, is reserved for those persons who cannot attend regular services, usually

due to hospitalization, sickness, or some other infirmity.
The fourth, An Order for Celebrating the Holy Eucharist, is
explicitly for irregular situations; the prayer book notes that it
is not intended to serve as a principal service for a worshiping
community.[1]

Second, note that the organization of the Rite I and II
Eucharists are not strictly linear—especially the Rite II
version. The Rite II Eucharist provides an outline of the
service giving much of the material but, afterward, adds on
five supplemental sections that may be used to fill in the
service. In other words, if you try to read through the Rite II
service starting on page 355, you will find yourself needing
to flip to several other sections to read along with the whole
service. So, what texts exactly are we missing here? Here's a
chart of the Rite II service:

Reading through the Service	Jumping to another Place
Entrance rite (pp. 355-356)	
Collect of the Day (p. 357)	Collects: Contemporary (pp. 211-261)
Lessons (pp. 357-358)	The [Eucharist] Lectionary (pp. 888-931)
Sermon (p. 358)	
The Nicene Creed (pp. 358-359)	
The Prayers of the People	**The Prayers of the People** (pp.383-393); The Collect at the Prayers (pp.394-395)
Confession of Sin (pp. 359-360)	
The Peace (p. 360)	
The Holy Communion	Offertory Sentences (pp.376-377)
The Great Thanksgiving: Eucharist Prayer A (pp. 361-365)	**Alternate Forms: Eucharistic Prayer B** (pp.367-369); Eucharistic Prayer C (pp.369-372); **Eucharistic Prayer D** (pp. 372-376)
The Great Thanksgiving [start]	Proper Prefaces (pp. 377-382)
The Breaking of the Bread (pp. 364-365)	
[Post-Communion Prayer and Dismissal] (pp. 365-366)	

On the surface, this way of arranging things looks crazy! Why do this? The collects and the Eucharistic lessons had always been a separate section; the real change here is the addition of all the material from the creed on. We'll look at the why of it in a second, but I need to observe an important point first: Just because the service or the prayer makes a jump doesn't necessarily mean that you need to follow it!

This may seem odd, but it's not once you spend some time with the material that we're jumping to. The Offertory Sentence is just that—a sentence. And there's no congregational response; the priest says it. Our response is to dig out our wallet for the offering plates. This is the same situation with the collect at the end of the prayers: The priest picks one, and we say, "Amen." The priest definitely needs to know where to find the Proper Preface—and we should read them over and be familiar with them—but it's a sentence fragment. By the time you have found it in the book, the priest is likely on to the next part of the liturgy.

You should be seeing a theme here by this point. One of the great strengths of *The Book of Common Prayer* from its beginnings is that it includes all of the words: Everything the priest says, and everything the people say. There are no secret parts. Yes, some priests might have devotional prayers that they say to themselves, heard only by God and the altar party, but the whole content of the common prayer is printed in black and white. As lay people and members of the Body of Christ, we have access to all of these. We should read, learn, and know them—and definitely inwardly digest their meanings. But we don't always have to read along in the book at the time of the service; we can just listen to some of the words. Priests often have one advantage over laity when it comes to these things: ribbons. It's a lot easier to flip back and forth between these various parts if they are all marked out beforehand with properly set ribbons attached to the spine of the book. Pew editions rarely have them; altar books always do.

The jumps that we need to follow are the ones where there is more than a sentence or two of content or we need to provide responses. There are two of these: the Prayers of the People and the Eucharistic Prayers (bolded in the chart on previous page). If you hang around the Church long enough, you will probably memorize the forms that get used the most—and I encourage that wholeheartedly—but until that time, these two jumps make sense. It might not even hurt to check the bulletin beforehand and mark these places so you are prepared. Who knows? You might even want to get yourself a couple of ribbons.

Having covered the logistics of these jumps, let's talk about the whys and wherefores.

One of the guiding principles of the revision that gave us our current prayer book is that diversity of form does not hinder unity in prayer. That is, we can pray using different forms and different words for the same service and still accomplish the same thing and express the same theology liturgically. Whereas in the past, a single service was given— actually, in the original English situation, it was *imposed* by means of the State with the full weight of law behind it—this revision multiplied options and enshrined diversity as a theological principle. Hence, Rite II gives us six different written forms for the Prayers of the People and four different Eucharistic Prayers.

Second, different prayers use different parts. Specifically, the Proper Preface changes according to the season or occasion in most of the Eucharistic Prayers, but not in Prayer C or Prayer D. They have their own fixed Proper Prefaces that are not meant to be swapped out.

Third, while Rite I and II are basically comparable in the Daily Office, the differences are more significant in the Eucharist. As with the Daily Office, Rite I retains a higher degree of continuity with the classical Anglican rites. To generalize, Rite I prayers tend to have a higher degree of penitential language—a greater acknowledgement of human sin and our need for grace—and also tend to draw closer connections between the Eucharist and the Passion of Christ than Rite II prayers. Conversely, Rite II prayers tend to emphasize the celebratory aspect of the Eucharist and to speak more broadly of the redemptive work of Jesus—they focus less on the Passion and include a greater sense of all of Christ's words and works.

Fourth, the six different Eucharistic Prayers should be seen as more or less complementary to one another. There are not great theological differences between them. Rather they should be seen as differing in emphasis. We'll talk about these emphases when we turn to the various prayers. On the whole, though, they should be seen as being in continuity with one another.

INTRODUCTORY MATERIAL

Rite I	Rite II	Required?	Variation
[Exhortation →]		Optional	None
Decalogue: Traditional	Decalogue: Contemporary	Optional	None
A Penitential Order: Rite I	A Penitential Order: Rite II	Optional	None

All of the Introductory material is technically optional. But there are perfectly good reasons to use it for specific occasions.

The Exhortation

The Exhortation is placed at the head of the Eucharistic material and, in a sense, serves as an introduction to all of it. While it is structurally placed alongside the Rite I material, it's not actually Rite I language. The introductory material doesn't give a very good sense of where it would be used, but a note within the services clarifies that it is used in place of the invitation to Confession.

The Exhortation exhorts the congregation to several different things, primarily to receive the Eucharist. It is well worth hearing or reviewing several times a year. After offering a brief reminder of the nature and purpose of the Eucharist, we are reminded of the dignity of the sacrament and the need for spiritual preparation for its reception. One of the concerns expressed in the move toward weekly communion was that people would see the sacrament as less precious if it were experienced more often. The Exhortation is a useful reminder of the need to view the Eucharist within the whole context of our lives and faith—and to remind us that the pattern of our lives ought to be worthy of the sacrament's grace. If you don't hear the Exhortation in church very often, it is worth seeking out on a regular basis to reflect upon it.

The Decalogue

The Decalogue is another term for the Ten Commandments. The Rite I Eucharist recommends either the Ten Command-ments or the Summary of the Law. This is a particularly Anglican feature—the Decalogue isn't used this way in the historic Western Liturgy. The original reason for its inclusion was to make sure that the Ten Commandments were used liturgically. From the earliest days of the Church, a minimum standard of knowledge about the faith was reckoned as the

Ten Commandments, the Apostles' Creed, and the Lord's Prayer. Even throughout the medieval period when the services were in Latin, Church councils reminded clergy that they were required to teach these three things to the congregation in their mother tongue. Of these, the latter two appear at both Morning and Evening Prayer. If you are following the prayer book's rule of life, you will say these quite a lot—but the Decalogue has no equivalent liturgical rehearsal. As a result, it was introduced (likely following other Reformation liturgies) in the 1552 prayer book revision as a means of making sure that congregations heard it and learned it from regular use. Its use in the American prayer books has become more optional over successive revisions, and yet it still deserves a place within our liturgical memory.

The Penitential Orders

The Penitential Orders are a means for transferring the Confession of Sin and related material from the middle of the service to the beginning. The title of this section makes the material sound more penitential than it actually is; indeed, if you take a good, hard look at the words, you'll note that we're not really adding much additional penitential material. The opening dialogue is the same as the regular Eucharistic opening; the text of the confession is the same as what ordinarily follows the Prayers of the People. The only addition is the option to include the Decalogue and/or the Summary of the Law or another scriptural sentence. While this element may sound penitential, it is simply a means of reordering what's already in the service and adding in one or more scriptural pieces. The key thing here is that this is the only rubrically permissible method for including the Decalogue within the Rite II service.

THE WORD OF GOD

*Italics indicates optional use.

Rite I	Rite II	Required?	Variation
[hymn, psalm, or anthem]	[hymn, psalm, or anthem]	Optional	Weekly
Opening Greeting/ Response	Opening Greeting/ Response	Optional	Seasonal
Collect for Purity	Collect for Purity	Rite I: Yes Rite II: No	
[Ten Commandments]/ Summary of the Law		Optional	
(Kyrie or Trisagion) and/or Gloria	Gloria or Kyrie or Trisagion	At least one	Seasonal
Collect of the Day	Collect of the Day	Yes	Weekly
The Lessons	The Lessons	At least one	Weekly
[psalm, hymn, or anthem]	[psalm, hymn, or anthem]	Optional	
The Gospel	The Gospel	Yes	Weekly
The Sermon	The Sermon	Yes	
The Nicene Creed	The Nicene Creed	On Sundays and Major Feasts	
The Prayers of the People	[The Prayers of the People]	Yes	
Confession of Sin	Confession of Sin	May be omitted occasionally	
The Peace	The Peace	Yes	

This section, entitled "The Word of God," is the first half of the Holy Eucharist. It is sometimes called the ante-communion where the Latin *ante* designates the portion before the communion. I'm not a fan of this term because it implies that these elements are merely the warm-up and not integral elements of Communion as a whole. But they are!

As we established earlier, the first half of the service offers us a direct encounter with the person of Jesus Christ who is the true Word of God. The highlight of this half is the exposition of the Gospel. This term can refer either to the sermon and its interpretation of the Word of God for a given congregation or, more narrowly, can refer to the act of reading the Gospel Lesson aloud in a language understood by the people. Indeed, sometimes it's necessary to go with the more narrow definition. Even when the preacher delivers a dud of a sermon, the Gospel is still heard in its proclamation.

The other elements of this half of the service are structured around the Gospel to help us hear and respond to it most fully. The collect should help to set the scene liturgically as would various seasonal additions or deletions. The readings before the Gospel give us a better context for its message within the scope of God's prior relationship with humanity and in the Early Church's own understanding of Jesus. After the Gospel we recite the Nicene Creed and once again remind ourselves of the Church's guide for the proper interpretation of the scriptures. Lastly, the intercessory prayers come out of our sense of the world's need and the divine capacity to meet that need.

The First "Hymn, Psalm, or Anthem"

An introductory hymn usually opens the service and gives a liturgical space for an entrance procession. This is not required but is quite common. As with all hymns and anthems appointed, the hymn is usually connected to the readings or the season, but this isn't always possible or feasible.

Opening Greeting

The prayer book offers three opening greetings at the start of the Eucharist: an ordinary use opening, then special options for Easter and for Lent/penitential occasions. It is good to remember, though, that a fourth opening greeting can be found in the service of Holy Baptism. The opening is the liturgical equivalent of saying "hello." As a result, there's no need for clergy to add a literal hello or some other sort of introductory greeting.

The rubrics on page 407 of the prayer book provide four possible spots for announcements: "before the service, after the Creed, before the Offertory, or at the end of the service." The opening greeting, therefore, is not the place for them.

The Collect for Purity

The Collect for Purity is a gem of Anglican devotion. In fact, it's important enough that it's worth quoting here:

> Almighty God, to you all hearts are open, all desires known, and from you no secrets are hid: Cleanse the thoughts of our hearts by the inspiration of your Holy Spirit, that we may perfectly love you, and worthily magnify your holy Name; through Christ our Lord. Amen (*The Book of Common Prayer*, p. 355).

Openly admitting to the God who knows our faults and shortcomings better than we do ourselves, we ask for the cleansing presence of the Holy Spirit that we might love and worship God rightly. It is appropriately one of our most beloved prayers. Originally a private prayer of the priest as part of the preparation for Mass in the Sarum missals, Archbishop Cranmer made an excellent choice in sharing it with the whole congregation. If you only memorize one collect in your life, this would be the one to pick. Rite I requires its use; Rite II leaves it optional.

Following the Collect for Purity in Rite I is space for either the Decalogue or Jesus' Summary of the Law. Rite II does not technically offer this same option unless the Penitential Order is being used.

The Gloria/Kyrie/Trisagion

The first principal element of the service is the song that appears at this point: the *Kyrie*, the *Trisagion*, or the *Gloria in Excelsis*. These are all hymns of praise sung or said corporately. Particularly when the Gloria is sung—but even when an alternative is used—this moment can be seen as the point where the gathered congregation purposely joins its voice to the great unceasing universal chorus of praise to God and to the Lamb. In this hymn, we stand alongside the angels who proclaimed "Gloria" at the birth of the savior in Bethlehem and the saints and martyrs whose prayers have been received before the throne of God. Some of the great choral settings of the *Gloria* directly evoke the experience of standing in the midst of celestial choirs, contributing to the solemnity of this moment.

The *Kyrie* is a simple cry to God for mercy that acknowledges our dependence upon divine grace. In its simplest form, it is the repetition of three brief sentences: "Lord, have mercy. Christ, have mercy. Lord have mercy." We have the option of using either English or Greek (*Kyrie, eleison*). This is a thoroughly biblical phrase. Suppliants ask for Jesus' help in the Gospels with these words, and the psalmists and prophets alike cry for help with them in the Greek translation of the Old Testament that was the Church's first Bible.

The *Kyrie* can be used as written in the prayer book, a simple alternation between priest and people, or it can be more elaborate: The Additional Directions allow its "threefold, sixfold, or ninefold form" (p. 406). The basic alternation written in the prayer book is the threefold form; in the sixfold, the priest or cantor sings a line and the congregation repeats it; in the ninefold, each line is said three times either in alternation or together before moving on to the next line. While this may sound complicated, it's not—the hymnal gives examples of the sixfold version in S85, S88, S94, and S95; the other settings represent the ninefold form.

The *Trisagion* means three-times holy because this Eastern acclamation names God as holy in three different ways. Like the *Kyrie*, it can be used alone or repeated three times. Unlike the *Kyrie*, when it is repeated, the whole unit is repeated three times rather than each line. Again, the hymnal contains settings for both: S102 gives it once; the other settings (S99-S101) use the threefold repetition.

We already touched on the *Gloria* during our discussion of the Daily Office. Beginning with the words of the angels from Luke, the *Gloria* flows into the words of the Church and serves as the preeminent vehicle for joining us musically with the full heavenly host. Permission is given to substitute another song of praise, but this should be done sparingly—if at all. If substituting, the best options would be a hymn paraphrase (like #421, "All glory be to God on high") or a canticle like the *Te Deum* or the *Benedictus es*.

The rubric for the *Gloria* indicates that it should be used "when appointed," but it doesn't give any clues as to where these instructions might be found. It's tucked away in the Additional Directions on page 406. As usual, the directions are fairly permissive, giving latitiude for local interpretation or practice. Here are the directions for use of the Gloria in tabular form alongside the historic use:

Season	Prayer Book	Historical Use
Advent	Omitted during this season	Omitted during this season
Christmas	Every day in this season	Every day in this season
Epiphany	"as desired" (optional)	Sundays/feast days only
Lent	Omitted during this season	Omitted during this season
Holy Week	Omitted during this season	Omitted during this season
Easter	All Sundays, every day of Easter Week; other weekdays "as desired"	Every day in this season
Post-Pentecost	"as desired" (optional)	Sundays/feast days only

Simply put, the *Gloria* is for our big celebrations. Thus, we use it throughout our festal seasons, we omit it during our more solemn seasons, and we use it for feast days in the seasons in between. The *Kyrie* and *Trisagion*, rather than being specifically penitential, are understood as the usual or default options.

When the *Gloria* is omitted, either of the other two songs will take its place in Rite II. Rite I gives the option of using the *Kyrie* consistently (or the *Trisagion*) and adding the *Gloria* when appropriate, following traditional Anglican use.

The Collect of the Day

At this point, the Collect of the Day is prayed. As discussed earlier, the collects provide a great unifying moment that connects this particular Eucharist to the larger superstructure of Episcopal devotion. Sometimes the collect may establish a theme for the day's liturgy. However, between the reshuffling of collects in this prayer book and the introduction of the Revised Common Lectionary, themes in the collects rarely align neatly with the scriptural texts anymore.

The Lessons

Following the collect comes the Lessons, which offer quite a lot of variety. At the most basic, at least one non-Gospel Lesson is needed, along with a psalm or music, and a Gospel Lesson. Earlier prayer books had only one non-Gospel reading, almost always from a New Testament Epistle, and some Rite I services use one Epistle reading in continuity with this practice. However, since the introduction of the latest prayer book with its Eucharistic Lectionary—and especially with the adoption of the Revised Common Lectionary—most Eucharists include an Old Testament reading, a selection from a psalm, a New Testament reading, and a Gospel reading.

Some parishes include a hymn between the New Testament reading and the Gospel, but an Alleluia verse is also common, frequently serving as music for a procession if the Gospel is read from the midst of the congregation.

Just as we spent some time exploring the pattern of the Daily Office readings, it is worth discussing the pattern of the Eucharistic readings and about the purpose behind them.

In the Daily Office, we encounter biblical texts in the form of *pericopes* (pronounced per-i-ko-pees) or short sections. Nevertheless, the basic unit of encounter is of a book. That is, the Daily Office moves through entire books piece by piece—or at least hits the major representative points of each book—in sequential order. In the Eucharist, the basic level of encounter has classically been the pericope rather than the book. In the superseded one-year lectionary of the historic Western liturgy essentially shared by Roman Catholics, Anglicans, and some Lutherans, the Gospel and Epistle readings were selected based on how appropriate they were to a given liturgical occasion, the Gospels being selected without regard from all four Gospels. The orienting pattern was the liturgical year, not the narrative sequence of the book.

Consider a moment what this means. A Eucharistic liturgy that picks small sections out of scripture on the basis of appropriateness is not a tool suited for basic education in the scope of the scriptures; its primary purpose is not teaching the breadth of scripture. This is compounded by the fact that there were only two readings—an Epistle and a Gospel. The Old Testament was heard much more infrequently. Often there was a thematic correspondence within the two readings. The Epistle would serve in some way to illuminate something within the Gospel.

The reason for this difference in structure comes down to purpose. The purpose of the Daily Office Lectionary is catechetical—it serves to teach the breadth of scripture and to give worshipers a familiarity with scripture on a basic level. The purpose of the Eucharistic Lectionary is mystagogical—it serves to delve deeply into one particular aspect of the mystery of Christ, usually one singled out or at least suggested by the season of the liturgical year. The two lectionaries were originally designed to work in intentional combination with one another. The Daily Office taught the broad scope of scripture, while the Eucharist focused on particular moments of encounter with Christ and assumed a prior familiarity with scripture gained from the Office.

The reformers of the liturgy in the mid-twentieth century chose to substantially overhaul the Eucharistic Lectionary. Instead of a one-year cycle that repeated year after year, the reformers moved to a three-year cycle. Instead of pulling the Gospel readings from all four Gospel books, they focused each year of the cycle on a single primary Gospel—either Matthew, Mark, or Luke—and reading them in sequence whenever possible and interweaving John across the three for festivals. Instead of a single non-Gospel reading, two were selected, one (usually) from the Old Testament, the other from the New Testament Epistles. In order to convey the scope, the Old Testament readings in the Season after Pentecost moved sequentially through a particular type of Old Testament book, a type that complemented the character of the year's selected Gospel. Anglicans and Roman Catholics eschewed an entirely sequential approach to the Old Testament, though, and developed another set of readings that connects the Old Testament Lessons to the Gospel pericope. Hence, we now speak of two tracks for the Season after Pentecost: a sequential set of Old Testament readings and a complementary set keyed to the Gospel.

Consider what is going on here: It is an attempt to be both catechetical and mystagogical, at the same time. Whether it's actually possible to achieve both at the same time is an open question. If we criticize the two-year Daily Office Lectionary for missing quite a lot of scripture, it is mathematically obvious that a three-year Eucharistic Lectionary is going to miss a whole lot more. Furthermore, the attempt to structure the Gospel pericopes sequentially for the main part of the year obscures the liturgical principles for selecting them in other parts of it.

On the other hand, this form of three-year lectionary recognizes the reality that most people in our congregations are not praying through the scriptures in the Daily Office. It also gives the average person in the pew a broader familiarity with the Old Testament and lifts up some of the classic Bible stories that are disappearing from the vernacular of Western culture.

The Revised Common Lectionary is anchored around the Gospel reading. The three-year cycle appoints a primary Gospel for each year: Year A uses Matthew, Year B uses Mark, and Year C uses Luke. The Gospel of John appears on significant feasts and fills out a section of the summer of Year B to compensate for the shortness of Mark's Gospel. The First Reading is usually an Old Testament Lesson. Matthew, often considered the most Jewish of the Gospels and written in a rabbinic spirit, is paired with readings from the Old Testament Law—Genesis and Exodus. Mark is paired with readings from the historical books of Samuel and Kings. Luke, with its emphasis on social justice, is paired with the prophets, particularly Jeremiah. The chief exception to the First Lesson being from the Old Testament rule is Easter time; we hear from the book of Acts in this season, the events that happened to the Early Church after the time of the Ascension of Christ. The Second Lesson is always from a New Testament non-Gospel text—usually an Epistle, but Acts gets mixed in at points as well.

The Sermon

When the Early Church realized that it needed to formally expand its canon beyond the Old Testament, it addressed the issue by means of this question: What books do we read publicly in worship? This was the guiding criterion by which the dispersed church communities assessed the books that would be gathered into the New Testament and into our scriptures. This criterion underscores that, for Christians, our paradigmatic encounter with scripture is hearing it in the liturgy. Don't get me wrong: I think we need to read it, and we have to read it outside of worship in order to truly learn it and gain the most from it. But our most important encounter with scripture is hearing it proclaimed in the midst of the worshiping community. We hear it most completely for what it is in this context.

The sermon, then, should flow naturally from the presence of the scriptures within the liturgy. There are as many different approaches to preaching as there are preachers. However, a few basic principles should remain consistent across them. First, the sermon is a part of the liturgy, not a distinct and separate event apart from it. The sermon is located within a liturgical setting. The sermon and liturgy should inform one another or—at the least—not contradict one another. It follows from this that the sermon usually has some direct continuity with its liturgical surrounding. Typically, Episcopal sermons comment on the scriptures appointed for the day, especially the Gospel. Second, if the sermon is part of the liturgy, then it should try to accomplish the same basic thing as the rest of the liturgy. Whether the sermon emphasizes interpretation of the scriptures, teaching, or something else, its underlying aim should be mystagogical. That is, it should seek to open our eyes and hearts to some aspect of the mystery of

Christ. It should show us the work and person of Christ—for us, with us, in us, and through us.

In some traditions, the sermon is the service—or at least the greater part of it. That is not our tradition. The success of the service does not stand or fall on the sermon. The sermon is one element in the whole scope of the liturgy. That is no excuse for poor preaching, of course, but even if the sermon is a flop, the worship of God still goes on.

The Creed

The next element in this portion of the service is the Nicene Creed. As we have said before, the creeds (whether the Nicene or the Apostles') belong in relation to the scriptural readings and their interpretation because they are guides for the Church's interpretation. At this point, no matter how well or poorly the sermon was preached, we are reminded of the basic framework of our faith: the Triune God, Christ who took on our nature that all creation might be reconciled with God, and the ongoing work of the Spirit in the Church.

There are always a few who look askance at the presence of the Nicene Creed because it was not part of the fourth-century Eucharist and was a later introduction to the service. I know some clergy who omit it even when the prayer book requires it (all Sundays and other feast days), but I think that's a mistake. When I read through the missionary preaching that swayed Europe and brought it into the Christian fold, one of the fundamental patterns of proclamation was a rehearsal of the creed. In my corporate job, executives like to talk about the importance of an elevator pitch: a succinct summary of a product or a position. This is ours; the creed is, in essence, a Christian elevator pitch. It is not designed to persuade—that is not its function. Rather the creed conveys the heart of the Christian belief in a quick, easy-to-memorize framework. In an increasingly secular culture, the creed stands as a great tool for thinking through how we answer questions about what Christians believe. Saying it weekly in the Eucharist establishes in us the fundamental framework of the faith.

The Prayers of the People

The Prayers of the People are a response to the Gospel call that we heard in the readings, the sermon, and the creed. Furthermore, the prayers also enact one of the central roles of the gathered community. As Christ both interceded for and directly intervened to address the ills of his people and the world, his gathered Body continues to raise these same concerns and to identify the broken and hurting places of God's world that cry for attention.

In order to ensure that our span of prayers is properly comprehensive, the prayer book establishes six areas of concern that must be addressed:

> The universal Church, its members, and its mission
>
> The nation and all in authority
>
> The welfare of the world
>
> The concerns of the local community
>
> Those who suffer and those in any trouble
>
> The departed (with commemoration of a saint when appropriate) (*The Book of Common Prayer*, p. 359).

Rite I provides a prayer in continuity with past prayer books that covers all of these areas. It feels more communal to me when, following the direction at the bottom of page 328, the leader ends each paragraph with "Lord in your mercy," allowing for a congregational, "Hear our prayer."

The six forms given between pages 383 and 393 incorporate these concerns as well and may be used in either rite, adapting the language for Rite I. These forms are examples, and they can be freely adapted—if desired—to reflect the situations of local communities or to more closely connect them to the liturgical situation, provided they continue to cover all six of the required areas named on page 359.

Local adaptations should be done with care. I have heard some that were preachy—it seemed the priest was trying to fit into the prayers extra material that didn't make it into the sermon. Others turn to the gossipy, especially when the "concerns of the local community" are amplified with excessive detail. Still others can come across as consciousness-raising exercises where particular causes seem to dominate. The root problem with all of these is that the worship of God has taken a second place; the prayers have become speech to the gathered community rather than the gathered community's speech to God.

Confession of Sin

The invitation to Confession in Rite I serves as a great introduction to the next elements of the service: Confession, Absolution, and the Peace. The invitation calls for people to commit to making three changes in their lives:

To "truly and earnestly repent you of your sins,"

To be "in love and charity with your neighbors,"

To "intend to lead a new life, following the commandments of God and walking from henceforth in his holy ways" (p. 330).

In the earlier prayer books, members of the congregation could leave at this point, and only those who desired to receive Holy Communion remained for the Confession and the Eucharist. Thus, this call was formerly extended to a self-selected set of the congregation. In its current location, the invitation encourages the whole congregation to these three disciplines, which are put into practice with what follows.

The Confession of Sin is a response to the Gospel proclamation no less than the prayers are. The classic human response to an experience of the holy is to draw near with wonder. An inherent secondary response is to draw back in recognition of our own limitation and sin—signs of our separation from the holy. The Confession gives voice to this experience. Too often penitence has been structured or explained as the religious process of feeling bad about ourselves. This is not the point of the exercise at all. Instead, the Confession gives voice to a realistic appraisal of who we are in the face of the Holy God. The Confession in Rite II (there is also a Rite I version) is structured in a very specific way. At its center, the Confession is an exact reversal of the Summary of the Law. In the summary, we hear the words of Jesus exhorting us to, "Love the Lord your God with all your heart, and with all your soul, with all your mind, and with all your strength" and "Love your neighbor as yourself" (*The Book of Common Prayer*, p. 351). In the Confession, we acknowledge that we have not done this; we acknowledge the reality of our human situation. We ask not only for forgiveness but also for the grace to do better. But note how we phrase this hope of doing better: It is not an intellectual change—it is not about knowing. Instead this hope is about embracing God's will with joy and then walking in his ways. This is a long-term, full-body response. It is not just thinking or doing; it is the whole body responding in faith using words that recall to us the vision of the faithful laid out in Psalm 15 and Psalm 26.

The Absolution is the Church's response to our congregational confession. The difference in wording between Rites I and II are worth exploring. The Rite II Absolution is characterized by certainty. There is nothing conditional here; it is a straightforward assurance of pardon: "Almighty God have mercy on you…forgive you…strengthen you…keep you…" (p. 360). The Rite I Absolution begins differently: "Almighty God, our heavenly Father, who of his great mercy hath promised forgiveness of sins to all those who with hearty repentance and true faith turn unto him, have mercy upon you…pardon and deliver you…confirm and strengthen you… bring you to everlasting life" (p. 332). The relative clause that identifies God names a promise with certain requirements, namely that forgiveness is given to "all those who with hearty repentance and true faith turn unto him." We hear this absolution best when both versions are kept in mind. As we hear the Rite I version, we need to remember the assurance of pardon. As we hear the unconditional pardon of Rite II, we need to remember our duty to conform to the Confession we have just said and enact the pardon we have received.

The difference between the rites continues. Rite I follows the Absolution with one or more lines from scripture, referred to as the "comfortable words." These New Testament passages emphasize Christ's victory over sin on behalf of the whole world. They explicitly name the promises alluded to earlier.

The Peace

The final element in this part of the service is the sharing of the Peace. The significance of this action is much deeper than shaking the hands of the people around you; rather, we enact being "in love and charity with [our] neighbors." The Confession and Absolution have reconciled us with God; now we share active signs of our own reconciliation with our neighbors. Two Gospel passages should float through our heads at this point. The first is a direct reflection of what has just occurred. In Matthew's parable of the forgiven debtor (18:23-35), a king forgives a servant who owes him ten thousand talents (a ridiculous amount of money, like saying a billion dollars today), but the servant turns around and demands from a fellow servant a hundred denarii (a much more reasonable sum, roughly a couple hundred dollars). The king then throws the first servant back in jail and demands the full amount because he has failed to learn the lesson of mercy. In the same way, our recognition of the forgiveness given to us by God demands a similar action on our part. The classic summary of this concept comes from a version of the Lord's Prayer: "Forgive us our debts as we forgive our debtors."

The second passage that should run through our heads leads us toward the next major portion of the service. Near the beginning of the Sermon on the Mount, Jesus says, "So when you are offering your gift at the altar, if you remember that your brother or sister has something against you, leave your gift there before the altar and go; first be reconciled to your brother or sister, and then come and offer your gift" (Matthew 5:23-24). We are at that point. We are about to offer our gifts at the altar. Jesus is reminding us that reconciliation with God is not a personal endeavor; it is social, communal. Our reconciliation with God is incomplete if we aren't actively seeking reconciliation with those around us.

To be honest, we tend not to emphasize this union between the Confession and the Peace very much, and there's a good reason for that—it's hard work! As much as I wish the hyperbolic overstatement in Psalm 51 were true—"Against you [God] only have I sinned and done what is evil in your sight" (*The Book of Common Prayer*, p. 656)—it's not. An honest confession of our sin reveals that we have sinned—in what we have done and in what we have left undone—against those around us and particularly against those to whom we are the closest. The sign of peace, whether an actual kiss, a hug, or shaking of a hand, ought to be a sign of our deeper commitment to set things right and to honor, value, and love those closest to us. John's first Epistle neatly—and uncomfortably—concludes this for us: "Those who say, 'I love God,' and hate their brothers or sisters, are liars; for those who do not love a brother or sister whom they have seen, cannot love God whom they have not seen. The commandment we have from him is this: those who love God must love their brothers and sisters also" (4:20-21).

THE HOLY COMMUNION

Rite I	Rite II	Required?	Variation
Offertory	Offertory	Yes	As desired
[hymn, psalm, or anthem]	[hymn, psalm, or anthem]	Optional	Weekly (by service)
The Great Thanksgiving	The Great Thanksgiving	Yes	By prayer
The Lord's Prayer	The Lord's Prayer	Yes	None
The Breaking of the Bread/ Fraction Anthem	The Breaking of the Bread/ Fraction Anthem	Yes	As desired; by season
Prayer of Humble Access		Optional	
Distribution	Distribution	Yes	As desired
[hymn, psalm, or anthem]	[hymn, psalm, or anthem]	Optional	Weekly (by service)
Post-Communion Prayer	Post-Communion Prayer	Yes	By occasion
Blessing	Blessing	Optional	As desired; by season
Dismissal	Dismissal	Yes	As desired

Let me give you an initial perspective to frame our discussion as we move into Holy Communion. Gregory Dix, an Anglican Benedictine monk, in his monumental work, *Shape of the Liturgy,* gives us a key entrée into the spiritual heart of the Eucharist as a result of his study of countless Eucharistic prayers of the Eastern and Western Churches. No matter what else they might do or have, they all had these four fundamental actions in common: take, bless, break, give. On a basic structural level, it's easy to align these with the elements in the chart above. In the Offertory, the congregation brings offerings to the altar including the bread and wine. Then, the Eucharistic prayer is the blessing of these elements. The bread is broken at the Breaking of the Bread/Fraction Anthem, and then both elements—bread and wine—are given to the people at the Distribution.

The real genius and spiritual meat of Dix's observation, though, only comes with reflection. It's easy enough to match up his four actions with parts of the service. But to leave it at that misses deeper opportunities for reflection and growth. You see, no one action exhausts any particular element of the Eucharist. If we stop at the structural level, we fail to notice that these four actions tend to operate in each individual part of the Eucharistic act. There's a continual flow of these actions around and through the various parties enacting the Eucharist: When the priest gives the consecrated bread, we— the congregants—are taking (receiving) Christ's own blessing. To just call this Distribution or to say the bread is given limits us to a clerical perspective. The priest is giving, but what are we doing, what is Christ doing, where is the Spirit moving?

Likewise, within the Eucharistic prayer, when we join with the priest in blessing, we are also in the act of giving—our very souls and bodies. And in so doing, Christ is taking while the Spirit is also blessing. As you engage in the Eucharistic meal, the Eucharistic practice, you will see different aspects come to the foreground as you are ready to see them and as you need to see them. What is required is a sense of the four fundamental actions in order to be attentive to them.

The Offertory

The Offertory is the point when the gathered community offers its material possessions for the good of itself and the world around itself. Despite what you might think, scripture—the New Testament in particular—has far more to say about possessions and what we do with them than it does about sex. Proper stewardship and the sharing of resources has been a hallmark of Christian teaching from the beginning (the book of Acts in particular makes this quite evident). This element gives us an opportunity to literally put our money where our mouth is. In the act of the Offertory, the congregation's gifts are received and then brought forward to the altar to be dedicated to God.

The Offertory Sentences explore the ideas of offering and sacrifice primarily through a lens of stewardship. What we have is what we have been given whether directly or indirectly by God in creation. Some priests raise the elements and say a prayer over them at this point; this isn't a pre-blessing but rather a prayer of thanks to God for giving us bread, wine, and sustenance that we are privileged to offer back. This prayer recognizes the inherent circularity in the act of giving a part of creation as a gift to the Creator.

The Great Thanksgiving

We now come to the pinnacle of the second part of the service, the great Eucharistic prayer. One of the most common ways of breaking down the prayer is dividing it into constituent parts. That is, there are subsections within the various Eucharistic prayers that have certain roles that can help us understand what we're hearing and doing. A lot of writings on the Eucharist spend time on these subsections and on their historical development. As a result, when priests teach about the Eucharist, this part often gets emphasized—maybe even overemphasized—because this is how they were taught. It is easy to trace these parts and to see literary dependence between different kinds of Eucharistic prayers.

But fundamentally, the Eucharist isn't about literary dependencies. It is not about the history of the development of the text of the prayer either.

The Eucharist is a whole-body, multisensory experience where we remind ourselves who God is for us, in which we praise God in awe and wonder, and ultimately, we taste and see that the Lord is good. We receive Christ into ourselves so that we (all of us, together, the whole company of faithful people) may be received more deeply into him.

And that is why we look at the parts of the prayer—so that we can more clearly perceive within ourselves the fruits of his redemption.

These are the chief parts of the prayer (sometimes called the *anaphora* or *canon*):

The Opening Dialogue

The Thanksgiving (Preface)

The Sanctus (Holy, Holy, Holy) [stuck in the midst of the Thanksgiving]

The Words and Deeds of Jesus (Institution Narrative)

The Remembrance (Anamnesis)

The Offering (Oblation)

The Invocation of the Spirit (Epiclesis)

The Final Blessing (Doxology)

The Opening Dialogue

The Opening Dialogue is a brief interchange between the priest and the congregation. It is a ritual exchange where we acknowledge what we are about to do and make public profession of our unity in what follows. This dialogue begins with the standard exchange that is the normal liturgical greeting and response: "The Lord be with you"/"And also with you [And with thy spirit.]"

The call to "lift up your hearts" only appears in the Eucharist. There are a few different ways to understand this call. One is to see this phrase as a metaphor that invites us to be joyful. By lifting up our hearts, we are metaphorically lifting them from sadness and putting them into a more acceptable place proper for rejoicing. Another, favored by John Calvin among others, takes the phrase in a *spirito-spatial* sense. He understood this to be a reference to lifting our hearts upward into heaven and into the presence of the enthroned Christ.

The final exchange establishes an agreement about what we are all about to do together: In Greek, to give thanks is the verb *eucharistein* from which our word "Eucharist" comes. The response, whether it's the Cranmerian, "It is meet [fitting] and right so to do" or the modern phrase, "It is right to give him thanks and praise," is a word of agreement. In essence, the priest says, "Let's Eucharist now!" and our response is, "Yes, let's!" From this point on, the priest continues, but we are all committed to the words the priest says and are united in the priest's prayer. The priest is praying on our behalf and in consonance with our own silent prayers. We are not observers simply because we are not talking; we are full participants—or at least certainly should be. This is part of the agreement we are making. Another way to consider this is that, in the final exchange, we as the people of God are extending our permission for the priest to give thanks to God in the midst of all of us on behalf of all of us. Even though the priest alone is talking, the Eucharist is never the act of a single person; in our church there is no such thing as a Eucharist offered by a priest alone. At least one other person is required. It is as the gathered Body of Christ that the Eucharist is offered, even if only a small group is gathered.

The Thanksgiving

The Eucharist is an experience, but it is not a strictly subjective one; we can't make it into whatever we think it ought to be. Instead, the priest begins with an act of thanks that reminds both God and us of the extent of our relationship up to this point. We are reminded of the intrinsic character of the God whom we are thanking.

Since we have just finished giving the priest permission to start thanking, the prayer logically proceeds in that vein. In most of our prayers, a Proper Preface is inserted at this point. (Again, these are gathered on pages 344-349 for Rite I; pages 377-382 for Rite II). Most seasons have their own Preface; on Sundays during green seasons there are three alternating options—Of God the Father, Of God the Son, and Of God the Holy Spirit. Some occasions get their own Prefaces—baptisms, marriages, ordinations, a few classes of saints, the dead. On regular weekdays, the prayer is written so the Preface can simply be dropped out. The Proper Prefaces thank God from a particular perspective and emphasize some special aspect of our relationship with God. The Seasonal Prefaces emphasize something that pertains to the season, using images, biblical allusions, or referring to biblical events prominent in the season's readings, tying the Eucharist back to the Calendar.

However the Preface goes—or even if it's left out altogether—it always concludes the same way. Our thanks turns to praise, and we join our voices with the whole heavenly chorus.

The Sanctus

A joke was making the rounds a while ago when I was in seminary that went something like this:

> A Southern Baptist minister and an Episcopal priest ran into each other at the post office on Monday morning. The Baptist turned to the Episcopalian and said, "We had such a great day yesterday! We had over 300 people show up. A famous foreign missionary came and gave us the message. And that was just our Seeker Service!"
>
> "Wow, congratulations," his Episcopal colleague responded.
>
> "So, how'd you do?" the minister prompted.
>
> "Let me think…" said the priest. "We had the Maxwells, the Murphys and their kids, and Bill and Joe. Old Miss Wordward was there and so was her driver. And we had nine ranks of angels, 144,000 sealed out of the tribes of Israel, and then a great multitude that no one could number from every nation, tribe, people and language. Our Lord Jesus Christ came and gave us himself. And that was just our 8 a.m. Low Mass!"

In addition to poking gentle fun at denominational rivalries, I have always remembered this joke because it expresses something deeply true about our understanding of worship—especially sacramental worship.

The *Gloria* is the first angelic song of our service. The *Sanctus* is the second. Coming right after the invitation to "lift up our hearts," the *Sanctus* reinforces the notion that the Eucharist is occurring in a different spiritual space than our normal lives. We are now existing in a geography peopled by saints, angels, and the hosts of the blessed dead. Or—better yet—it reinforces that there is something richer and deeper going on all around us of which we are usually unaware.

The word *Sanctus* is Latin for holy, and the text of this song comes from Isaiah's great vision of God in the temple recorded in Isaiah 6. In his vision, this was the song of the seraphim as they flew about the person of God: "Holy, holy, holy is the LORD of hosts; the whole earth is full of his glory" (6:3). Significantly, Saint John the Divine records a similar song from the four living creatures about the throne of God: "Holy, holy, holy, the Lord God the Almighty, who was and is and is to come" (Revelation 4:8). This second part of the song from Revelation conceptually leads into the second half of the *Sanctus*: "Blessed is he who comes in the name of the Lord."

A few things are going on here. First, it allows the liturgy to return to the song heard in Isaiah and to amplify it with the song heard in Revelation. These final words of the *Sanctus* take an incarnational turn: The coming of God in flesh names specific ways in which God's glory fills all of creation.

Second, these words are quoting Mark 11:9 and Matthew 21:9, which refer to Jesus. If Jesus hasn't already been brought into the picture by the Proper Preface, now he has. In our great act of communal blessing and thanking God as part of the greater chorus, our praise makes reference—if only indirectly, to the person of Jesus and reminds the priest to say more about him. Sure enough, the prayer usually takes a more Christological turn after this point. We are blessing him who will shortly come and bless us in his sacramental presence.

Third, in the Gospels, these words are from the lips of the crowd at the triumphal entry of Jesus into Jerusalem. This provided an ideal point of connection for the patristic and medieval interpreters who allegorized the Eucharist according to the life of Christ; at this point Jesus enters the holy city to be sacrificed.

And the Thanks Keep Coming

Some liturgical scholars speak of the Post-*Sanctus*. On one hand, the name makes sense because this is the part that literally comes after the *Sanctus*. However, this naming can cause confusion about what's actually going on.

Here's the problem that I have with it: The title, Post-*Sanctus*, creates the sense that we're doing something different now than what we were before—and that's not the case. The priest is still engaging in the same basic act of thanks. Furthermore, when we start breaking things up into elements, it can appear like we have three separate things: A Thanksgiving, the *Sanctus*, and the Post-*Sanctus*. When we see these three as a conceptual unity (which they are), then we better understand that the *Sanctus* too is an inherent part of our complete act of thanksgiving.

As prompted by the congregational reminder in the second part of the *Sanctus*, the object of thanks focuses on what God has done for us specifically in and through the person of Jesus. God's work of creation often appears here, but the real move is to the person of Christ.

The Words and Deeds of Jesus

At this point we shift from Jesus in general to a vignette of Jesus in particular. The previous section invoked the broader work of redemption, largely centered on the cross. Here, we focus on the pivotal moment at the dinner Jesus shared with his disciples before his death.

We know this part goes back to the very beginning of what Christians do together. Of all the writings that we have, the letters of Paul are the earliest. While dating the writings of the New Testament is a fairly tricky business, we know that Paul was writing in and around the year 51 CE. Indeed, as best as we can tell, his letters were committed to paper ten to twenty years before the Gospels themselves were being circulated. As a result, the earliest, still-surviving, written testimony we have to Jesus Christ, who he was, and what he did on this earth, is preserved for us in 1 Corinthians:

> For I received from the Lord what I also handed on to you, that the Lord Jesus on the night when he was betrayed took a loaf of bread, and when he had given thanks, he broke it and said, "This is my body that is for you. Do this in remembrance of me." In the same way he took the cup also, after supper, saying, "This cup is the new covenant in my blood. Do this, as often as you drink it, in remembrance of me." For as often as you eat this bread and drink the cup, you proclaim the Lord's death until he comes (11:23-26).

This moment is central for who we are and for who we are together. It's easy for us to become numb to certain words and actions, and these are no exception. We become used to hearing them and lose sense of how radical they are. If I had to focus on a single word to rekindle the wonder that lives within it, it would be covenant. In classical Hebrew, you don't make a covenant. Instead, the proper turn of phrase is to cut a covenant. Genesis 15 shows Abraham cutting a covenant with God, and it involves cutting animals in half as part of the ritual action! Covenant-cutting is part of what God does. God commits reconciliation with creation by means of covenants, solemn promises between the divine and the created (including humans). Here at dinner, Jesus commits to a new covenant cut in his own blood, by means of his blood. The symbolic action will become literal in a few short hours. And yet the great movement to which all of this is driving is not fundamentally about blood and death but about consummating a reconciliation.

But this is the covenant that I will make with the house of Israel after those days, says the LORD: I will put my law within them, and I will write it on their hearts; and I will be their God, and they shall be my people. No longer shall they teach one another, or say to each other, "Know the LORD," for they shall all know me, from the least of them to the greatest, says the LORD; for I will forgive their iniquity, and remember their sin no more (Jeremiah 31:33-34).

And I saw the holy city, the new Jerusalem, coming down out of heaven from God, prepared as a bride adorned for her husband. And I heard a loud voice from the throne saying, "See, the home of God is among mortals. He will dwell with them; they will be his peoples, and God himself will be with them; he will wipe every tear from their eyes. Death will be no more; mourning and crying and pain will be no more, for the first things have passed away" (Revelation 21:2-4).

As Christians, we stand as people, witnesses, of this new covenant. In these words, we hear this new covenant proclaimed week after week. And yet our struggle is to hear it again and again, to take its call to heart again and again, to step into the world that it offers us at our fingertips, closer to us even than our hands and our feet.

The Remembrance

Having heard again the words of Christ, we are struck by the repetition of remembrance. After the bread, after the wine, Jesus enjoins his disciples gathered with him—and that is us too—to do this, the act of taking, blessing, breaking, and giving, in memory of him. Accordingly, we echo in return an act of remembrance. But what exactly are we remembering? Nothing exact, if our prayers are anything to go by. That is, we are not just remembering a poignant moment before he died; we're not just remembering his death. Rather our memory encompasses in a flash the whole sweep of the Great Three Days. It includes not just his death, not just his descent among the dead and his redemptive work there, but also his resurrection and ascension, his promise to come again, as well as the totality of who and what he was, is, and will be for us.

The Offering

Here we speak in prayer what we acted out at the start of this particular movement. In a choreographed moment (the Offertory) that we initially labeled as a take, the prayer reveals it to be a give, but—oddly—in the act of giving, we shall receive, and it will be a blessing.

In the Offering, the priest prays the elements back to God and, in doing so, lays bare what we're really offering here: ourselves. At the end of the day, this isn't about bread and wine. It's about the greater transformation into the fullness of God. It is about us being transformed. But not just us, either. It's about the whole created order being transformed back toward the image and ideal in and through which it was created in the first place. It's that reconciliation business yet again.

The Invocation of the Spirit

The invocation of the Holy Spirit should remind us of where we find ourselves. Remember, in a very real sense, we have been invited into the interior dialogue of the Holy Trinity. As members of the Body of Christ and incorporate within him, we are participants in his own self-offering to the Father through the Spirit. Sometimes—and here especially—

our invocation of the Spirit isn't truly an invoking in the proper sense. To invoke is to call; we're not actually calling the Spirit; the Spirit is here! Rather, we are being proper in acknowledging one in whose presence we stand. And again, because it's proper, not because we control it or direct it, we request the Spirit to do what it does in sanctifying the gifts and us.

The Final Blessing

We conclude the prayer with a final note of thanks. Acknowledging what we are doing, we attempt to wrap words around the Triune confluence of Father, Son, and Holy Spirit within which we have been privileged to participate. We have some fun with prepositions as we struggle to adequately describe our perception of the glory of Christ toward the Father—"by him, with him, in him." And of course the Spirit of whom we have just spoken is unifying and binding the act into a worthy garland of praise.

The prayer comes to an end with a great "Amen." This Amen is our collective assent to the communal prayer that the priest has just voiced. Just as the prayer begins with agreement that it is by all, for all, though through the mouth of one, so the Amen confirms the unity of our collective prayer. These amens are the only ones in the prayer book printed in all caps. They remind us visually of their importance and the emphasis that they deserve.

On that Ping Moment

Now that we have finished the run-through of the Eucharistic prayer, we have to pause. We have to talk about the "ping."

This is something liturgists love to fight about.

When do the elements, the bread and wine, really become Jesus? When is the moment at which the sacramental presence becomes present in a way that it wasn't before? A favorite professor of mine liked to call this the ping moment. So, where do we look?

There are three good options: 1. The words of institution when the priest recalls Jesus' own words over the bread and wine, 2. the invocation of the Spirit, and 3. the final Amen. Naturally, different groups have lobbied for different options.

The Western Church typically goes with the first option. The whole reason that the host is elevated in the Roman Catholic Mass at the words of institution is so the congregation can adore Christ who is then present in a way he wasn't before. When Martin Luther reformed the Mass, he basically took out everything except the words of institution, and for generations, this was the only part of the classic prayer that Lutherans used. For Luther, it was all about the promise of Christ to be present when the Word of the Gospel is joined with the elements: That's when the magic happens.

The Eastern Church tends to go with option two. The invocation of the Spirit is what accomplishes the change, they will tell you. The priest doesn't make anything, God does; therefore, it's the action of the Spirit that effects the fundamental transition into the fullness of the Eucharistic presence.

A classic Anglican position likes the third option. If we didn't need the whole prayer, why would we have the whole prayer? Besides, consecration is a function of celebration, not a mechanical action. As a result, the whole prayer should be seen as a collective and coherent act of consecrating the elements.

Thankfully, although faced with an array of three possible options—all with good reasons to back them up—I can give you the single correct answer: It fundamentally and truly doesn't matter.

Or more accurately: It doesn't matter **when** it happens; it matters **that** it happens.

We honestly don't know when the ping happens, and it's not worth fighting over. What is much more important is that we locate a movement of the greater presence of Christ in our midst at some point within this action. If it helps you to see it at a particular point, then by all means, embrace that. If it doesn't matter to you, leave it at that. For me, I'm an option one kind of guy. A good friend who was raised Pentecostal will always be a number two. And that's fine. Neither of us can prove our point and for the sake of our own devotion and the sake of growing more deeply into the mystery of Christ, we don't need to prove it. The when is not as important as the connection itself. The lack of a definite when can become an opportunity. You are open to explore this yourself: Which moment—or set of moments—feels most powerful and holy to you? When do you feel Christ or the presence of the Spirit most fully? Listen for that. Be attentive. And know that it doesn't have to be one point for all time either: You might find it at different places as you proceed in your spiritual journey.

THE LORD'S PRAYER

As a fitting conclusion to our great prayer of the service, we then pray together the Lord's Prayer. A standard element in most Christian services, we shouldn't be surprised to find it in the Eucharist. The question, though, is why here? Why now? Why not at the end of the Prayers of the People, as in the Daily Office? In one sense, we are continuing the theme of Christ's conversation with the Father. We, as the Body of Christ, are praying his own prayer. But I think something more particular is going on with its placement. When we pray this prayer at this moment in the service—after the prayer but before the distribution—it changes the way we hear the line at its center: "Give us this day our daily bread." An obvious association is made between the petition for bread and the Eucharist, the bread from heaven.

The question is: How long afterward will this meaning linger? Does saying the prayer at this point and experiencing this particular interpretation of the text alter it for us and become our instinctive understanding of the line? It's hard to say. Perhaps we might understand it this way: This placement certainly suggests a meaning. While not closing off other interpretations of the line, it invites us to see the request being fulfilled within the Eucharist.

THE BREAKING OF THE BREAD/FRACTION ANTHEM

Now we come to the worst-kept moment of silence in The Episcopal Church.

After the heading "The Breaking of the Bread," the prayer book gives two short sentences as directions: "The celebrant breaks the consecrated Bread. A period of silence is kept." After fifteen years of attendance at Episcopal services, I can't recall more than a few when the time between the breaking of the bread and the start of the Fraction Anthem could justifiably be referred to as a period. Most of the time, there is no pause—one sentence runs right into the other. And that's a shame. This is one of the few places where the prayer book actually mandates silence, and it is a good point for reflection.

At this point we have the words said or sung around the breaking of the bread. This is often called the Fraction Anthem. It's quite common to have a double anthem at this point. The priest says, "Christ our Passover is sacrificed for us," and our response, "Therefore let us keep the feast," is an anthem; however, it's common to immediately thereafter have either a choral or a congregational fraction anthem, perhaps a version of "Lamb of God" or another sung fraction. From a technical perspective, this is redundant. On the other hand, two different ideas are being expressed. Indeed, the Rite I service includes both texts—the Christ our Passover and the *Agnus Dei*—even though the Rite II text only contains the Christ our Passover.

The Christ our Passover anthem holds together the notion of the sacrificial meal. It underscores the notion of sacrifice—as controversial as that still remains in Protestant circles—but proceeds immediately to the meal. The fact of the sacrificial death does not end the sacrificial act; harking back to the Homeric, the meal needs to to follow.

The Lamb of God anthem, on the other hand, contains the concept of sacrifice but makes the turn toward the expiation of sin. It's a more introspective response but one that deserves to be heard in relation to the other.

The prayer book doesn't contain any other Fractions, although it gives permission for others; the hymnal, on the other hand, has quite a few more. In addition to the two already mentioned, it also has:

The disciples knew the Lord Jesus (S167)

My flesh is food indeed (S168-9)

Whoever eats this bread (S170)

Be known to us (S171)

Blessed are those who are called (S172)

All adaptations of New Testament readings, these additions give us more perspectives into the meal that we are about to receive. There can be a practical purpose for these as well—particularly when several patens and chalices need to be prepared or a large altar party communed before moving to the rest of the congregation. These anthems help us reflect and focus on what we have done and are about to continue while allowing time for the elements to be made ready.

PRAYER OF HUMBLE ACCESS

Rite I offers the Prayer of Humble Access (p. 337) as an option; Rite II does not mention it at all. In a very real sense, this prayer has become something of a litmus test for those who either champion or decry the liturgical shifts away from the 1928 status quo. For fans of the new approach, the Prayer of Humble Access seems overly penitential. With its bald assertion that "we are not worthy so much as to gather up the crumbs under thy Table" (*The Book of Common Prayer*, p. 337), the prayer seems to dismiss the real consequences of grace, redemption, and reconciliation. Others, conversely, see its absence as a sign of spiritual arrogance and as the Church's capitulation to a culture of entitlement that believes it deserves anything it wants. The proper question focuses around the we—who is this we? Is this the we before, after, or apart from God's grace?

Two things here: First, I must say, reading the troublesome line in context helps. The sentence right before it—the one with which the prayer opens—is this: "We do not presume to come to this thy Table, O merciful Lord, trusting in our own righteousness, but in thy manifold and great mercies." The first line, therefore, draws a contrast between humanity's own efforts toward righteousness and the abundant mercies of God. The next sentence is logically read to mean that by our own efforts and merits, we don't measure up. As Cranmer penned this prayer in the sixteenth century, I'm sure he heard echoing in his ears Martin Luther's teaching on original sin: that it consists of the basic inability to love, fear, and trust God as we should. Therefore, Luther taught, even if we outwardly act in accordance with all of the commandments, we will still fail to satisfy them if we are not loving, fearing, and trusting with our whole hearts. That's the intention here and the ground of our unworthiness apart from the grace of God.

Remember, though, the first sentence ends with the reminder that we don't have to measure up. We don't come to the table on our own nor do we have to earn our spot. Rather, we are called by the "manifold and great mercies" of God. The first sentence has a balance to it that starts with our efforts and moves to God. Classically, our next two sentences were one sentence connected together that echoed the structure of the first moving, again, from us ("We are not worthy…") to God ("Thou art the same Lord whose property is always to have mercy").

Pulling the line out of context is a perfect recipe for misunderstanding the concept and the theology behind it.

Second, I want to remind us of Rudolf Otto's discussion about the human experience of the holy. An inevitable part of that experience is the impact caused by a recognition of the gulf between Creator and creature. This language of unworthiness is part and parcel of trying to wrap human language around the experience of finding oneself in the presence of the Holy. Like all attempts at this kind of language, it falls short. When this inadequacy is coupled with an atrophied sense of the holy, the prayer's language can feel unnaturally or improperly penitential. Our greatest remedy to overcoming the obstacle is not to chuck the prayer but to recognize and embrace its diagnostic function as a guide back to cultivating our own sense of the holy.

I understand that this sixteenth-century wording collides with the late twentieth-century conversation about the psychological importance of self-worth. I'm all for healthy self-confidence. But, as with Confession, the point of the prayer comes back to the reality of the human condition, especially when it is put in perspective with the reality of God. We have sinned. We do sin. We hurt ourselves and the people whom we love. We have not lived up to our covenant promises to God. And yet the God who reveals himself at the table and in the breaking of the bread is revealed to be a God of manifold and great mercies who will not stop calling us back to himself and will not rest until we evermore dwell in him, and he in us.

Third, the reference to the crumbs is another multivalent scriptural reference. We are borrowing the words of the Syrophoenecian woman in Mark who acknowledges her unworthiness to receive the benefits of Jesus and who turns his heart.[2] It also reminds us of the many leftovers in the great feeding stories—crumbs that fill entire extra baskets. Further, there is even a faint echo of the manna gathered by the Children of Israel as they wandered in the deserts, the bread from heaven that saved them from perishing in their exile. This prayer, with its reference to crumbs, draws on that rich scriptural tradition and ties the central act of Eucharist to the entire arc of salvation history.

DISTRIBUTION

At this point, the priests and the congregation receive the consecrated elements. There are various phrases that can be used, all of which emphasize a special sacramental presence of Christ in the moment.

> The Body (Blood) of our Lord Jesus Christ keep you in everlasting life. [*Amen.*]
>
> The Body of Christ, the bread of heaven. [Amen.]
> The Blood of Christ, the cup of salvation. [Amen.]
>
> The Body of our Lord Jesus Christ, which was given for thee, preserve thy body and soul unto everlasting life. Take and eat this in remembrance that Christ died for thee, and feed on him in thy heart by faith, with thanksgiving.
>
> The Blood of our Lord Jesus Christ, which was shed for thee, preserve thy body and soul unto everlasting life. Drink this in remembrance that Christ's Blood was shed for thee, and be thankful.[3]

The words aren't the main thing here. The main thing is receiving the sacrament.

Thanks to the opening title sequences of the TV show, *Iron Chef*, my family is well-acquainted with the crowning quotation from French lawyer, politician, epicure, and early theorist of a low-carb diet, Jean Anthelme Brillat-Savarin: "Tell me what you eat, and I will tell you what you are."

It's that moment. If ever that phrase had a deep, philosophical, existential reference, it is this point.

Tell me what you eat, and I will tell you what you are.

WHAT DO YOU FEEL?

So, what should you feel when you receive Communion?

My mother told me as a child that if you didn't feel anything, you hadn't spiritually prepared yourself. Now that I'm a grown-up and have lived with this for quite some years, I don't think that's quite right. (Sorry, Mom!)

It's not a question of how you should feel. We get into danger when we start placing emotional requirements onto religious experiences. When we do that, we start creating expectations. If these expectations somehow aren't met, or if we question whether they were met enough, then we can spiral into some unhealthy territory while we attempt to sort through what we did wrong. We start asking why God doesn't like us enough to let us feel what we are supposed to feel.

Conversely, having specific emotional expectations of the experience leads to the creation of tactics to either meet them or to exploit them. We can fall into this trap ourselves, but it gets even worse when worship leaders decide that they need to make sure everybody feels the appropriate feeling. Then we slip into various forms of emotional and spiritual manipulation.

The better question isn't "what *should* you feel" but "what *do* you feel?"

For me, the time after receiving Eucharist is a moment for awareness and for, literally, communion. What am I feeling? What am I thinking? How is God speaking to me in the midst of this very intimate experience? These are very real questions. Because I am a thinking-oriented person by nature, I generally don't take enough time with exploring my feelings. But this is precisely the time to do that.

The prayer book allows hymns, psalms, or anthems during the administration of Communion. Some people say that the whole congregation should participate in this sung element—and that this is preferable to an individualistic act of prayer. Don't be pulled into others' expectations. This is your time of communion with God whom you have taken into yourself. If you are moved to sing along, do so. But sing because you want to and because it's expressing where you are, not because you have to. If you feel called to stay in prayer, do it.

My practice is usually to kneel and feel for a bit, then to pray the prayer appointed for After Receiving Communion:

> O Lord Jesus Christ, who in a wonderful Sacrament hast left unto us a memorial of thy passion: Grant us, we beseech thee, so to venerate the sacred mysteries of thy Body and Blood, that we may ever perceive within ourselves the fruit of thy redemption; who livest and reignest with the Father and the Holy Spirit, one God, for ever and ever. *Amen* (*The Book of Common Prayer*, p. 834).

Note that this prayer isn't about what we feel. Instead, it asks God to give us the grace to properly venerate the sacrament. Venerate here means to hold it in honor, to respect it in all its forms, and to give it the full attentiveness the sacrament deserves as a central mystery of our faith. The result of this veneration is that we might be enabled to perceive the fruits of Christ's redemptive work within ourselves. Notice here what we're saying. We are not asking for grace to be redeemed. Nor are we asking for grace to **feel** redeemed. Instead, we are asking for a grace of perception. The prayer acknowledges that whether we feel it or not, whether we perceive its fruits or not, Christ's redemption is already at work in us. We are asking to be allowed to see the products of the work of inner transformation that Christ is already working in us.

Brillat-Savarin's quote was paraphrased in the 1920s by nutritionist and salesman Victor Lindlahr into its more common form: "You are what you eat." There's a subtle difference between the original and this form, and I think this one works better here.

Between the bread of life, the cup of salvation, and the fruits of redemption, it's shaping up to be quite a meal.

POST-COMMUNION PRAYER

There are two forms of the Post-Communion Prayer in Rite II, one of which is a direct descendent of the prayer used in Rite I. Depending on which one you're praying, they weave together many of the themes that we have touched on (and will talk about again later in the book). The prayers have two main components. First, they give thanks for what we have received. We give thanks for the gift of the sacrament and for what that means corporately—that we are part of the household of God. Second, they acknowledge that we have to go out and act like the household of God. God has given us work to do—his own work of reconciliation—and in this meal we are strengthened to go forth and accomplish it. In doing so, we demonstrate with our lives our connection with the household of God, that we are board-mates with Christ. Showing up on Sunday and coming to the table isn't the point; doing the will of the One who sends us is the point.

BLESSING

The blessing either by the priest or bishop moves this thought along. If our Acclamation at the beginning of the service was the priest's liturgical hello, this is the priest's liturgical goodbye. Properly and appropriately it comes in a Trinitarian formula, and there are seasonal variations available in *The Book of Occasional Services* and elsewhere.

DISMISSAL

The deacon—in places where there is one—also has an official liturgical goodbye. Like the priest's blessing, like the post-communion prayer, the Dismissal has two key aspects: We are God's, and he has some work for us to do. Our work in worship is directly connected to our work in the world.

Our response, "Thanks be to God," is our liturgical goodbye. It also stands as an act of thanks, an act of praise, and an acknowledgement of the charges that we have been given. In Easter, extra alleluias are added in consonance with Easter's general theme of rejoicing; during Lent the more sober, "Let us bless the Lord," is suitable.

CHAPTER 10
THE BODY OF CHRIST

Disciplining yourself to exercise regularly is an effort. As an effort, as a discipline, we need to have reasons and purposes to keep at it: to crawl out of bed at an entirely unreasonable hour; to pause in the middle of our day to sweat; to push through that last set of repetitions that our muscles scream against. There are many reasons why people push through those obstacles to exercise. Too, there are many reasons that people tell themselves why they do it. (The "why" and the "what we tell ourselves" aren't always the same—the human mind is like that.)

Let me be clear. I tell myself that I exercise for my health, to maintain stamina, and to keep a well-functioning body as I move through middle age. But I would be lying if I said that how I look in the mirror in a semi-clothed state has nothing to do with it. I know vanity is not really a praiseworthy motivation. As somebody who studies this stuff, I realize the irony of being motivated by one of the classical vices. However, even without that perspective, there are a couple of good reasons why vanity is not a great motivator.

First, appearances can be deceiving. As we are well aware, a slender body (or a buff one, for that matter) does not automatically equate to a healthy body. All sorts of unhealthy behaviors can mimic health in the body's appearance. A host of supplements and pharmaceuticals—legal and otherwise—promise improved results with less efforts, while at the same time tearing down the body's health.

Second, vanity falls into the perception trap. I am always amazed by the guys in the gym who seem to focus only on the chest and the biceps. Since that's what they notice, they assume that's what everyone else notices. But that's not the way the body works. Muscles are parts of interlocking and interdynamic systems—you exaggerate one part of the system to the peril of the rest of it. Your perception of the health of the whole system becomes skewed.

Wiser heads point to the notion of functional fitness rather than appearance: Does the body do what you need it to do? Do the parts work together? Is the system stronger, healthier, more efficient? Do the habits promote the health of the entire system—not just the most noticeable bits?

Vanity can be an effective motivator—a helpful reminder that you have some work to do—but it should never be the only motivator. And vanity always fails as a goal or an effective measure of progress. This is just as true of spiritual fitness as it is of physical fitness.

There is a temptation in the spiritual life to be spiritual for the sake of praise. It's vanity of the soul; it's the exact spiritual correlation of vanity of the body because it is driven by the exact same motivation: We want praise from others because of their perception of us. As with vanity of the body, vanity of the soul promotes unhealthy practices. Just as the perception trap leads to crazy imbalances in the body, it does so with the soul as well. On one hand, it can lead to the adoption of only those spiritual habits that can be seen (and appreciated and approved of) by other people. That is, we engage in something only if it means other people can see it and observe how very spiritual we are. On the other hand, just as pernicious is a loss of perspective: We see ourself more than anyone else and come to the conclusion that we are the most important part of the system. Spirituality becomes about my spiritual journey, about my spiritual experience, about my spiritual fulfillment.

But it's not.

Authentic Christian spirituality is a team sport, not an individual endeavor.

And this is how we get back to the Eucharist. At the very heart of the Eucharist is the incontrovertible fact that it's not just about me and that we are all in it together. Literally. There's a key phrase that is at center of our Eucharistic practice and theology: the Body of Christ. Two little words in Greek (*soma Christou*), three in English, this term has several interrelated meanings that lead us deeper into our consideration of the Eucharist, into the sacraments as a whole, and into the identity of the Church. In essence, it takes us full circle, back to our initial discussion of what spirituality is all about, and we will end by considering from a new perspective some of the topics with which we began.

Language around both the Body of Christ and the presence of Christ—particularly Real Presence—are deeply related. In the simplest terms, where your body is located is where you are present. As a result, I'd like to take a look at some of the ways that the scriptures and the Church talk about the Body of Christ—and in some cases the presence of Christ without necessarily using the phrase Body of Christ. This isn't intended to be exhaustive, but suggestive. Instead of locking ourselves into a single literal sense of the term, I want us to think about all of the multiple meanings that this term can—and does— have. Then, we will talk a bit about what that means for how we understand the Eucharist.

THE PHYSICAL BODY OF CHRIST

This is the absolute starting place; any proper discussion of the meaning of the term, Body of Christ, has to start here—with the physical blood, guts, bones, and bile of Jesus. His was a historical body that lived, occupied space, sweated, smelled bad, and performed all of the physical functions of a body. The letter of 1 John affirms this body by taking the physical encounter with it as its literal opening point:

> We declare to you what was from the beginning, what we have heard, what we have seen with our eyes, what we have looked at and touched with our hands, concerning the word of life—this life was revealed, and we have seen it and testify to it, and declare to you the eternal life that was with the Father and was revealed to us—we declare to you what we have seen and heard so that you also may have fellowship with us; and truly our fellowship is with the Father and with his Son Jesus Christ (1:1-3).

And here we hit on our first key point concerning this body. The Johannine perspective, found both in this letter and in the Gospel of John, emphasize that this body is simultaneously the Word (of God, of Life) and a real body. The most paradoxical aspect of John's hymn-like start to his Gospel becomes the great antiphon of Christmas encircling it, encapsulating it, and proclaiming it: "And the Word became flesh and lived among us, and we have seen his glory, the glory as of a father's only son, full of grace and truth" (1:14).

Here we assert the perennial teaching of the Church: that Jesus Christ was fully human and fully divine. In his body, born from his mother Mary, he was both completely human and completely God. We all know that 100 percent plus 100 percent doesn't add up to 100 percent! Countless explanations have attempted to fix the equation ranging from all human pretending to be God (0 + 100) to a human body but a divine soul (50 + 50) to all God pretending to be human (100 + 0). At each explanation, the Church has looked, sniffed it a few times, and said, "No, this isn't it." The best answer that we have come up with is a mystical union. The Word of God united to physical flesh is both God incarnate and a true human being.

This is the body that got weary from walking up and down the hills of Galilee; this is the body that became exhausted after nights spent in prayer rather than sleep; this is the body that took bread, blessed it, and broke it, saying, "This is my Body, given for you." This is the body that was nailed to the cross, died, and rose again.

THE RESURRECTED BODY OF CHRIST

We affirm that it was the physical Body of Christ that died and was raised. And yet, the resurrected Body did things that normal living bodies do not. On the other hand, it also did things that only normal living bodies can do. John goes to great pains in his Gospel to affirm a direct and fundamental continuity between the physical Body of Christ and the resurrected Body of Christ; as proof of his identity, the Risen Jesus shows the disciples his hands and side (John 20:20). The story of Thomas serves to hammer this point home: "Unless I see the mark of the nails in his hands, and put my finger in the mark of the nails and my hand in his side, I will not believe" (John 20:25). Of course, when Jesus comes to the disciples again, he invites Thomas to do just that: "Put your finger here and see my hands. Reach out your hand and put it in my side. Do not doubt but believe" (John 20:27). The wounds that Jesus received in his physical Body remain in his resurrected Body.

Furthermore, Jesus uses this resurrected Body in very physical ways. He breathes on the disciples (John 20:22). He cooks fish for them, with the clear implication that he ate some of it as well (John 21:9-14). And this isn't just a John thing either; Luke spends some time with this also. Jesus walked and talked with the men on the road to Emmaus. He took, blessed, and broke bread with them (Luke 24:13-35). He specifically invites the apostles to touch him, including his hands and feet, and asks for some broiled fish to eat in their presence (Luke 24:41-3).

On the other hand, both John and Luke record the resurrected Body doing things beyond the ability of physical bodies—entering locked rooms (John 20:19), appearing suddenly among them in a manner that seemed like that of a ghost (Luke 24:36-7), and ascending into heaven (Acts 1:9). Furthermore, disciples who knew him well—including Mary Magdalene—had a hard time recognizing him by sight in both Luke and John.

So, as Luke and John tell it, the resurrected Body is fully continuous with the physical Body but is beyond it in some quite important ways.

THE ASCENDED BODY OF CHRIST

The ascended Body seems to be continuous with the resurrected Body and is thus linked to the physical Body as well. This is the Body that we confess in the creeds to be "seated at the right hand of the Father." In the New Testament, we seem to have three separate references to this mode of Christ's presence with a strong common thread: They are all visionary, ecstatic experiences by individuals.

In Acts, the dying Saint Stephen turns his eyes to heaven, "and saw the glory of God and Jesus standing at the right hand of God. 'Look,' he said, 'I see the heavens opened and the Son of Man standing at the right hand of God!' " (7:55b-56). The point is that Christ in his ascended state was fully present with Stephen within his martyrdom.

Similarly, Saint Paul receives an experience of Jesus in Acts 9:3-6, which is later retold in Acts 22 and 26. While Paul speaks of "heavenly visions" in Acts 26:17, the experience is consistently described as a blinding light accompanied by the voice of Jesus speaking to Paul. There is certainly no question in Paul's mind that Jesus was fully present.

The third is the vision of Saint John in the book of Revelation. There is an initial vision where John is "in the spirit on the Lord's day" (Revelation 1:10) and he both sees and hears Jesus who, in dramatic fashion, dictates letters to seven churches in Asia (modern Turkey). John's words convey a sense of full-on bodily presence—like when he passes out in fear "at his feet" and is revived when Jesus "placed his right hand on me [John]" (Revelation 1:17). John then discloses a more traditional enthronement scene clearly located "in heaven" (Revelation 4:2) where the Lamb appears at the right hand of God following the standard creedal image.

The key aspects of this mode of presence seem to be twofold: First, it is a very intense mode of presence; second, it is located spatially in heaven.

THE PNEUMATIC BODY OF CHRIST

With the ascension of the resurrected Body, and its enthronement—literal, metaphorical, symbolic—at the right hand of God, we pass into various post-physical modes of the Body of Christ. The lines between some of these are admittedly fuzzy but are worth mentioning, including the pneumatic Body.

From the Greek word *pneuma* (spirit), this is the Body that is mediated to believers by the Holy Spirit. I find this mode in particular when Jesus promises, "For where two or three are gathered in my name, I am there among them" (Matthew 18:20). This seems to be the mode of presence that Paul invokes at the start of 1 Corinthians 5 when he tells the Corinthians that he is present with them spiritually: "When you are assembled, and my spirit is present with the power of our Lord Jesus" (5:4b).

Just as there is a special continuity between the physical and resurrected bodies, this mode of the Body of Christ has a certain continuity with the next two as well.

THE MYSTICAL BODY OF CHRIST

The mystical Body of Christ is best captured in a single verb: abide. This is the mode of mutual indwelling where Christ dwells in us and we in him. Scripture speaks of it in a variety of ways:

> [Jesus said:] I am the true vine, and my Father is the vinegrower. He removes every branch in me that bears no fruit. Every branch that bears fruit he prunes to make it bear more fruit. You have already been cleansed by the word that I have spoken to you. Abide in me as I abide in you. Just as the branch cannot bear fruit by itself unless it abides in the vine, neither can you unless you abide in me. I am the vine, you are the branches. Those who abide in me and I in them bear much fruit, because apart from me you can do nothing. Whoever does not abide in me is thrown away like a branch and withers; such branches are gathered, thrown into the fire, and burned. If you abide in me, and my words abide in you, ask for whatever you wish, and it will be done for you. My Father is

glorified by this, that you bear much fruit and become my disciples (John 15:1-8).

By this we know that we abide in him and he in us, because he has given us of his Spirit. And we have seen and do testify that the Father has sent his Son as the Savior of the world. God abides in those who confess that Jesus is the Son of God, and they abide in God. So we have known and believe the love that God has for us. God is love, and those who abide in love abide in God, and God abides in them (1 John 4:13-16).

I have been crucified with Christ; and it is no longer I who live, but it is Christ who lives in me. And the life I now live in the flesh I live by faith in the Son of God, who loved me and gave himself for me (Galatians 2:19-20).

Perhaps most telling is this last selection, which is one of my favorite passages in the Pauline letters:

Set your minds on things that are above, not on things that are on earth, for you have died, and your life is hidden with Christ in God (Colossians 3:2-3).

Particularly significant here is the means by which our death occurs: "...you were buried with him in baptism..." (Colossians 2:12).

When we are baptized, we are baptized into the Body of Christ and become partakers of the divine life of God. Specifically, this is the Body of Christ that we are baptized into. And, being baptized into Christ, we are linked with all those who share that baptism. This is the Communion of the Saints spoken of in the creeds. We share a common life in Christ through our connection in him.

THE SOCIAL BODY OF CHRIST

The social Body of Christ is the visible institution of the Church. There is a lot of overlap between the mystical Body of Christ and the social Body of Christ; perhaps in a perfect world they would be identical, but in this present age that is not to be. The distinction is that the social Body is a human society, reinforced with human rules and administered by human beings. While we truly believe that the Church is of divine origin and receives divine guidance through the Spirit, the Anglican tradition acknowledges the fallibility of such institutions.

We cannot be Christians properly by ourselves. Our binding into the Body of Christ obligates us to gather with one another into the visible institution of the Church. Both the scriptures and the witness of the Early Church legislate particular forms of church life that include bishops, priests, and deacons alongside the main body of the faithful. As an Episcopal church—that is, one whose name includes the Greek word for bishop—we believe that these structures are important and necessary channels for the maintenance and proclamation of the faith.

Furthermore, the Church has been granted means of grace as sure and certain channels of the grace of God. Chief among these are the sacraments and various sacramental rites. Baptism, Eucharist, Confirmation, Reconciliation, Anointing, Marriage, Ordination: these rites and others like them connect individuals, families, and communities deeper into the life of the Church, the social Body, and—hopefully—deeper into the mystical Body as well.

This social Body is one of Paul's favorite uses for this multivalent term. In several of his Epistles, he makes reference to this metaphor, particularly to speak of the nature of the Church and its essential interdependence:

For just as the body is one and has many members, and all the members of the body, though many, are one body, so it is with Christ. For in the one Spirit we were all baptized into one body— Jews or Greeks, slaves or free—and we were all made to drink of one Spirit. Indeed, the body does not consist of one member but of many. If the foot would say, "Because I am not a hand, I do not belong to the body," that would not make it any less a part of the body. And if the ear would say, "Because I am not an eye, I do not belong to the body," that would not make it any less a part of the body. If the whole body were an eye, where would the hearing be? If the whole body were hearing, where would the sense of smell be? But as it is, God arranged the members in the body, each one of them, as he chose. If all were a single member, where would the body be? As it is, there are many members, yet one body. The eye cannot say to the hand, "I have no need of you," nor again the head to the feet, "I have no need of you." On the contrary, the members of the body that seem to be weaker are indispensable, and those members of the body that we think less honorable we clothe with greater honor, and our less respectable members are treated with greater respect; whereas our more respectable members do not need this. But God has so arranged the body, giving the greater honor to the inferior member, that there may be no dissension within the body, but the members may have the same care for one another. If one member suffers, all suffer together with it; if one member is honored, all rejoice together with it.

Now you are the body of Christ and individually members of it. And God has appointed in the church first apostles, second prophets, third teachers; then deeds of power, then gifts of healing, forms of assistance, forms of leadership, various kinds of tongues. Are all apostles? Are all prophets? Are all teachers? Do all work miracles? Do all possess gifts of healing? Do all speak in tongues? Do all interpret? But strive for the greater gifts. And I will show you a still more excellent way (1 Corinthians 12:12-31).

That's long, but the passage is worth citing in full. The reason is because here we see Paul talking about differentiation within the Body; not everybody has the same job—nor do they need to. Not everyone fulfills the same role, but all roles are important even if some are more visible than others. Differentiation and the hierarchy or potential for hierarchical ranking emphasizes the social character of the Church, particularly as it grapples with the ways that the Church both is and is not (or should not be) like other human social groupings.

Continuing with the theme of differentiation within the Body causes us to return to where we began. When we started speaking about the purpose of Christian spirituality, we began with Paul's use of the body metaphor in Ephesians:

> There is one body and one Spirit, just as you were called to the one hope of your calling, one Lord, one faith, one baptism, one God and Father of all, who is above all and through all and in all. But each of us was given grace according to the measure of Christ's gift....The gifts he gave were that some would be apostles, some prophets, some evangelists, some pastors and teachers, to equip the saints for the work of ministry, for building up the body of Christ, until all of us come to the unity of the faith and of the knowledge of the Son of God, to maturity, to the measure of the full stature of Christ. We must no longer be children, tossed to and fro and blown about by every wind of doctrine, by people's trickery, by their craftiness in deceitful scheming. But speaking the truth in love, we must grow up in every way into him who is the head, into Christ, from whom the whole body, joined and knit together by every ligament with which it is equipped, as each part is working properly, promotes the body's growth in building itself up in love (4:4-7, 11-16).

Paul goes to great lengths to emphasize the unity of the Body without insisting on uniformity but also makes clear that being the Body is not enough. The Body of Christ is not yet fully matured. It is in the process of becoming filled out and strong but is not there yet. The Body of Christ—this social Body—does not yet fully possess the Mind of Christ. Only when the Body grows into full unity will it most fully be what it is.

THE MARGINAL BODY OF CHRIST

Another mode of presence that exists in partial relation to the previous ones is made explicit in one biblical passage (although others allude to it). This is Matthew's famous parable of the sheep and the goats. Set at the moment of Judgment, all peoples are gathered before the throne and judged based on how they treated Christ. The whole crowd—righteous and unrighteous alike—is confused and asks the same basic question: "'Lord, when was it that we saw you hungry or thirsty or a stranger or naked or sick or in prison...?'" (Matthew 25:44). He responds: "'Truly I tell you, just as you did it to one of the least of these who are members of my family, you did it to me'" (Matthew 25:40).

Scholars argue over exactly what group Matthew and Jesus are referring to with "the least of these who are the members of my family." Is this the Church specifically, or is it broader than that? At the end of the day, when we are wrestling with this passage's call on our lives and actions, it fundamentally doesn't matter to whom Matthew was referring. Scripture makes clear God's concern for those at the margins, those who get the short end of the social stick no matter how society is structured. To put a finer point on it, the more that the social Body overlooks or deliberately ignores the marginal Body, the further from the presence of Christ it is.

THE ESCHATOLOGICAL BODY OF CHRIST

Eschatological is a fancy word that simply pertains to final things. Theologians use it when referring to the ideal future state where all of God's plans have come to fruition, and humanity and creation are finally and ultimately reconciled with God and one another. One way of grasping the great eschatological vision appears in Isaiah's prophecies about the coming messianic rule:

> The wolf shall live with the lamb, the leopard shall lie down with the kid, the calf and the lion and the fatling together, and a little child shall lead them. The cow and the bear shall graze, their young shall lie down together; and the lion shall eat straw like the ox. The nursing child shall play over the hole of the asp, and the weaned child shall put its hand on the adder's den. They will not hurt or destroy on all my holy mountain; for the earth will be full of the knowledge of the LORD as the waters cover the sea (Isaiah 11:6-9).

Isaiah speaks of entire ecosystems being fundamentally realigned in order to communicate the radical nature of this idyllic state and to contrast God's perfect image of reality with our current situation. This is a new Eden. Everything is as it was in the garden, full harmony between Creator and creation.

Humans are included in this vision too, and a passage from Isaiah uses similar imagery, combining it with undertones of the sacrificial meals in his description:

> On this mountain the LORD of hosts will make for all peoples a feast of rich food, a feast of well-aged wines, of rich food filled with marrow, of well-aged wines strained clear. And he will destroy on this mountain the shroud that is cast over all peoples, the sheet

that is spread over all nations; he will swallow up death forever. Then the Lord GOD will wipe away the tears from all faces, and the disgrace of his people he will take away from all the earth, for the LORD has spoken. It will be said on that day, Lo, this is our God; we have waited for him, so that he might save us. This is the LORD for whom we have waited; let us be glad and rejoice in his salvation (25:6-9).

We'll return to this image a little later—I'm sure you've noticed that it has some interesting interpretive angles—but the key point I want to make is that this is a comprehensive gathering of **all** people.

So, what does this have to do with Christ?

In the Stoic philosophy of the time, the term *Logos* (word) was used to speak of the logic or pattern underlying the universe. It's likely that when John's prologue speaks of Jesus as "the Word," it is tapping into this sense of a cosmic pattern. Paul certainly has this notion in mind in Colossians:

[Jesus] is the image of the invisible God, the firstborn of all creation; for in him all things in heaven and on earth were created, things visible and invisible, whether thrones or dominions or rulers or powers—all things have been created through him and for him. He himself is before all things, and in him all things hold together. He is the head of the body, the church; he is the beginning, the firstborn from the dead, so that he might come to have first place in everything (1:15-18).

Imagining the fullness of time, all creation is reconciled back to Christ the Logos within the eschatological Body. All creation is conformed, in joy and perfect freedom, to the pattern intended for it by its shaper. Romans alludes to this when it speaks of creation's groaning in anticipation of God's birthing of the new age:

For the creation waits with eager longing for the revealing of the
children of God; for the creation was subjected to futility, not of
its own will but by the will of the one who subjected it, in hope
that the creation itself will be set free from its bondage to decay
and will obtain the freedom of the glory of the children of God.
We know that the whole creation has been groaning in labor
pains until now; and not only the creation, but we ourselves, who
have the first fruits of the Spirit, groan inwardly while we wait for
adoption, the redemption of our bodies (8:19-23).

This, then, is the eschatological Body—looking forward
in hope to the point when Christ is all in all. This mode of
Christ's presence exists for us now as a future state. It is
something that our present activities can point toward but
cannot be fully realized until the consummation of all things.

THE SACRAMENTAL BODY OF CHRIST

Finally, we arrive at one of the most common—and most
argued over—uses of the term. When the consecrated
Eucharistic bread is distributed from the altar, the priest never
just gives it silently. The prayer book gives three phrases to
choose from:

"The Body of our Lord Jesus Christ keep you in everlasting life."

"The Body of Christ, the bread of heaven."

[Or the expansive form found in Rite I] "The Body of our Lord Jesus
Christ, which was given for thee, preserve thy body and soul unto
everlasting life. Take and eat this in remembrance that Christ died
for thee, and feed on him in thy heart by faith, with thanksgiving."

Whichever version your priest happens to go with, one
thing is left abundantly clear: The Church makes the claim

that the piece of bread being put into your hand at that moment is in some important way the Body of Christ.

How, exactly, do we mean this? Well, that's part of the genius of the Anglican system. Our formularies and liturgies are quite careful not to say exactly how we mean it, which permits a variety of acceptable interpretations and neatly sidesteps one of the greatest and most pressing religious differences in the Western Church from the time of the Reformation to the present: the mode and means of how Christ is present in the Eucharist.

One way to understand this mode is as a memorialist position. This theology suggests that the phrase Body of Christ is a metaphor and that the consecrated bread reminds us to remember Christ's death on our behalf and to nourish ourselves and our faith through this fundamentally mental act of memorial. Another way of understanding takes the identification of the bread with the Body of Christ literally and believes that Jesus is—somehow—truly and fully present in the bread. Different Anglicans have understood the mode of Christ's presence in the Eucharist in a variety of ways; some advocate a memorialist position, some speak of a purely spiritual presence, and others speak of a real presence. Still others explain by means of minor nuances how their view differs from transubstantiation, a theory of Real Presence explained by means of Aristotelian metaphysics, which was officially forbidden under the English 39 Articles of Faith.

I'm not going to try to persuade you one way or another; as I said, the prayer book permits quite a range. What I must insist upon, however, is that every one of our Eucharistic prayers includes the words of Jesus at the Last Supper when he tells his disciples, "Take, eat, this is my Body, which is given for you." These words require every theory of Eucharistic presence be grounded in Christ's own words. There is an unavoidable continuity between the physical Body, the resurrected Body, and the sacramental Body. Likewise, all of the prayers forge a direct verbal connection between the bread of the rite and the Body of Christ:

> Prayer I: "we, receiving [these thy gifts and creatures of bread and wine] according to thy Son our Savior Jesus Christ's holy institution, in remembrance of his death and passion, may be partakers of his most Blessed Body and Blood" (p. 335).

> Prayer II: "bless and sanctify these gifts of bread and wine, that they may be unto us the Body and Blood of thy dearly-beloved Son Jesus Christ" (p. 342).

> Prayer A: "Sanctify [these gifts] by your Holy Spirit to be for your people the Body and Blood of your Son, the holy food and drink of new and unending life in him" (p. 363).

> Prayer B: "send your Holy Spirit upon these gifts that they may be the Sacrament of the Body of Christ and his Blood of the new Covenant" (p. 369).

> Prayer C: "Sanctify [these gifts] by your Holy Spirit to be the Body and Blood of Jesus Christ our Lord" (p. 371).

> Prayer D: "sanctifying [these gifts] and showing them to be holy gifts for your holy people, the bread of life and the cup of salvation, the Body and Blood of your Son Jesus Christ" (p. 375).

It is difficult to interpret all these in a purely metaphorical sense; the language seems to recommend something more substantial. The practice of reserving the sacrament—keeping leftover consecrated bread within a special box in the chancel (ambry) or on the altar (tabernacle)—within many Episcopal churches follows the logic of Real Presence. After all, if the bread is only a reminder or a metaphor, there is no reason to put it in a special box.

No matter how we understand it or what the mechanics are, our prayers emphasize that the consecrated bread is the Body of Christ—this is the faith of the Church.

The Church has always taught that the fullness of both the Body and Blood of Christ subsist in each of the elements. That is, the Body of Christ is not restricted to the bread or the Blood of Christ to the wine; to receive one of the elements is to receive the fullness of Christ's Eucharistic presence. Those who cannot drink wine or cannot eat gluten are not thereby excluded from it.

REAL PRESENCES

The classic argument over the Eucharist is about the Real Presence of Christ within it. I can't help but think this is the wrong way of asking the question. It's not: is there a Real Presence of Christ in the Eucharist? Rather, I ask: How many modes of Real Presence are we experiencing simultaneously within the Eucharist? Or—to phrase the same question another way—how many dimensions of the Body of Christ and modes of Christ's presence are operative within a given rite?

I argue that, quite frequently, several of these dimensions are active in most anything that we do. As we walk down the street, go to work, or cook dinner, we function as members of the Body of Christ. We are participants—however passively at the moment—of the mystical Body of Christ through the basic fact of Baptism. When we pause with our families to say grace over dinner, we add a further dimension of the pneumatic Body as we unite in the Spirit through the act of prayer. When we pray the Daily Office, we connect to the social Body as well as the mystical Body and the pneumatic Body as we express prayer as a habit of the Church, whether gathered together or dispersed.

But it is in the Eucharist that we have the greatest possible confluence of the multiple senses of the Body. As members of the mystical Body of Christ, we have been invited to participate within the interior life of the Trinity and to experience the self-offering of the Son to the Father through the Spirit. We physically gather with the social Body to raise our collective voices in praise and thanksgiving. Our spirits mingle in the pneumatic Body as we share in the one Spirit that leads us. We are invited to lift our hearts up heavenward to the ascended Body as we begin our great act of thanksgiving. We receive into ourselves the sacramental Body—however we choose to understand Christ's presence within the elements. And, together, as people gathered from all nations around the meal with God, we foreshadow the eschatological Body when Christ will be all in all and the reconciliation of Creator and creation will be complete.

It is easy to get stuck in binaries. For a long time, the argument focused around the exact nature of the bread and wine: Was he really there or wasn't he? In more recent years, the focus has changed to a fixation on the worshiping assembly as the Body of Christ to the relative exclusion of other meanings. Instead of proposing a narrow set of mutually exclusive binaries, it seems to me that we engage in the spirit of the Eucharist most fully when we experience it as a solemn and holy game of hide-and-seek where we keep our eyes out, ever attentive, ever watchful, to locate the presence of Christ within it in a way that we had not expected or suspected before.

Furthermore, I suggest that our liturgies ourselves point us to this perspective. Within them we find deliberately interwoven, intentional ambiguities, double-meanings, and turns of phrase designed to call to mind the many simultaneous modes of Christ's presence. One of the reasons I love the Rite I liturgies is the way these Eucharistic prayers subtly reinforce the aspect of the mystical Body while making explicit reference to the sacramental Body. It begins most overtly in the Oblation of Eucharistic Prayer I when we ask that "we, and all others who shall be partakers of this Holy Communion, may worthily receive the most precious Body and Blood of thy Son Jesus Christ, be filled with thy grace and heavenly benediction, and be made one body with him, that he may dwell in us, and we in him" (p. 336). The theme appears again in the Prayer of Humble Access, where we ask: "Grant us, therefore, gracious Lord, so to eat the flesh of thy dear Son Jesus Christ, and to drink his blood, that we may evermore dwell in him, and he in us" (p. 337). It appears once more in the post-communion prayer—but not alone. Perhaps in recognition that an overemphasis on this aspect can lead to an unhealthy individualist attitude of "just Jesus and me," the post-communion prayer deftly ties this aspect to three others. Here's a section of the prayer:

> ...we most heartily thank thee for that [A] thou dost feed us, in these holy mysteries, with the spiritual food of the most precious Body and Blood of thy Son our Savior Jesus Christ; and dost assure us thereby of thy favor and goodness towards us; [B] and that we are very members incorporate in the mystical Body of thy Son, [C] the blessed company of all faithful people; [D] and are also heirs, through hope, of thy everlasting kingdom (*The Book of Common Prayer*, p. 339).

Starting with [A], the prayer invokes the sacramental Body that we have just received. Then in [B], the mystical Body is brought in. However, this is immediately qualified and diverted from an individualistic focus in [C] with a nod toward the coexistence of the mystical and social Bodies.

—— [313] ——

Finally, this chain concludes in [D] with a move toward the eschatological Body.

The other Eucharistic prayers are equally as rich in meaning. If we have an expectation that there is only one place where the Body can be, one form in which it can be found, and one mode through which we can experience it, we close off a host of potential meanings and insights concerning the nature of God and God's interaction with his creatures.

THE EUCHARIST AS A GIFT TO THE CHURCH

As we move into and through the Christian life, there is an order—a progression—through which we pass. Not all do it the same way, of course, but history and experience have shown that there is a regular channel that the Church has identified as the ordinary path of the means of grace. In this channel, some experiences of the Body of Christ are more foundational than others; there is a logical order. If one mode of the Body of Christ should be selected to hold the primary place among the rest in our experience as Christians, it should be the mystical. The mystical Body is the means by which we as individuals are plugged into the life of God, are welcomed into the interior dialogue of the Trinity, and, in that connection, are united to our fellow brother and sister believers without regard to time and space, becoming heirs of the hope of the ultimate victory of love and life in the final consummation. Our entry into the mystical Body serves as the great gateway into the full experience of life in God. The writings of the New Testament emphasize the rite of Baptism because it is the means revealed for achieving this connection. Matthew's grand ending pushes this point home as it encompasses the mystical, social, pneumatic, and eschatological Bodies in the words of the Great Commission:

"Go therefore and make disciples of all nations, baptizing them in the name of the Father and of the Son and of the Holy Spirit, and teaching them to obey everything that I have commanded you. And remember, I am with you always, to the end of the age" (28:19-20).

Baptism stands as our point of entry into the mystical and the social Bodies of Christ. The other sacramental rites proceed from and assume the mystical Body as a foundation for everything else.

The Eucharist did not appear one day, out of the blue, in the middle of a Galilean sidewalk. Rather, it is a rite that was bequeathed to the Church. It was given to the mystical Body as a deliberate act enacted by the social Body. The sacramental Body of Christ is given context as an act of the social Body on behalf of the mystical Body as a sign of and for the eschatological Body.

As the Church, we don't own the Eucharist; it is not ours. And yet, we are called to be stewards of it, meaning that we should faithfully celebrate it under the conditions in which it was given to us. It is an act of the Church that provides grace for the Church as the Body of Christ to be transformed more completely into the Mind of Christ. Outside of the Church, and outside of the company of the baptized, it loses a host of meanings because the multiplicity of Bodies participating within the rite are not present in the same way.

There are voices within the Church that urge the communion of the unbaptized as a sign of hospitality. It is hard to be against hospitality. And, indeed, we never should be. However, there is more present and at work in the Eucharist than simply that. The mystical Body is the foundational Christian reality that sheds light upon everything else that we do together. To be intentionally welcoming, our hospitality should focus upon welcoming the curious and the seekers into the mystical Body of Christ. They should be given the opportunity to perceive the context of the Eucharist for themselves—to see it as a culmination of Real Presences that bind us deeper into the life of God into which we were planted in Baptism.

Saint Augustine, the fourth-century Bishop of Hippo, offered an invitation to the Eucharist in one of his sermons that captures the mechanics at work here. In speaking with reference to the Eucharist elements, he exhorts his listeners: "Be what you see; receive what you are!" He invites them, as the gathered Church, to receive the Eucharistic elements, then to enact the victory of life and love. He invites them to receive the sacrament, then to be the Church, to be the consecrated—set apart—Body and Blood of Christ in and for the world. This is the Eucharist's true home; this is where it makes sense.

PERCEIVING THE BODY

With physical fitness, checking yourself in the mirror is not—cannot be—your sole means for assessing progress. Sure, it can be one metric among many. That is, if you're looking at how your shape changes over time, you can assess certain things. You can get a sense of how weight loss or gain is going (although a scale is a more objective measure). You can see if you're making progress with certain muscle groups (although a measuring tape is a more objective method). It can help give you a sense of proportion. So, yes, there is value. And, again, it can be an effective motivator.

However, it can't tell you about your heart health. The mirror can't tell you about your lung health. It can't tell you about your own fitness over and against other people's health. And I say this as a guy who has watched many people far less lean than myself blow past me at mile eleven of a race. Going strictly off of looks, I would have judged myself to be in far better shape. But where the sneakers meet the road, I learn otherwise to my chagrin. When we put it in these terms, it seems obvious that other measures and motivators ought to be in on the game.

So how do we assess the spiritual fitness of the systems we're in? If we take the Body of Christ seriously, what kind of things ought we be concerned about?

As in physical fitness, it's easy to get sucked into judging by appearances. How is the Body doing? Well, our congregation, our local outpost of the social Body of Christ, must be doing great because it looks good on Sunday mornings!

Really?

I'm going to suggest that appearance—how things look, how things seem to be going—is only one part of assessing spiritual health.

No matter what it looks like, we must ask: How is it functioning? Is your local experience of the social and mystical Body of Christ being the Body of Christ in **all** of its potential dimensions in a wounded world? Is it manifesting Christ's care to the marginal and the forgotten? Is it caring for those within it and those outside of it? Is it forging connections to bring other people, other communities into the pneumatic Body as you pray and work and witness together? Is your community baptizing new people into the mystical Body? Is it enriching the connection into the deeper life of God through provision of the sacramental Body and Blood? These are important measures of the functional fitness of the Body of Christ.

Is the Body of Christ as a community growing and inhabiting more deeply the Mind of Christ?

And is your individual spiritual journey contributing to that growth and benefiting the whole Body? Are you doing your own thing for your own reasons by your own self, or is your journey simultaneously an act of service to those around you, building up the Body in all of its facets?

These are the questions we need to consider as we perceive the Body as it manifests around us and within us.

CONCLUSION ON THE EUCHARIST

The Eucharist is the main event in the liturgical life. This is the moment when the local worshiping community embodies and enacts the Body of Christ more fully, more completely, than any other time in its life together. The Eucharist is the sacrificial meal of reconciliation, Christ's own great self-offering to the Father. In the proclamation of the Gospel and in the meal at the altar, we are invited to take in Jesus through all our senses and to be converted—spiritually, emotionally, physically—into the God who calls us to be reconciled to himself and to the whole creation. As we are reconciled, we experience the corporate dimension of this sacramental reality when we truly reconcile with with those around us and extend that reconciliation to those who have not heard its Good News.

NOTES

1   General Convention passed a resolution in 2015 allowing a Eucharist of this type to be conducted at a principal service if the text has been approved beforehand by the bishop.

2   Mark 7:25-30.

3   *The Book of Common Prayer*, p. 338. The final option is found only in Rite I.

AFTERWORD

AFTERWORD

I ran across a quote a couple of years ago that I liked well enough to print out in big letters: "Discipline is remembering what you want." The internet attributes it to a David Campbell, identified variously as the founder of Saks Fifth Avenue or perhaps a Canadian politician. Whoever said it, the statement certainly rings true for me. I would like to say that I hung that sign over the place where I keep my running shoes, but I'm pretty sure it is buried in a pile of papers in my office.

Tying on my running shoes and hitting the pavement is an act of discipline. Sometimes I run because I am able to keep the big picture goal in mind: to enjoy good health with my family for as long as I can. I hope, decades from now, to be able to play and run around with my children's children as a result of embracing healthy habits now. Keeping this goal in mind helps me get out the door. But sometimes it's a lesser, more frivolous reason that gets me going. Like vanity, I run when I realize that the scale numbers are starting to creep up as beach season is drawing near or pride, as I realize that my wife's race times are getter better and better and mine aren't. Or sometimes I simply feel the need for a break: to stop what I am doing and immerse myself in something different, to feel the sun on my face and the wind on my back. And, although I thought I would never say this, sometimes I run because I find it fun, something to be done for its own sake.

Picking up my prayer book, or firing up my tablet, for Morning Prayer is likewise an act of discipline. Sometimes I can see the end goal far off: a life drenched with the presence of God, a way of being where the recollection of God is a near-constant experience. Awareness of that presence lends a dignity, grace, and wisdom to my daily dealings and relationships. On my clearest days, I aspire to draw ever closer to the Pauline goal of praying without ceasing. But sometimes the lesser goals keep me on the path. Like trying to keep a good streak with the number of times I have said Morning and Evening Prayer without missing. Or dragging myself out the door to church despite the beautiful weather because I know I should, because going provides a good example for my daughters, and because I will enjoy seeing my friends at the parish. And yet the prayer book itself draws me to it as well: the poetry, the rhythms, the spiritual depths, the organic continuity with generations of Christians who have prayed these words before me. Truly the prayer book services are something that I love for their own sake, too.

Hopefully what we have done here together is a beginning. Hopefully it will inspire you to pick up your prayer book more frequently, more attentively, and with a deeper understanding of its ways and riches. With a clearer sense of why we do the liturgies, what those liturgies communicate to us, and what strategies they employ to draw us further into the life of God, we may move toward a deeper communion with one another and the God who calls and reconciles us.

At the end of the day, that is what all of this is about: more perfectly embodying the Gospel of Christ in love and patience and good cheer to those around us and encouraging them in the same path, so that the whole Body of Christ might—together—possess the Mind of Christ.

ABOUT THE AUTHOR

Derek Olsen is a biblical scholar and an active layman in The Episcopal Church. He earned a master of divinity degree from Emory University's Candler School of Theology and a master of sacred theology degree from Trinity Lutheran Seminary. He served as pastoral vicar of a large Lutheran (ELCA) church in the Atlanta suburbs before beginning doctoral work and being received into The Episcopal Church. He completed a doctorate in New Testament in 2011 from Emory University under the direction of Luke Timothy Johnson.

His chief areas of interest are in the intersection between scripture and liturgy, the history of biblical interpretation—particularly in the Church Fathers and the Early Medieval West—and liturgical spirituality. He served as the liturgical editor of the recent revision of *Saint Augustine's Prayer Book,* published by Forward Movement.

An information technology professional in the corporate sector by day, Olsen maintains an active online ministry of teaching and programming; he writes the *St. Bede Blog* at www.stbedeproductions.com and is the creator of the *St Bede's Breviary* (breviary.stbedeproductions.com), a highly praised online resource for praying the Daily Office. He has written for *The Episcopal Café* and *Grow Christians* blogs, and his work appears regularly in *The Anglican Digest* and *The Living Church* as well. He is also one of the celebrity bloggers for *Lent Madness,* an online formation resource.

He currently serves on The Episcopal Church's Standing Commission on Liturgy and Music.

Olsen lives in Baltimore, Maryland, with his wife, an Episcopal priest, and their two daughters. In his spare time, he enjoys running, martial arts, cooking, and reading anything he can get his hands on.

ABOUT FORWARD MOVEMENT

Forward Movement is committed to inspiring disciples and empowering evangelists. While we produce great resources like this book, Forward Movement is not a publishing company. We are a ministry.

Our mission is to support you in your spiritual journey, to help you grow as a follower of Jesus Christ. Publishing books, daily reflections, studies for small groups, and online resources are important ways that we live out this ministry. More than a half million people read our daily devotions through *Forward Day by Day*, which is also available in Spanish (*Adelante Día a Día*) and Braille, online, as a podcast, and as an app for your smartphones or tablets. It is mailed to more than fifty countries, and we donate nearly 30,000 copies each quarter to prisons, hospitals, and nursing homes. We actively seek partners across the Church and look for ways to provide resources that inspire and challenge.

A ministry of The Episcopal Church for eighty years, Forward Movement is a nonprofit organization funded by sales of resources and gifts from generous donors. To learn more about Forward Movement and our resources, please visit us at www.forwardmovement.org (or www.venadelante.org).

We are delighted to be doing this work and invite your prayers and support.